D1275836

Instructor's Manual to Accompany Cases in Strategic Management and Business Policy

SECOND EDITION

LAWRENCE R. JAUCH

Northeast Louisiana University

JAMES B. TOWNSEND

Kansas State University

McGraw-Hill Publishing Company

New York   St. Louis   San Francisco   Auckland   Bogotá   Caracas
Colorado Springs   Hamburg   Lisbon   London   Madrid   Mexico
Milan   Montreal   New Delhi   Oklahoma City   Panama   Paris
San Juan   São Paulo   Singapore   Sydney   Tokyo   Toronto

Instructor's Manual to Accompany
CASES IN STRATEGIC MANAGEMENT
AND BUSINESS POLICY
Second Edition

Copyright ©1990 by McGraw-Hill, Inc. All rights reserved.
Printed in the United States of America. The contents, or
parts thereof, may be reproduced for use with
CASES IN STRATEGIC MANAGEMENT
AND BUSINESS POLICY
Second Edition
by Lawrence R. Rauch,
and James B. Townsend
provided such reproductions bear copyright notice, but may not
be reproduced in any form for any other purpose without
permission of the publisher.

ISBN 0-07-032356-9

1 2 3 4 5 6 7 8 9 0 WHT WHT 8 9 3 2 1 0 9

CONTENTS

PREFACE

This manual accompanies CASES IN STRATEGIC MANAGEMENT AND BUSINESS POLICY. Since its purpose is to provide maximum assistance to the instructor, we wrote it with the instructor always in mind. We reason that the more helpful we are, the more effective the instructor will be because we have lightened the demands on him in preparing for this most complex of all business courses. We regard it as the most complex not so much for its depth but for the fact that it deals consistently and essentially with that most complex of all mental qualities, judgement.

We have broken the manual into two parts. Part I is general in nature. It sets forth our philosophy, indicates how our cases might be used, and tries to answer some of the questions that have bothered us all from time to time. We suggest you read Part I so that you can better appreciate both the teaching notes and the casebook.

Part II contains teaching notes for each case. Their format is nearly always identical, and we feel that they are comprehensive. Each note has seven parts. First, the teaching objectives which we believe can reasonably be attained. Second, our thoughts on how and when the case might be used, its length, and its complexity. Third, a brief synopsis. Fourth, the outcome of the case, if we were able to ascertain it. Our students so often wonder what happened to X, and it is always nice to be able to tell them. Fifth, teaching approaches to the case. How many times we have wondered as we entered a classroom if we were going to go about things the right way! We have described what worked for us, or we have asked the case writers for their experiences. Ours is certainly not the way, it's just a way. Sixth, case analysis. We have analyzed each case comprehensively and followed the model proposed in the introductory chapter of the text. We have tried to leave no stone unturned in trying to make class discussion go that much more smoothly. Seventh, recommended discussion questions. We have supplied answers, but we caution that what appears is not necessarily the answer. It is our answer from a standpoint of logic, and we freely admit that answers are influenced by one's values and perceptions.

In preparing our teaching notes, we have been fortunate to have had the willing and enthusiastic assistance of the case writers themselves. Nearly all provided us their own notes along with permission to use those notes. Whenever asked, they also revised and commented on the note we had prepared. We are grateful to them all, for without their help there would be no such publication as this. And we are acutely aware that without the loving forbearance of our wives, Cathy and Betty, and the genius of our typists, we would still be in the idea stage.

Instructor comments on either teaching notes or cases are invited. We welcome your views.

Larry Jauch
Beidenharn Professor
of Management
Northeast Louisiana Univ.
Monroe, LA 71209

Jim Townsend
Department of Management
Calvin Hall, KSU
Manhattan, KS 66506

PART I

INTRODUCTION TO

INSTRUCTOR'S MANUAL

ACCOMPANYING

CASES IN STRATEGIC

MANAGEMENT AND

BUSINESS POLICY

We write this because we think it important that you know our basic considerations in preparing this casebook.

It is a sign of our times that every strategic management text seems to have an inevitable half-life of 18 months or two years. In not over two years perfectly good texts are usually retired, not because the text itself is dated but because the solutions to cases are widespread on the campus. The answer is obvious: no solutions are returned for permanent student retention. That is easier said than done, unfortunately, and even doing that is no guarantee of solution security. So we select another text, not necessarily for the superiority of its narrative text nor for its teachability, but because its cases are new. Back to the desk - new lesson plans, new time blocks, and a lot of frustration. Some intellectual shine is inevitably lost when we start over again, and the points which needed to be stressed and fitted so well now have to be forced into a new mold. That's not our idea of fun, and neither we nor our students are any the better for the process.

We personally like Jauch-Glueck, 5th edition, *Business Policy and Strategic Management*. (Larry is especially fond of it.) We consider it incredibly rich and very long lived. We think it the best on the market today from a standpoint of logic and teachability, and of course we admit our prejudices. We didn't want to retire a book we like, just because its cases were shopworn, so we thought of a casebook. We know the field of strategic management is dynamic, but we reasoned we could live with the text part because new developments in our field are well the reported in the *Strategic Management Journal, Long Range Planning*, the *Academy of Management Journal or Review*, etc. If we complemented what we had, we could still use the text we preferred. And we would still be able to use our favorite cases in the 5th edition for illustrative purposes because their solutions are not that material.

We hold that the same is true for any user - he is able to use his favorite text and cases if he has a casebook at hand. But what sort of casebook? While designed for use by those who might reluctantly be leaning to adopt a new text with cases, we thought it should be capable of being used as a standalone casebook with other standalone texts. It had to provide students with the opportunity to use strategic management concepts in a comprehensive and integrated manner, so we wanted to rule out issue - specific, operational cases. Rather than overwhelm students with extremely complex cases and raise the instructor's classroom frustration quotient still higher, we wanted cases that students could reasonably grasp without getting bogged down. We thought cases should be relatively recent whenever possible and cross as much of the business spectrum as possible. And we didn't want to group them by conventional headings such as formulation of strategy, since nobody will do that for our graduates.

We believe we hit a balance that will appeal to most instructors. The Table of Cases following shows that we aimed at cases long and short, simple and not so - simple, service and manufacturing, profit and non-profit, and entrepreneurial. Mindful of AACSB's injunction to teach "worldwide," we included a part on multinationals, and we touched on some of the issues that will confront our graduates for a long time to come. We aimed for maximum instruction flexibility without losing that all important student interest. And last but not least, we wanted to produce a truly helpful Instructor's Manual, written as we would like one to read.

STRUCTURING THE COURSE

We write with some assurance that users already have an idea of how they want to put a course together, so we don't want to pretend to a superior knowledge that we don't own. What we can say is that a recent survey of BPP Division professors in the Academy of Management examined how that group taught the Business Policy/Strategic Management Course [1]. Case analysis occupied about 52% of classroom time, lecture and discussion of strategic concepts and theory 25%, computer games 7%, and 15% otherwise.

We don't know how many cases you should assign because that number is a product of innumerable variables, plus your own objectives. We indicate in the Table of Cases the length and complexity of a case and believe that the Table will serve you well. Part One of the Casebook should be assigned reading. The inevitable question, "Why do we use cases?" has caused us to place J. Philip Wernette's fine answer to that question at the end of this Part.

We are frequently asked and it is often debated whether one should examine theory and illustrate it then with a case, return to theory and go to a case again (the TCTC method), or if it is wise to teach until one has exhausted the text and then go the cases (the TTCC method). In the abstract it should matter because that is how we learned mathematics, for example. What we know flies in the face of logic, because apparently it doesn't matter. An SIU paper presented at the Academy of Management several years ago was unable to establish the superiority of either method. That may permit more flexibility in how you decide to structure your course.

If you are contemplating adding a management simulation game, you have company. About a third of those in the BPP survey [1] reported computer games as one of the course activities used to determine student grades. We have been told that the most popular games by survey [2] are *The Executive Game* (Henshaw and Jackson, R.D. Irwin, 29%), *The Executive Simulation* (Keys and Leftwich, Management Resources Associates, 19%), *Tempomatic* (Scott and Strickland,

TABLE OF CASES

Cases are listed alphabetically with indications of length, complexity, usage, organization type and size, and strategic issues. All cases are suitable for class discussion. (Also see facing page).

CASE	LENGTH	DIFFI-CULTY	WHEN TO USE	HOW TO USE	SIZE	TYPE	MAJOR ISSUE(S)
Apple Computer	M	3	L	L	L	M	Formulation
Bartles & Jaymes*	S	1,2	M,L	I,S,L	L	M	Reformulation
Bavarian Motor*	S	1,2	E,M	I,S,L	L	M	Env analysis, Reformulation
Bennett's Machine	M	1,2	E	S,L	S	E	Formulation
Burger King	M	2	M,L	I,S,L	L	S	Implementation, Reformulation
Citicorp*	L	2	M,L	S,L	L	S	Formulation, acquisition analysis
Designs	M	1,2	E,M	S,L	S	E	Strategic choice
Drexel Burnham	M	2,3	L	S,L	M	S	Formulation, Reformulation
Electrolux*	M	3	L	S,L	L	M	Implementation
Environcare	S	1	E	I,S	S	E	Env analysis
GM of Canada*	M	2	L	S,L	L	M	Negotiation, Formulation
Inner City Paint	S	1	E,M	I,S	S	M	Survival
Jenny Stuart Med.	S	1	E,M	I,S	M	N	Formulation
Kraft*	M	2	L	S,L	L	M	Env analysis, Implementation
McDonald's*	M	2	M,L	I,S,L	L	S	Reformulation, Implementation
Nucor*	L	3	L	S,L	L	M	Reformulation
Ozark Glass*	S	1,2	E,M	I,S	S	M	Formulation
Printech	M	1,2	M,L	S,L	S	E	Values, strategic choices
PS Golf Car	S	1	E,M	I,S,L	S	E	Strategic advantage profile
Saunders System	M	2	M,L	S,L	L	S	Reformulation
Springfield Reman	S	2	E,M	S,L	M	M	Reformulation
Springfield Ballet	M	1	E	I,S,L	S	N	Strategic management
Turner Broadcast	L	2	E,M	I,S,L	L	E	Formulation
Zarembo*	M	2,3	M,L	L	S	S	Strategic choice

LEGEND

*: International in whole or in part, or have international aspects
Length: S-short, 0-10 pages; M-medium 10-20 pages; L-Long, 20- pages+
Difficulty: 1-easy, 2-moderately difficult, 3-complex
When to use: E-early in course, M-middle, L-later
How to use: I-inclass exam, S-short report, L-long report
Size: S-small, M-medium, L-large
Type: E-entrepreneurial, N-not for profit, M-manufacturing, S-service

TABLE OF CASES (CONT'D)

Cases by length

	Short	Medium	Long
	Bartles & Jaymes	Apple Computer	Citicorp
	Bavarian Motor	Bennett's Machine	Nucor
	Environcare	Burger King	Turner
	Inner City Paint	Designs	
	Jenny Stuart	Drexel Burnham	
	Ozark Glass	Electrolux	
	PS Golf Car	GM of Canada	
	Springfield R	Kraft	
		McDonalds	
		Printech	
		Saunders System	
		Springfield Ballet	
		Zarembo	

Cases by difficulty
(may appear twice)

	Easy	Moderately difficult	Complex
	Bartles & Jaymes	Bartles & Jaymes	Apple Computer
	Bavarian Motor	Bavarian Motor	Drexel Burnham
	Bennett's Machine	Bennett's Machine	Electrolux
	Designs	Burger King	Nucor
	Environcare	Citicorp	Zarembo
	Inner City Paint	Designs	
	Jenny Stuart	Drexel Burnham	
	Ozark Glass	GM of Canada	
	Printech	Kraft	
	PS Golf Car	McDonald's	
	Springfield Ballet	Ozark Glass	
		Printech	
		Saunders System	
		Springfield Reman	
		Turner Broadcast	
		Zarembo	

Cases by time of usage
(may appear twice)

	Early	Middle	Late
	Bavarian Motor	Bartles & Jaymes	Apple Computer
	Bennett's Machine	Bavarian Motor	Bartles & Jaymes
	Designs	Burger King	Burger King
	Environcare	Citicorp	Citicorp
	Inner City Paint	Designs	Drexel Burnham
	Jenny Stuart	Inner City Paint	Electrolux
	Ozark Glass	Jenny Stuart	GM of Canada
	PS Golf Car	McDonald's	Kraft
	Springfield Reman	Ozark Glass	McDonald's
	Springfield Ballet	Printech	Nucor
	Turner Broadcast	PS Golf Car	Printech
		Saunders System	Saunders System
		Springfield Reman	Zarembo
		Turner Broadcast	
		Zarembo	

Cases by size of organization

	Small	Medium	Large
	Bennett's Machine	Drexel Burnham	Apple Computer
	Designs	Jenny Stuart	Bartles & Jaymes
	Envinroncare	Springfield Reman	Bavarian Motor
	Inner City Paint		Burger King
	Ozark Glass		Citicorp
	Printech		Electrolux
	PS Golf Car		GM of Canada
	Springfield Ballet		Kraft
	Zarembo		McDonald's
			Nucor
			Saunders System
			Turner Broadcast

Houghton Mifflin, 13%), *The Business Policy Game* (Cotter, Reno Games, 10%), *The Business Policy and Strategy Game* (Bates and Eldridge, W.C. Brown, 6%), and *The Business Management Laboratory* (Jensen and Charington, Business Publications, 6%). The same survey [2] reported roughly half of its respondents did use simulations and two thirds of those had used simulations previously. We do not enter it here, but if you want information on grading, weights, and so on, we will be happy to talk with you.

Other activities in a course can include <u>films</u>. Strategy films are unfortunately hard to come by. What the film trade would like to regard as filling the bill does not because what we have seen belongs almost entirely in the OD field. (Possible) exceptions are the documentaries from Zipporah Films, (One Richdale Avenue, Unit #4, Cambridge, MA 02140, (667-576-3603), the Peter Drucker series on strategic management from BNA Communications (9401 Decoverly Hall road, Rockville, MD 20850, (301-948-0540), and Harvard's new but limited video material (in the HBS *Directory of Course Material,* HBS Case Services, Morgan Hall, Harvard Business School, Boston, MA 02163 (617-495-6117).

In passing we should note that additional cases are listed in Harvard's *Directory of Course Material.* HBS Case Services also supplies the *Directory of Management Cases* which provides information about cases from other institutions.

We would be remiss not to mention <u>class discussion</u>, the true cornerstone of any policy/strategy course. We do not blush to append Ram Charan's classic on classroom teaching. He says what we would say, but he says it much better. We were not surprised to see the BPP survey learn that class discussion was used to the greatest <u>extent</u> to evaluate undergraduates, a finding reflective of a conclusion reached earlier by others [3]. We emphasize extent in pointing out the use of class discussion in determining grades is not related to its <u>weight</u>.

GRADING

Again, we cannot tell you what to do, but we can indicate directions others have taken and provide some mechanical aids.

Boyd, Kopp, and Shufeldt [3] profiled the typical Policy Course and found that individual case studies, exams over theory, group cases, and class participation, in that order, made up 75% of the reported undergraduate grade. (The graduate aggregate was 73%, ordered as individual cases, exams, group cases, and class participation.) The BPP survey [1] was reported differently in that it showed <u>extent</u> (how many respondents used that factor in grading) rather than <u>weight</u>. Most used criterion to evaluate undergraduate performance was class participation, followed by individual cases, exams, and then group cases. Graduate evaluation was not asked.

Given the importance of cases in grading, the BPP survey [1] looked at the criteria used in grading written case analyses. Conducting an analysis and providing support for recommendations was most used, followed by the appropriate use of recommendations, identification of alternatives, applying theory, and developing an implementation plan. A spring 1983 survey of 300 randomly selected BPP professors [4] tallies closely but with slightly different nonmenclature. In order: Problem recognition/conceptualization, logic and clarity of problem analysis, application of theory, development and evaluation of alternatives, detailed plan of action, etc.

Grading oral case presentations is a different matter. We stress the oral communication of results because the world moves on briefings. Part One of the casebook addresses the subject but not its evaluation. We use Charles Hofer's format and find it quite satisfactory. A copy follows Ram Charan's masterpiece. Since our point of view is not a contemporary point of view, we ask that peer groups also comment on what they have heard. That form is attached, too. Some of the remarks we have seen are those we would all like to make but by virtue of office are prohibited from making. We do not use peer comments for grading purposes, but we have noted that the presenting group is _always_ interested in how its peers perceived it. We should add that we videotape student presentations and then critique that tape privately with its participants before attempting Hofer's form.

FRAMEWORKS FOR CASE ANALYSIS

We believe that our graduates must communicate equally well on paper, and we tend to require a goodly amount of penmanship. We stress that this is what the real world is like, and one who is unable to communicate effectively will have ample chance to update his/her resume. Students at KSU write a career plan (we'll provide details on request), report on a visit with a manager (if you're going to be a manager, go see what one does), and a 2000 word minimum paper on a topic of their own choosing. We also require 4-5 case briefs per semester in the form given at the very end of the Part.

We argue that a manager's time is his most precious commodity. It is irreplaceable. Don't waste it. We recall being told once that President Eisenhower would never take more than two thirds of a page on a subject. Secretary of Defense MacNamara would read no more than two pages, but he would devour the backup, even if it had to be wheeled in in a grocery cart. We're impressed, so we stress brevity.

For in-class exams we limit students to one side of one page. We don't let them drown the issue in a sea of words. Problem, solution, rationale. We drive that into them because of its constant applicability in the working world, and we require "executive briefs" from _Business Week_ with that format. If it's an exam and we are using a case, we let them use their books, their notes, a calculator, and anything else they can carry. They'll have access to all that in the manager's world, so why be different if the requirement is to solve a business problem? Practically, we encourage this brief form for its future utility and its implicit demand that the student think. You have to choose your words wisely when you are limited to one side of one sheet.

Not everything fits in the same mold. We know that, and we want our students to be able to do more if required, and to do so in logical fashion. The attached format was given to us once upon a time and is attributed to Charles Summer. We think it is just great. Short reports then run from 500 to 1250 words.

Halfway through the semester, we assign the final problem. We permit the use of any resource, but we do bar calling casewriters. Construction problem? See the experts in the College of Engineering. Money? Try the Finance Department. We encourage students to work in groups, because so much of the effort in business is by small groups. The problem is long and complex and we expect (and receive) up to 2000 words. The format for such a comprehensive report follows that described in Part One of the casebook.

NOTES

(1) "How Academy Members Teach the Business Policy/Strategic Management Course," Larry Alexander (VPI), Hugh O'Neill (Univ. of Conn.), Neil Snyder (UVA) and Jim Townsend (KSU), a paper presented to the Business Policy and Planning (BPP) Division, Academy of Management annual meeting, Boston, 1984.

(2) Letter, June 25, 1984, to Lawrence R. Jauch from Michael Keefe, Department of Management, University of Arkansas, reporting on the results of simulation survey made in April, 1984.

(3) "Grade Determination in the Business Policy Courses: A survey of Professors," Charles Boyd, Daniel Kopp, and Lois Shufeldt, Southwest Missouri State University, a paper presented to the BPP Division, Academy of Management, Boston, 1984.

(4) "Case Analysis in the Business Policy Course: Concepts, Formats, and Evaluation Criteria," Charles Boyd, Daniel Kopp and Lois Shufeldt, Southwest Missouri State University, a paper presented to the BPP Division, Academy of Management, Boston, 1984.

THE THEORY OF THE CASE METHOD

J. PHILIP WERNETTE
The University of Michigan

Professors of business administration naturally are interested in the methods utilized in the teaching-learning process. They, however, are not alone in this interest. Many business executives have (and others should have) the same interest. These executives are the men who are responsible for educational or training programs for staff members at all levels--from the humblest job-holders up through executives. In addition to these responsible executives, the people who serve as instructors in these programs are (or should be) interested in the same subject.

One of the many techniques of instruction is the one called the "case method."

THE IMPORTANCE OF KNOWING THE THEORY

The case method, properly handled, is an excellent way of teaching business administration. The usefulness of the method is increased if both teacher and students understand the basic theory of the method--what it aims to do for both teacher and students, and how it goes about doing it.

If the <u>teacher</u> does not grasp this basic theory, he is unlikely to get maximum results from use of the case method.

If the <u>students</u> do not understand this basic theory, they are likely to become bewildered and discouraged, and their progress will be delayed.

If, contrariwise, both teacher and students understand the method, the teaching-learning process is speeded and improved.

Reprinted from the *Michigan Business Review*, January 1975, pp. 3-6 (Ann Arbor, Mich.: The University of Michigan, Graduate School of Business Administration, Division of research), by permission of the publisher. Copyright 1975 by The University of Michigan. All rights reserved.

The purpose of this article, therefore, is to assist in understanding the fundamentals of the system by (a) explaining the basic theory of the case method, (b) indicating the respective roles of instructor and students in the classroom, and (c) suggesting how to study and recite.

This article might be assigned to students for study and class discussion, either at the start of a case course, or after one or a very few cases have been discussed.

Those who understand the use of the case method in <u>law</u> courses should be informed that the case method as used in <u>business</u> courses is quite different, although it appears similar. No business experiences and no written cases based on them have the authority of a law case decided by a high court. Moreover, since many of the business experiences are written in the form of problems without solutions, rather than complete statements which carry a business story through to its end, the method might more accurately be called "the <u>problem</u> method" than "the <u>case</u> method."

UNDERSTANDING THE METHOD

The first step in understanding this method of teaching is to realize that there really are two completely different methods of teaching by the use of business cases or problems. One may be called the <u>lecture method of case instruction.</u> In this method, the teacher assigns problems for study. He may or may not open the class by asking some student a question. Even if he does so, he does not permit the student recitation to last long; then or at the very opening of the class, he starts to lecture, basing his lecture on the assigned problem or problems. This method of instruction is not without its merits, but they are not those of the second method; they are those of the lecture method.

The second method is the <u>class recitation case method.</u> In this method, the instructor talks very little. He evokes discussion from the members of the class and they do most of the talking. He may pit members of the class against one another with respect to their opinions, or he may question the students himself. Key questions in this method of instruction are likely to include these: What do you consider to be the real problem in this case? What do you consider to be the important questions to answer in the problem? What would you do if you were the business executive responsible for making a decision or preparing a plan in this situation? Why would you make this decision, or select this plan instead of doing something else? In this kind of questioning, if there are any relevant accounting, statistical, or mathematical calculations, the teacher expects the students to have made them, and to be prepared to state clearly the nature and content of his calculations.

The significant characteristic is that the students are required to analyze the problem, and be prepared to present and defend their analysis in the classroom. They know this in advance and, therefore, they understand that the method of preparing for the class is to analyze the assigned problems thoroughly.

It is clear, of course, that students cannot reason effectively about business problems unless they have a satisfactory background of understanding in connection with the problem. The statement of the problem may include background information, or it may be obtained from a standard declaratory textbook.

BENEFITS TO STUDENTS

The pedagogical theory of the case method of instruction can be described as <u>acquiring vicarious experience</u>. Since it is not possible for the students to work in all of the various business firms involved in dozens of cases, this teaching method figuratively brings the firms into the classroom, and lets the students, in imagination, occupy the chairs of business executives. An adage says that experience is the best teacher, if it does not cost too dear. The case method is one way of providing the experience at modest cost. If, for example, a student makes a poor decision, which in real life would have cost millions of dollars, he will learn about his error in the classroom without the massive loss.

The significance of experience, of course, is that few problems are absolutely unique, and skill in handling them can be acquired by experience. There are certain common characteristics of problems and of the ways of going about solving them. If this were not true, it would make no difference to a patient whether he was operated on by a surgeon performing his first operation, or by a doctor performing his thousandth operation. So it is with business and other forms of human activity that involve action by a person. Experience enhances applicable skills.

Another way of describing the pedagogical theory is to say that it is a kind of daily practice in wrestling with problems. A man cannot learn to wrestle physically merely by reading an excellent book on the subject. The book may help; but there is no substitute for practice. The members of the wrestling team practice daily so as to improve their performance in each contest.

The problem method of studying business administration provides this daily wrestle with problems. This daily exercise supplies not only information and understanding about specific types of business problems but also provides practice in the technique of solving problems.

IT'S THE EXERCISE THAT COUNTS

If students understand that this daily wrestle with problems is the purpose of this method of instruction they are likely to cease to be bothered by something that puzzles and bewilders many serious students, accustomed as they have been to declaratory textbooks and definite lecture statements. In a case course, the students find that often the discussion and analysis of the business problem do not produce any "answer." The problem is discussed pro and con. Various considerations and relevant aspects of the situation are analyzed. In the end, a good argument can be made for one decision or the other, or one program or another. When the class discussion concludes at this point, the student may feel confused and perhaps even cheated.

The fact is that for this kind of teaching-learning process, the type of problem just described is frequently ideal. The reason is that a business problem whose analysis leads to a clearcut, definite, and positive solution is likely to be so simple and, therefore, so easy to analyze as not to present much of a challenge to keen students. Just as a hopelessly one-sided question does not provide a suitable subject for interscholastic debates, so a business problem to which the solution is really clear is unlikely to provide much mental exercise in reaching the solution. The important thing for the student to understand is that it is the <u>hard exercise that counts rather than reaching a</u> <u>"right answer."</u>

All this applies, of course, to the classroom. In actual business life, business executives have to bat higher than professional baseball players. An average substantially above .500 is necessary for business success. In legal circles, it is said that hard cases make bad law. They probably do. But in the study of business administration, hard problems--those without plain and clear solutions--provide the toughest exercise, and raise the later business batting average.

VARIETIES OF CASES

Lest the impression be given that there is but one standard pattern of cases--in terms of their nature, objectives, and use--let it be emphasized that this is not true. Some cases are short--perhaps a page or less. Other cases are longer and some of them are very long, running to scores of pages. Some are simple, some are complex; and the short ones are not necessarily the simple ones nor the long ones the complex. In some cases the issue or problem in the business situation is clearly defined. In other cases--ordinarily the longer ones--the point of the case is to discover what the problem is and then to proceed to discuss solutions. In such a case the description of the situation is likely to be lengthy and to contain much information that is irrelevant.

RECORDING THE "LESSONS OF EXPERIENCE"

The effectiveness of the case method can be enhanced considerably by engaging in a type of exercise which seems to be rather rare. This exercise is that of drawing from each case some <u>principles</u> in the form of currently useful generalizations or rules of action, or ways of thinking. In order to do this, it is necessary simply that at the end of the discussion, class members be invited to suggest the principles that can be learned from the problem that has been analyzed. Each principle that is suggested should be subjected immediately to scrutiny by other class members in order to determine whether they agree that the principle is, in fact, sound. This discussion itself is illuminating. Moreover, it is likely to be surprising how many useful generalizations the members of a class can derive from a problem, and can agree on as being valid. To the ones suggested by class members, the teacher may wish to add some of his own. In any event, if at the conclusion of the discussion, members of the class write down the generalizations thus agreed upon as the "lessons of experience" they increase the definiteness of what they have learned from this kind of study.

THE TEACHER'S ROLE

Since the class recitation case method involves very little talking by the teacher, it might be supposed that this type of teaching is easy, and requires little preparation. Not so. It is a very different kind of activity from lecturing. For one thing, it requires intense concentration on the part of the instructor on what the student is saying. Inasmuch as it is important to permit--perhaps even to require--the student to go ahead with a suitably lengthy statement discussing the question that he has been asked, the teacher may even find it necessary to take notes on what the student is saying so that he will not have forgotten points on which he wishes to comment, or wishes to secure comment from some other student, by the time the student has finished his statement. Successful teaching by this method requires that the teacher study the case thoroughly in advance, work through the analysis completely, plan the questions to be asked, and the reactions to be sought, depending on the type of responses obtained from the students. If the instructor is undertaking to record grades on oral recitations, he may find that notes taken on the various student comments will help him to determine the grades to be assigned as he ponders the discussion in his office, after class.

The case method of instruction is valuable in helping the teacher to avoid a graduate retreat into an academic ivory tower. First, teaching actual business cases keeps his thinking practical. Second, if he, himself, gathers and writes cases, this activity brings him into contact with businessmen and business firms, and provides firsthand acquaintance with their problems. Third, preparing cases from classroom use sharpens the teacher's concept of the use of cases as a pedagogical method, and helps him to clarify the objectives of his instruction and the aims of his course.

CLASSROOM TECHNIQUES IN TEACHING BY THE CASE METHOD

RAM CHARAN
Boston University

Since the pioneering of the case method at the Harvard Business School in the 1920's, several authors have written extensively on its use in teaching management courses. Most of this literature deals with the adequacy and inadequacy of the case method and gives helpful hints on case writing, course design, preparation of course outlines, and selection of course material. This article builds on that foundation and describes one approach to conducting successful classroom discussions in teaching business policy courses. This approach is also applicable to other areas such as marketing and finance. Since many management professors seem to prefer teaching by cases, this discussion may stimulate teachers to examine their total teaching proces and to discover new insights.

The proposed classroom techniques do not preclude the use of other classroom methods such as lectures, group projects, negotiating sessions, management games, audio-visual presentations, and student-run simulations of actual management situations. Nor is the proposed technique the only way to teach cases. To an extent, teaching is a function of individual style, but a course requires more than a teacher with an amusing or charismatic personality; behind an effective course is a strong organizational framework. The longer the course, the more necessary this framework becomes. If the case method is to be used effectively, an instructor must go through three organizational steps: (a) course design; (b) class preparation; and (c) method of conducting class discussions.

COURSE DESIGN

The success of each class session depends in part on the strength of the course design and clearly delineated operational objectives. Development of course design involves making decisions regarding the selection and sequencing of materials, the speed at which they are to be covered, the pace of each

---

This remarkable essay appeared in the July 1976 issue of the *Academy of Management Review.* Permission for its reproduction has been granted by the Academy of Management. Copyright 1976 by the Academy of Management.

session, and the nature and extent of the assignments. A successful course outline should be structured around a framework that satisfies the objectives in a manner the students can grasp. It is useful to divide the course into three to five conceptual blocks per twenty session term. These blocks help to establish the pace and continuity of the course and to aid an instructor in selecting appropriate points in the term to summarize and relate the various concepts. By drafting a course outline session by session, an instructor will have a clear picture of those insights and concepts which students should master in each session, and how each session will build on the previous session.

The instructor should select and sequence the case materials carefully, recognizing that if students find the cases interesting, they will more readily absorb course concepts. Students seem to prefer short cases regarding recent situations. In selecting materials for assignments, the teacher must consider how much class preparation time is available to the students. If an instructor significantly over- or under-estimates the students' preparation time, course effectiveness is likely to suffer. The nature and timing of written assignments is crucial for feedback. A requirement of two or three single-page answers to assignments early in the term will encourage students to internalize relevant concepts and to receive feedback about their progress. Moreover, the instructor will receive feedback on how effectively he or she is teaching and pacing the course.

In constructing the course outline, the teacher must know how the material relates to the curriculum and what courses the students have completed. In a business policy course, for example, the instructor can estimate on the basis of information from the registrar if there are students who are weak in marketing, accounting, or finance, and offer catch-up lectures or background readings for these students.

Seating arrangements and acoustics are important in case teaching. Too many permanently empty seats can inhibit discussion, and a classroom that is too large will distort voices. Limited blackboard space can cramp an instructor's teaching technique. Other distractions, such as a prominent clock over the blackboard, should be avoided. It is the teacher's responsibility to get the right type of classroom, large enough to seat everyone comfortably, but small enough for spirited debate in a friendly, informal atmosphere.

PREPARATION FOR CLASS

The instructor who is to be an effective discussion leader must have a thorough knowledge of the case to be taught. The instructor should begin by preparing the case as a student would, carefully reading, analyzing, and re-reading it and projecting as many significant dimensions of the case as possible. But he or she must go beyond knowing the case well; the instructor should internalize the case to the extent of being prepared to conduct class without having to rely on notes. Contacting the case writer, who often knows far more about the situation than appears in the final version of the case and its teaching notes, is an excellent way to gain additional insights. Discussing the case with colleagues who have taught it previously or who might be interested in the case situation, may lead to other insights. Further information about a company can be found in its annual reports and in publications such as *Fortune* or *The Wall Street Journal.* An added perspective might be gained by inviting to class an executive of the company being discussed.

Developing assignment questions for students and projecting possible responses will assist the instructor in keeping the session running smoothly and logically. Because it is not possible to foresee all responses, and because it is desirable to encourage originality and spontaneity, the assignment questions should serve as an outline for discussion rather than a script to which the instructor is tied.

Assignment questions should be consistent with course and session objectives, starting from questions which only require the student to draw together case data, and building to those which require making a judgment and developing an argument in its support. Assignment questions are useful as the "key" to starting class discussion or as the "opener" to introducing central concepts. Questions should be designed to fit objectives, rather than relying on questions presented in the teacher's manual.

It may be helpful in preparation and teaching to approach each class session in terms of sequential segments; for example, in a business policy session there might be key environmental trends, strategy definition, criteria for evaluating strategy, and recommendations for action. These segments will help the teacher effectively organize the concepts on available blackboard space and maintain control over the flow of class discussion. In projecting the segments, the teacher prepares the session objectives in terms of one or two central concepts and supporting ideas. The central concepts should be the focus of discussion in the classroom and should be related to concepts learned in previous cases. If classes are prepared in overlapping sets of two or more, session-to-session movement will be smooth, and continuity among sessions assured.

CLASSROOM PEDAGOGY

Administrative matters usually take up a significant part of the first class session. On the first day each student should be asked to fill out a card to provide relevant data about age, academic background, business experience, area of special interest, and career goals. The class cards are a convenient tool for learning to list names and faces, and for recording a student's contribution through the term as well as his or her progress and need for improvement. The cards should be reviewed before each class to see who might possess a particular competency in the case situation to be taught and might be a good candidate for opening the class discussion. At the conclusion of every session, each student's contribution should be recorded on his or her card. The process allows the instructor to freshen his or her memory of each student and to assign individual grades for class participation which generally account for as much as 40 to 50 percent of the final grade. The process helps the instructor to identify students who may require more challenge, more encouragement, or private counseling. As the term progresses, the instructor's sensitivity to class composition and to the students' progress may lead to further modifications in pacing and sequencing teaching material.

A permanent seating arrangement should be established on the first day of class, to help students and instructor connect names with comments. A seating chart and a list of each student's address and phone number should be distributed to class members in order to encourage the discussion of materials and written assignments outside of class.

All students should have name plates, to increase free interchange and heighten the students' sense of responsibility for participation. If the school does not provide name plates, the instructor could make paper and felt tip markers available to make them. The teacher should address students consistently by either first name or last, since class members might misinterpret varying forms of address as favoring some students and slighting others.

The instructor must explain rules governing homework preparation, attendance, class participation, written assignments, and examinations at the outset of the course. It is helpful to students when one is specific about the nature and timing of written assignments and examinations described in the syllabus distributed on the first day. Conflicts with requirements in other courses can then be dealt with far in advance of deadlines.

In the first session the instructor would also find it worthwhile to explain grading procedures, being frank about the system of rewards and impressing upon students that they will be expected to study the cases thoroughly before coming to class so that they are prepared to participate in the discussion. Skill in case analysis is developed through regular preparation and defense of one's views, rather than occasional massive doses of overwork that examination-based lecture method courses frequently encourage.

On the first day, students should be asked to form small study groups which meet weekly to discuss cases prior to class. These groups of six to eight members may be given guidance on how to conduct their business, what is expected of them, and how they might aid in the growth and development of individual members to achieve a high quality of class discussion. Carefully designed group assignments should promote intra-group cohesiveness. The instructor may visit each group or join its members for lunch during the first three to four weeks of the term. This will assist the instructor in getting to know the students and indicate commitment to the groups.

Consistent with insistence upon careful case preparation, the instructor should spend the remainder of the first class session discussing the assignment prepared for that day. In most instances assignments can be included in registration case packets. This first class discussion sets the tone for the remainder of the term by demonstrating that assignments must be prepared and how they must be prepared.

ARRIVING EARLY

The instructor should arrive in the classroom a few minutes before each class session to talk with early arrivals, to assess the class mood, to determine if students thought the case was especially difficult, and to determine if an important event might have kept some students from preparing. This makes it possible to adjust the presentation before class begins, by changing the series of questions or by presenting case data to begin the discussion. The blackboard should be clean and there should be adequate teaching aids such as chalk, erasers, and when necessary, a movie projector. Color chalk might be useful during the class discussion to highlight and coordinate important points. Comments written on the blackboard can be emphasized by underlining and can be related by circling in the same color.

THE BLACKBOARD

The instructor should enter the classroom with a clear picture of how the blackboard should look when a session ends. Blackboard space should be divided into several sections, one for each sequential segment of the class session. This will facilitate the recording of important concepts that may not emerge in a logical order. Students should be encouraged to take notes from the blackboard to help retain information and to aid in class preparation. Judicious use of the blackboard can increase the level of class discussion. The recording of worthwhile comments becomes reinforcing to the students. It is wise to move periodically to the rear of the classroom to make certain that one's handwriting is legible.

CONDUCTING CLASS

By using one or more of the following approaches, the direction of the class discussion can be structured.

Discussion Question Format - When the class begins, the instructor may call the names of the two students who have been chosen to open the class (the students chosen normally do not know the instructor's choice ahead of time). Each is asked a separate question drawn from the prepared assignment. By having initial questions limited to those assigned, students learn that homework preparation pays off.

The quality of the opening is of primary importance, because a good initial contribution made by well-prepared students can substantially improve the depth of the class session. The instructor can help insure a successful opening by carefully choosing the two students who begin each class, reviewing the class cards and seating chart to identify the most appropriate choice.

Two criteria are helpful in selecting these two students. First, their backgrounds should be different, if not opposite. If they have widely divergent experience and perspectives, they are likely to set the broadest possible foundation for subsequent class discussion. Second, they should be sitting far enough apart in the classroom that they physically seem to envelop most of the class. The ideal arrangement, which is not always possible, is to have the two students and the two edges of the blackboard form the four points of a large quadrangle, surrounding most of the class within its imaginary bounds. Since the opening contributors become the focus of the class session they initiate, it is not a good practice to select the same students to open discussion more than once or twice in the term.

After the opening contributors are designated and appropriate questions asked, the students are given a few minutes to collect their thoughts, while the instructor summarizes what had been accomplished previously and relates it to what will follow in a way that provides the opening contributors a natural lead. The instructor then turns the floor over to one of the two students, who makes his or her presentation on the assigned question(s). The opening contribution can be recorded on the blackboard according to the instructor's predesigned segmentation of the class discussion and the corresponding segmentation of the blackboard space. Opening contributions are seldom interrupted unless there is a need to clarify. Then, the second student is told to build on the contribution of the first and note any disagreements with the position; other class members are encouraged to join in, and the discussion progresses to other assignment questions.

It is important to demand excellence of two opening contributors, challenging their supported statements and encouraging them in order to test their capacities. The instructor should make the contributors excel without embarrassing them, and through insistent and incisive questioning, let the other students know that their own preparation and presentations will also be closely scrutinized and that outstanding work will be rewarded. This understanding will lead to improved preparation, which will inevitably improve the quality of class discussion.

If the student originally called upon to open class discussion is unprepared, the instructor should quickly call on another student. Embarrassing a student in front of the class wastes class time and is a sure way to tune a student out for the rest of the term. The instructor should discuss the situation privately with the unprepared student and decide on an appropriate way for the student to make up the missed assignment. The instructor must make it clear that unprepared students will not be rewarded.

The instructor should also think of subtle ways to reward a student for a strong opening contribution, so that the good student will not lose interest. One should return to the good points made, relate them to the theme of the session, and remind the class of who made them. A student's excellent work should be rewarded in front of peers and poor work should be punished in privacy.

The Vote Format - Some cases lead to clear cut "yes" or "no" decisions. A few may lead to three or four mutually exclusive or clear cut decisions. In such situations the instructor can heighten the students' commitment to a decision by having them vote. During the vote, the instructor should take note of those who are taking an "unpopular" view or who are on the minority side as well as those who are abstaining. The instructor usually draws a laugh upon asking, "Who are the diplomats? Who did not vote?"

The two opening contributors can then be chosen on the spot, usually a student representing the minority viewpoint as the first opener and the second contributor from the majority. The tone of the discussion is then set and contributors are encouraged to argue persuasively in order to influence peers to change their positions on the issue. Some students will change their minds, and their explanations for the change often prove to be a tremendous learning experience. Before class is concluded, the teacher should take another vote to determine whether the class is shifting its position.

Role Playing Format - Prior to class or spontaneously, class members can be assigned different managerial roles and asked to discuss a case from the viewpoint of their assigned roles. Such an approach is likely to bring out the interpersonal aspects of the situation more effectively than other formats. While role playing is often exciting, it may be inefficient because it is extremely time-consuming. For this approach to be effective, the instructor should summarize or ask students to summarize the key insights and concepts derived from such a class discussion.

Audio-Visual Format - Another format which is especially useful toward the end of the course is to have small study groups tape their case analyses. The tapes can be evaluated either by the group that made the tape or by the entire class. Such presentations provide students an opportunity to work in groups, supplement the preparation they must do for the comprehensive written analysis of cases, and improve their presentation skills. In the absence of audio-visual taping equipment, the same objectives can be achieved by having students make flip-charts or slide presentations for class review.

Additional techniques that are useful in facilitating class discussion include the following:

Use of Data - If a case being studied is particularly complex, the level of analysis can be improved by recording selected rudimentary or partially processed data from the case on the blackboard before the discussion begins. The students then can begin analysis immediately without rehashing the case data. This technique is particularly helpful toward the end of the term. By this time, the class has demonstrated its capacity to identify, relate and discriminate key facts and evidence from the case.

Leading Discussion - The instructor must exercise judgement in encouraging reticent participants and curbing over-zealous ones. When a discussion is being monopolized, the teacher should tactfully revitalize waning interest by intensively questioning the monopolizer until that student recognizes the fallacy of his or her arguments, or by stopping the individual, asking him or her to restate a point succinctly, and then asking another class member to respond to that point. Debate around the same or another question can then continue, with increased alertness of the entire class and with students encouraged to contribute by listening as well as by speaking.

In leading discussion, the instructor should avoid speaking in a dull monotone. By changing the volume and pitch of one's voice at appropriate points, one can hold the attention of the students and orchestrate the movement of class discussion.

Summarizing - To keep the discussion flowing, the instructor should summarize periodically and introduce carefully planned questions to highlight certain concepts. For example, when one of the conceptual blocks has been completed, the instructor should summarize what has been accomplished up to that point in the term and what is to come next. This imposes substance and continuity on the course design. During each session there should be an opening summary, a body, and a concluding summary. The concluding summary is particularly important, for it provides a sense of where the class has been on a given day and where it is going.

Toward the end of a session, the instructor may ask the student who opened the class, "Where have we been? What do you think about that now? Has your decision changed?" Sometimes a reversal on the part of a class opener, combined with the stated rationale for the changed position, can be an effective teaching device.

Pet Answers - While the instructor has thought through most of the relevant issues which might surface during the class discussion and has a conceptual understanding of an overall flow of the discussion, he or she should be careful not to "fish" for pet answers. Otherwise students might sense that they are being manipulated.

Sample Student Papers - During the early part of the term, the instructor might distribute and discuss several student papers concerning the case being discussed. Reviewing the work of their colleagues helps students understand what is expected of them on written assignments.

Dominant Pockets of Contribution - Occasionally, the class seating is such that, within two or three sessions, the instructor discovers that one geographical section of the class is more dominant in class contribution than the rest of the class. Regular geographical imbalance in class contributions or regular dominance of contribution by a few individuals tends to make class discussion less effective. The former should be altered by changing the seating arrangement and the latter controlled by posing to over-zealous participants difficult questions toward the end of the class, making them realize the value of listening.

THE ROUGH SPOTS

A frustrating session that is not progressing smoothly may be handled in different ways. First, the instructor may take an active role in case analysis in an attempt to rekindle interest by encouraging students to react to his or her statements. Another technique is to let a disappointing session run its course, summarize what was discussed and how the discussion could have been improved, and leave the class with the key question designed to lead to the instructor's original objectives. At the beginning of the next session, the same question may be raised to make certain that concepts imparted in the previous session were understood.

SPECIAL CASES

As the term progresses, cases will become more complex, and the instructor's role will be difficult. To avoid the type of systematic review of details which often occurs as cases become more difficult, the instructor should designate opening contributors ahead of time. In this instance, the opening contributors would present case data on the blackboard, quickly dispensing with rudimentary facts and allowing the discussion to proceed on a higher level of analysis. As an alternative, the instructor may choose to outline these data on the board or to devise the lesson plan so that factual data are elicited early in the class session.

When a case is so rich that it merits several sessions, the instructor should outline the pace of discussion at the beginning of the first session, describe how much material will be covered in each session, advise the students to take careful notes, and summarize the entire discussion at the end of the last session at which the case was discussed.

At the conclusion of each class, the instructor should review the discussion. While his memory of the session is still fresh, he or she should record on the class cards information about outstanding contributions made that day and take note of any new ideas the students presented.

In preparing a case for presentation to a new group of students, the instructor can benefit from having taught the case previously. But each time the instructor teaches a case, the entire process of case preparation should be repeated. One should not rely on old notes or assignment questions, for each term the makeup of the class will be different, the case's relationship to other materials may vary, and the environment may not be the same.

Finally, the instructor should be introspective with regard to his or her performance as a teacher. One should analyze the session's weak points and ask what concepts need to be reemphasized. One should consider whether or not teaching strategies need modification for the next session, as well as giving thought to which students need more probing, attention, or encouragement. In addition the instructor should evaluate the session and the materials used in the context of the conceptual block and overall course design to creatively rethink whether the case material, the course design, or the preparation for that session in the future need modification. At several points during a term, an instructor could question the effectiveness of integration among the three components: course design, class preparation, and classroom pedagogy.

CONCLUSION

Teaching by the case method is a continuing process in which the instructor is totally absorbed as initiator, director, participant, and motivator. To be effective in each of these roles, the teaching process must effectively integrate the course design, class preparation, and conduct of each class session, for the quality of each session is dependent upon the design and the classroom pedagogy.

CHARLES HOFER'S PRESENTATION ARRAY

	5	4	3	2	1	Weight	Total
Identification of Issues							
Accurate						3	
Complete						2	
Analysis of Issues							
Rationale provided						2	
Alternatives given						2	
Evaluation and choice						1	
Plan of Action							
Comprehensive						1	
Specific						1	
Time sequence indicated						1	
Consequences considered						1	
Workable						2	
Presentation							
Clarity and precision						1	
Organization						1	
Overall impact						2	

TOTAL $\overline{20}$

PEER EVALUATION OF ORAL CASE PRESENTATION

Student Evaluation of _____

(Case Name)

1. Was the presentation effectively organized?

2. Was the transition between topics smooth and orderly?

3. Were the significant issues discussed?

4. Were the conclusions supported with facts?

5. Does the strategy meet the objectives of the firm?

6. Was the proposed solution attainable?

7. Was the implementing plan sensible?

8. Were your questions adequately answered?

9. As the boss, would you have bought the package?

10. Rate each speaker as 1. Excellent; 2. Good; 3. Fair;
    4. Poor; 5. Lousy

	Appearance	Impact	Credibility	Knowledge
#1				
#2				
#3				
#4				
#5				
#6				

11. If the group were to make another presentation, what helpful suggestions would you offer them?

GUIDELINES FOR WRITTEN CASES

This class requires that you provide case analyses. These guidelines are intended to assist and direct you.

Generally, your analysis of any case should be written as a memorandum. Assume that we have a management consulting firm and that I am your immediate superior. For each case, I have asked you to review and analyze the situation of the case and to offer your recommendations for action. The purpose of the memorandum is to communicate your recommendations and reasons therefor.

In any case there is no perfectly correct answer. Your answer (recommendation) will come from your analysis. Thus, your grade is based upon (1) the clarity of the logic that underlies your recommendation, (2) the use of the facts in the case to support your recommendation, and (3) the use of appropriate course material in your outline.

FORM REQUIREMENTS

Because communicating your ideas is the basic element of the written analyses, and because the assumption of the assignment is that you are submitting a report to a decision -maker who has limited time to read and understand your recommendations, there are stringent requirements on your memorandum. These are:

1. Do not waste paper by having binders, title pages, cover sheets, or any other pieces of paper that are not a direct part of your memo.

2. Your memo must be typed. A handwritten paper will reduce your grade one full grade level.

3. The memo must not exceed 5 typed, double-spaced pages. Exceeding 5 pages reduces your grade one-third of a grade level for each page in excess of 5 pages.

4. Correct spelling and proper grammar are essential. Each group of five spelling errors and each group of three grammatical errors reduces your grade one full grade level.

5.Late papers will not be accepted unless prearranged in advance of the due date.

STRUCTURE REQUIREMENTS

Begin your memorandum with this basic information:

<u>Example</u>

DATE:
FROM: Your name
TO:
SUBJECT: Skyway Services Company

The opening paragraph should contain a brief and general description of the problem being considered, and at the end of the paragraph, a concise statement of your recommendation for resolving the problem, single spaced. For example:

This memorandum relates to the question of whether to expand or withdraw from our operations at Stewart airport. Our five year option as sales representative for Cessna (Beech or Piper) is nearing an end, and a decision at this time on our future activities at Stewart is imperative. <u>I recommend that we withdraw entirely from the Stewart airport.</u>

For emphasis, your recommendation <u>should be underscored</u> in the opening paragraph. Also in the opening paragraph is a statement of the "trigger" to the problem or decision (in the above example, the end of the five year option). In sum, then, the opening paragraph, not to exceed half a page, should contain:

(1) a brief and general statement of the problem or situation;
(2) the reason the decision is needed at this point; and,
(3) an underscored statement of your recommendation.

The remainder of your memo should consist of the reasons underlying your recommendation. Your reasons should be stated as a series of declarative statements which summarize your conclusions from and observations of the facts of the case. All conclusions should directly relate to your recommendation; they should support the resolution which you are suggesting. In terms of form, the conclusions should be <u>single-spaced</u> and <u>underscored</u> for emphasis.

Immediately following each conclusion should be the evidence (facts from the case) which led you to the preceding conclusion. Do not put opinions in this supporting evidence because opinions are conclusions. The only items to be included in supporting comments are facts which directly led to the particular observation. These facts should be <u>double-spaced</u>, and stated in complete sentence form.

Using the Skyway case as an example again, your first conclusion might be:

Without some major change in general aviation traffic the Stewart airport is not capable of supporting a profitable operation of our type.

After three years of exceptional growth, activity at the Stewart airport is now leveling off at approximately 140,000 plane movements per year. Traffic at Stewart grew 49%, 27% and 17% the first three years respectively but last year traffic increased only 2% (see Table on page 37). We have been continually losing $3000 to $5000 annually, so unless there is a major change in the level of traffic at Stewart, continued losses can be expected.

Notice that the conclusion is supported by the following facts and logic. Also, the conclusion goes back to support the recommendation.

The analysis then continues with a series of conclusion statements and the factual evidence that supports each conclusion. In total, the series of conclusions should present clear logic for your recommendation, and reading the evidence for each conclusion should provide adequate support for the conclusion.

As an optional part of the write-up, you can include a summary statement at the end, but do not sacrifice valuable space in order to make such as statement. Thus, your memo should be in the form of:

I. Basic Information
II. Opening Paragraph
III. Conclusions with Support
IV. Summary Statement (Optional)

PART II

TEACHING NOTES

ACCOMPANYING

CASES ON

ENTREPRENEURIAL

ORGANIZATIONS

BENNETT'S MACHINE SHOP, INC. (BMS)
TEACHING NOTE

TEACHING OBJECTIVES

This case follows an energetic, entrepreneurial engineer as he slides up and down the ladder of success without really knowing why. Specific objectives:

Visualize some of the problems endemic in many small companies.

Understand the need to carefully define one's business and mission.

See the necessity for strategic management in an entrepreneurial setting.

Determine possible courses of action.

USING THIS CASE

While lengthy, BMS has a writing style and flow which make for easy reading. Student interest should not be a problem. BMS is not suitable for an inclass exam but could support either a short report or a long report. It can literally be used anywhere in a course, depending on time available, instructor's desired depth of examination, or extent of coverage. It can be discussed in various settings. As a study in human behavior, it illustrates vividly how the values of management shape an enterprise, be it for better or for worse. It is a prime vehicle for illustrating the necessity to ask again the familiar question, what business are we in? It certainly belongs under the heading of formulation, with the conventional interplay of values, objectives, environment, and strategic advantage. It is not out of place in the implementation phase, when one can unravel happenings, functional elements, and luck to see how BMS has gotten to where it is. If used as a first case, it is moderately difficult; used otherwise, it should be a simple case.

SYNOPSIS

Pat Bennett, an engineer by education, by degrees moved into an automotive machine shop and repair business. Start-up is a struggle, but then came boom years, followed by the inevitable bust. Through it all there is really no plan, merely a reaction to events. It is true that no amount of planning beats a little dumb luck, but when luck runs out, the devil has his due. Pat flits from crag to crag, sometimes successfully, sometimes not, without ever fully realizing the cause of his ups and

---

This note reflects a prior Note by and conversations with the casewriter.

downs. Pat is so busy plastering up the cracks that one wonders if BMS will ever be able to level its bubbles.

OUTCOME

By January 1988 things were beginning to look up for Pat. He was able to extend his contract with Boeing, though at reduced rates. At the casewriter's suggestion, he began to focus more on his core business, engine rebuilding and installation. He actively supervised the operation, and his orders showed it. Emboldened, he decided to go into the repairing of cracked cylinder heads. One has to wonder if Pat is about to watch the replay of the same old script without even realizing it.

TEACHING APPROACHES TO THIS CASE

The instructor's problem here will be to try to turn student consideration back to the strategic issues. The word "problem" is used advisedly because the case reads so easily that it is hard to distinguish forest from trees, especially when there are so many interesting trees. Born tinkerers that Americans are, it is to get lost in wrist pins, machines, buildings, people and advertising without stopping to realize that all these fun things have to be joined together. Cater to the functional areas, and then ask how the problems in those areas arose. What do these problems prove? If nothing else, that BMS, like little Topsy, just grew. There was no coherent plan. If someone maintains to the contrary, ask for proof. Alternatively, ask for a statement of mission and definition of business, and then try to trace that or those. It can't be done very neatly. Or start with the Appendix and ask how the interview with Pat points up the problems in the case.

CASE ANALYSIS

STRATEGIC MANAGEMENT ELEMENTS:
MISSION, GOALS, AND OBJECTIVES

BMS has no enunciated <u>mission.</u> Pat states that "I already had this machine shop idea," but the idea is never fleshed out. What in effect that means is that Pat never has a plan, because if you don't know where you're going, it makes no difference how you get there. The other side of the coin says that's not all bad because Pat as an entrepreneur has no inhibitions-if it looks good and can be done profitably, why not? An implicit <u>goal</u> is survival and profitability, which means haphazard growth if that growth will help the bottom line. Pat talks vaguely in the Appendix about some free time for the things he wants to do and achieving a net profit of $70,000 to $100,000 a year. These are the only figures set as profits, and there seem to be no firm quantitative goals in any area. Viewed in the abstract, this is somewhat understandable because entrepreneurs of course want to operate profitably but are more taken with the physical manifestations of an idea than such mundane mattrs as quantitative goals. As we read BMS, there are no true _objectives_, and certainly nothing quantifiable.

STRATEGISTS

Pat Bennett is the obvious entrepreneur who will pursue an idea single mindedly without ever stepping back to examine the big picture. He is technically qualified, skilled at his work, honest, and not averse to long hours. He's a doer, however, not a true thinker, much more given to action than to thought, and prone to a direction without considering all factors. He has boundless selfconfidence and once seized with an idea, will pursue it tenaciously. He seems dedicated to quality work and apparently enjoys a good reputation, because he has never really had to contribute any equity funds to his business. He can make a tough decision and follow through without qualms. He has an ambivalence reflected in the Appendix - while he professes a loyalty to and concern for his workers, he wonders if his feelings are reciprocated, without stopping to realize that what he sees is a reflection of his lack of organization.

ENVIRONMENTAL ANALYSIS

SOCIOECONOMIC SECTOR. While BMS is in a somewhat impecunious area of Louisiana (Table 1 refers), the business seems relatively immune to economic fluctuations. Since its business is repair/rebuild, it can be argued that BMS enjoys a contracyclical effect: consumers are far more likely to repair in bad times than they are to replace. There are no deep social forces which pressure BMS; such forces as are are purely local, as when Pat's landlord complains of Pat's lack of good housekeeping.

TECNOLOGICAL AND GOVERNMENT SECTORS. BMS enjoys a rather stable technology. While motor technology is not static-witness transverse engines and computer controlled systems - the advances are not so great that BMS is left behind. There is enough skill and ingenuity in the company to profit from Boeing contracts. While defense appropriations will never decline precipitousely, it does not follow that money will automatically flow to Boeing. While Boeing work may be lucrative for Pat, it has no sure permanence; when work is bid rather than sole sourced, Pat may or may not be the successful bidder.

INDUSTRY THREATS AND OPPORTUNITIES. Quality work, decent _prices_ and rapid response have earned BMS a good reputation. It seems not to lack for _customers_, even though its marketing leaves much to be desired. Its market is not identified in any detail but is segmented by the company's type of work. Pat may not know it, but BMS has a very decent niche. Not realizing that, however, Pat is more given to chasing new opportunities than in taking care of the store. He was slow to realize that his business is highly personalized, hence requires more than just a modicum of passing attention. _Customers_ and _suppliers_ seem diverse and plentiful, and there appear no shortages of raw materials or labor. BMS recognizes some <u>competitors</u> for engine sales, but there is no local automobile service shop which rebuilds engines. Barriers to entry and skill requirements appear minimal, so there should be potential competitors. Here the case is silent, so we reason that Pat's entrenched position discourages local competition. While his customers are obviously mobile, it stands to reason that his work and pricing are such that customers will seek him out rather than look for other shops.

STRATEGIC ADVANTAGE PROFILE

<u>CORPORATE RESOURCES AND PERSONNEL</u>. BMS is well established and appears to have a solid reputation built on service and quality. It has almost succeeded in spite of itself since it lacks effective <u>organizational structure;</u> that is no wonder, since BMS has no <u>strategic management system</u>. <u>Employee</u> relations are satisfactory, apparently made so by a lack of local competition for the skilled labor the shop requires. Pat trains for his needs and compensates well enough to retain the personnel he has trained. The <u>personnel system</u> is what one would expect in a small, action-oriented business: minimal training, informal recruitment, no job standards, no appraisal apparatus, etc. It could be argued that the entire operation is so uncomplicated that informality should rule.

<u>FINANCE AND ACCOUNTING</u>. Pat boasts that from 1972 on, he contributed no equity funds to his business. Others were willing to finance his operations, and Pat claimed super-productive years with no money problems until 1985. After that the <u>lack of planning</u> showed itself, and the roof fell in. One could find no comfort in 1985's <u>current ratio</u> of .42 or <u>quick ratio</u> of .1, nor in the 1% <u>return on sales</u> in 1986. <u>Direct costs</u> 1985-87 do not seem to vary unreasonably, but <u>GPA expenses</u> rise almost 20%. The financial picture is glum as income tails off in 1986. Forgetting how he had succeeded-rebuilding engines-he loaded himself with debt in 1985 to branch off into engine installation. The lesson was costly, since retiring notes the next year drastically reduced net income and caused Pat to lose sight of his labor costs. Accounting is done on an acquaintance basis after Pat lost patience with his CPA firms. One has to wonder if the changes were effective: inventory, for instance, is pegged at $45,436 for three years. That borders on the incredible and raises questions about the effectiveness of whatever <u>inventory control</u> procedures exist. Fortunately, BMS succeeds in spite of itself when a lucrative Boeing contract falls into Pat's lap, obscuring the fact that Pat really can't divide his time effectively.

<u>MARKETING</u>. One could hardly accuse BMS of marketing. Pat realized early on that a new machine shop spelled opportunity in Lake Charles, and so it did. There is no indication of <u>marketing research,</u> just entrepreneurial hunch. Given the apparent lack of serious local <u>competition</u> and a combination of <u>good work</u> and a <u>fair price</u>, BMS practically sells itself. Pat runs television spots and does occasional radio advertising, but he seems not to

know how effective those efforts are. Discount specials, run in slow times, seem fruitful, but again Pat seems almost indifferent to the favorable results. Competitive prices and quality work, not any particular marketing expertise, bring in the trade.

PRODUCTION AND OPERATIONS. BMS rebuilds engines, removes and replaces engines, and in 1987 lands a Boeing contract to sharpen tools. Labor seems abundant, willing, skillful and well paid. Equipment, labor and supplies do not seem to limit operations. The same cannot be said of facilities. The shop gives the impression of a happening rather than an organized facility. Engines are not a "clean" business, and perhaps for that reason there is scant incentive to be orderly. One worker is described as searching through a "waist-high pile" of connecting rods and pistons, and another locates an engine among several thousand "piled here and there around the shop...." Job costing is problematical since there are no parts tally procedures. It would have been quicker for a harassed mechanic simply to buy a part from a parts supplier, and as Pat noted "We had a terrible, terrible parts situation...out of control...." An effort was made to stop the buy problem, but there is no mention of a parts inventory, inventory control, or a more orderly work place. Dirt doesn't breed efficiency, and Pat admits to at least one effort to clean up the shop. There seems a lack of formal procedures, but things do get done. However, effectiveness and efficiency do not necessarily equate.

STRATEGIC ALTERNATIVES

A strategy of stability would give Pat time to plan and to better organize his business. He doesn't have to work harder, but he should work smarter. Expansion is Pat's middle name-go for it and worry about the details later. Expansion matches his values and perhaps better promises the income he desires, but overreaching himself has been disastrous in the past. Retrenchment promises little unless Pat can convert unneeded inventory into cash. A combination strategy might capture the best of all worlds.

CHOICE

A combination strategy of stability, retrenchment and then expansion is most feasible.

IMPLEMENTATION

Stability - BMS above all needs a strong dose of strategic management. Pat has to curb his natural instincts to act rather than think, decide what business he is in, and provide himself with a sensible plan of operation. Pat has moved more by hunch than design: in 1985 he opened a new operation without even considering the requirement for TLC that any new undertaking requires. He shut it, and then seized on a Boeing contract that looked like salvation personified. In doing so, he again neglected his core business. Without stopping and considering where he is going, he is foreordained to repeat past blunders. He can't do everything well, despite his competence in some areas, but saying it and believing it are worlds apart. He needs to focus on his core business, clean up his act and his shop, set objectives, write and enforce policies, etc. To do so is probably anathema to a free spirit like Pat Bennett who detests detail, shrugs off things he doesn't enjoy like planning, and would rather dirty his hands than spend that time thinking about the future. <u>Marketing research</u> would not be out of place and could act to ensure an effective ad campaign. Some <u>IE advice</u> from the local university would do wonders for the efficiency of his facility. Just one dedicated partsman with the very cheapest of computers would be worth his weight in gold. Pat would do well to set <u>objectives</u> and <u>performance standards,</u> for reasons too obvious to state.

A <u>strategic plan</u> would be of inestimable use to Pat - work smarter, not harder. A plan should help him in deciding <u>organization</u>; a GE-type chart isn't needed, but something better than by guess and by God certainly is. If he can once tie things down - and there surely seems no lack of business-he can be an entrepreneur to his heart's content. A decent plan would help him to distinguish between opportunity and no-no's.

Some <u>retrenchment</u>, especially in inventory, should be indicated. Thousands of engines? Waist high piles of parts? This area needs a searching look.

With a good plan, sensible policies, some organization, and decent control, BMS could embark on a strategy of <u>growth.</u> As noted, marketing research will help and simply cannot help but pay dividends. When Pat has stuck to his knitting, he has done well. He must realize that he has some practical limitations and cannot ignore them. Good planning will give him ample opportunity to pursue his niche strategy.

RECOMMENDED DISCUSSION QUESTIONS

1. Describe Pat Bennett's objectives. Are they realistic?

2. Describe Pat personally, restricting your discussion to those points which most affect the fortunes of BMS.

3. Describe his current strategy.

4. Are any changes in functional areas indicated? If so, what?

5. What is BMS' greatest need?

6. What should Pat do?

7. To what should one attribute Pat's problems?

8. Should Pat continue to operate his firm under Subchapter S?

ANALYSIS AND DISCUSSION

1. Describe Pat Bennett's objectives. Are they realistic?

Pat's objectives are hard to isolate. Generally, what students will come down to is the desire to make a profit. That's fairly evident. But there is more. The more thoughtful students will say that he wants primarily to be an entrepreneur, for whatever that means. Those two objectives are realistic. At the same time he seems to want to do whatever attracts him - and that isn't realistic. He can't have his cake and eat it, too.

2. Describe Pat personally, restricting your discussion to those points which most affect the fortunes of BMS.

We think this is a good discussion question because it encourages students to try to see how very much entrepreneurial values here affect BMS. Pat dislikes detail, except that which pertains to technical work. This makes him content with the big picture without ever realizing the house is built on sand. He brushes aside what he doesn't like: bookkeeping, housekeeping, piles of parts, etc. This makes for pleasure but not for efficiency. What are a thousand engines worth? Better yet, are they really needed? Pat is mechanically inclined (good) and likes to putter (bad). When he comes to work early, he does whatever pleases him, like grinding a crankshaft, rather than carefully planning out the day. He is a man of action, not thought. That's fine for getting out the work, but who then is left to plan? BMS gets the job done and done well, but its products seem more the work of happenstance and hungry, interested mechanics than of conscious design. Pat is given to doing what he most likes. Understandably it is his football, and it is his game, but his penchant for the immediate and his interest in daily operations obscure the need to put together a coherent strategy. While likeable, Pat tends to be quick tempered, witness the pot of paint. That plus an autocratic manner tend to dampen the ardor of personnel for improving operations-get on with the job and stay out of the way.

3. Describe his current strategy.

In a word, he really does what he likes. BMS has followed a grand strategy of growth, but it has been growth by accretion rather than by plan. Rebuilding and installing engines are his livelihood, but he does whatever else meets the mood of the moment. Essentially, his strategy seems one of happy drift.

4. Are any changes in functional areas indicated?

This question is calculated to bring a myriad of responses, so many that we have omitted listing them here. We mentioned some in our discussion of the Strategic Advantage Profile. If there are no immediate replies, ask the cost of an electric box, remembering that Pat said he had grinding machines in different rooms simply to avoid rigging another box (Figure 1 refers). Could there be a better use of space than that of sheltering used engines?

5. What is BMS' greatest need?

The need is simply for a strategy which starts with a succinct definition of Bennett's business and progresses through a thoughtful plan of operations. No business, however entrepreneurial, is immune to the need for strategic management.

6. What should Pat do?

See our comments under Implementation.

7. To what should one attribute Pat's problems?

You will get every conceivable answer here, so you will be faced with the need to reduce all to some common denominator. To us it seems that he simply can't allocate his time and attention wisely. He's a "do" man rather than a "think" man, and besides, putting out fires is more fun than bossing a strategy. The casewriter notes also that if Pat were to focus on his primary business, there would be fewer fires to attend.

8. Should Pat continue to operate his firm under Subchapter S?

Table 2 footnotes that BMS is a Sub S corporation. Taxwise, it is simply an earnings conduit into the pockets of Pat and Cheryl, who presumably file a joint return. The Sub S advantage to them is to be able to pay retirement, life insurance, health insurance, dental insurance, and the like (fringe benefits) out of pretax dollars and so doing, to lower their taxable income. Table 2 notes "Earnings reinvested." It is not clear, but presumably any funds left after withdrawals are plowed back into the business. Someone will point out that Sub S corporations cannot retain earnings and then draw attention to Table 3. Whatever earnings are depicted as retained cannot be in cash. A non-S corporation can retain earnings; if the figure becomes large, it can be justified on the grounds of business purposes - new plant, set asides for new equipment, etc. Without evidence to the contrary, Pat seems well advised to retain his Sub S designation until such time as a need to retain earnings in liquid form exists; he can drop the election at that time and become a straight corporation, but his tax picture will be quite different. Commencing in 1987, S corporations look better because individual tax rates will be lower than corporate rates in 1988. Further, S corporations escape the new corporate alternative minimum tax and also will be permitted to use the cash method of accounting.

DESIGNS, INC. (DI)
TEACHING NOTE

TEACHING OBJECTIVES

This case depicts two successful partners in a new women's sportswear business who complement each other well but find themselves at odds over which way best to continue their success. Specific objectives:

See how distinctive competence affects enterprise success.

Understand the reasons for success in a highly competitive business.

Differentiate between strategic and operational problems.

Be able to enumerate DI's strategic options.

Select the most appropriate option.

USING THIS CASE

DI is of medium length and can be regarded as moderately difficult. It flows easily and grips the average reader. The subject is not commonplace but again, it is not arcane. It is a success story which is guaranteed to hold student interest. It is suitable for either a short report or a long report and equally would make a good final problem for the instructor who prefers a case to the more traditional exam. It is an excellent case for discussion because it demonstrates that the immediate, easy decision is not necessarily the right one. The case can be used early in a course to help students sort out the real from the imagined in distinctive skills or it can be used in the middle of a course as an exercise in the formulation of strategy.

SYNOPSIS

Steve Cohen grew up in the garment business and in 1984 started a one man manufacturing operation. Since his background was in production, he teamed up with Robert Freeman, 21 years his senior, a marketer. They early discovered that private label work was profitable. They copied fast selling garments first for department stores and specialty shops and later for discount stores, too. They ran a lean and mean operation with enough finesse and skill to guarantee their customers considerable profit on popular items. Sales boomed.

This note draws on a prior Note by and conversations with the casewriter.

While both agree that DI should increase sales 50% annually over the next three years, they disagree as to how to achieve those increases. Freeman prefers to go as is, looking forward to DI's eventually being acquired by one of its customers. Cohen has no objection to selling but feels that DI has to diversify if it is to be an attractive acquisition.

OUTCOME

Freeman's ace in the hole was his list of contacts, a list never shared with Cohen. On a social occasion Freeman dropped dead of a massive heart attack. Cohen labored for two years to return DI to the position it had enjoyed at the time of Freeman's death. Business fell off badly but gradually came back. DI today is highly successful, doing what it always did. Cohen countered the problem of excess inventory, generated by fabric maker pressure, by starting a highly successful retail operation in his building.

TEACHING APPROACHES TO THIS CASE

DI is excellent for class discussion, and it lends itself to role playing. You can split the class, or you can let the class sort itself out as students identify with either Cohen or Freeman. Alternatively, you can play the devil's advocate, or since most tend to identify with the younger partner, you can either assume the role of Freeman or designate a student for that role. The casewriter suggests leadoff questions to stimulate role playing such as: Imagine for a moment that you are Steve Cohen (Robert Freeman). You are driving home late one evening and mulling over in your mind what you should be concerned about in terms of Design's future. X(Y), what would you be most concerned about and why? This will require some quick integration of the main points covered in the discussion questions. A good answer will uncover some of the problems or opportunities which ought to be considered. Another approach is to march through the discussion questions. Still another is to ask about DI's strengths and weaknesses. This approach has as its objective an analysis of DI's distinctive competence, which goes beyond a mere recital of facts. Having done this, pose the partners' dilemma against the analysis. This should split the class into two camps. After discussing the pros and cons of each side, ask what would happen to DI if Steve Cohen were suddenly mowed down by a drunken driver. The casewriter suggests that the usual conclusion is something like "too bad, inconvenient, but Freeman can easily find a replacement." Conversely, if Freeman were struck by lightning, then what happens to DI? Consensus usually is that DI will fail in not over two years if Cohen cannot find a replacement for Freeman.

CASE ANALYSIS

STRATEGIC MANAGEMENT ELEMENTS: MISSION, GOALS AND OBJECTIVES

DI's <u>mission</u> goes unstated, but we infer it is to make private label women's sportswear for discounters, department stores, and chain specialty stores. Its <u>goals</u> are more detectable and are simply to increase sales 50% each year by selling well made products. There are no quantitative <u>objectives</u>. One partner, Cohen, would like to see DI "upgrade a bit" with its own label, making a mark somewhere and becoming better established with its customers. Freeman, the other partner, sees it differently. Both agree in principle to the <u>long term objective</u> of being acquired. Uncertain of what terms would be attractive and unsure of how big DI should grow in order to be attractive to a buyer, the partners disagree greatly over which way DI should go in the interim.

STRATEGISTS

Both partners are well grounded in the garment business, although each knows it best from a different viewpoint. Cohen at 37 is the younger of the two. He is the "inside man," responsible for production. He is a detail man, and it is right that he should be. He can be decisive in small matters but views large matters with less precision. For instance, he believes DI operates too much at the low price end of the scale and therefore should seek to upgrade by putting its own label on items. But what items in what markets is unclear. Both men are realists. Both have a good sense of DI's market. While they may appear conservative, they exhibit a tolerance for the risk inherent in the garment business. Freeman, 58, is the "outside man" who sells. He sells shrewdly and intelligently. He learns in a hurry, and because he does, DI literally lives by its wits. Freeman is the idea man, intuitive, almost instinctive, well known, widely acquainted, and versed in the finer points of the industry. Major decisions are jointly made; while responsibilities tend to overlap, this seems no detriment to DI.

<u>SOCIOECONOMIC SECTOR</u>. It is apparent that the fortunes of DI rise and fall with the <u>economy</u>. During the period of the case the economy trended upward, employment rose, inflation slowed, and interest rates fell. Garments are a DPI item - in hard times, one makes do. In good times, garments tend to sell well. DI has an attractive, almost can't miss circumstance. DI chose its customers wisely, department stores and chain specialty stores, because these are able to attract most of the middle class women, DI's ultimate consumers. DI's pricing, quality and "knockoff" (copy) techniques cover the waterfront. The numbers of working women are on the rise, so DI profits from inherent <u>social pressure</u> to dress as well as one can for the workplace. Population centers provide large potential markets; distances are short, so response times to capitalize on trends can be short.

TECHNOLOGICAL SECTOR. Change is dictated by the tastes of the American woman, not by sparkling new processes or materials breakthroughs. Since DI by virtue of its custom tailoring is spared the necessity to design, it can forego the requirement to continually update processes. DI is not immune to change, since Cohen notes that new designs have required the use of specialized equipment, for instance to sew elastic. DI does have an option, however: do the work inhouse, buy necessary equipment for a contractor to use, or find a contractor who has that capability. At the same time, since DI contracts its sewing and pressing, it seems unlikely to be overpowered by technological innovation. Its own operations are stable, state-of-the-art, and almost commonplace. There are no obvious equipment or material limitations.

GOVERNMENTAL SECTOR. Not a factor in this case.

INDUSTRY THREATS AND OPPORTUNITIES. The case is silent on competition, other than that there are large manufacturers. Of course there are, many of them, and there are just as undeniably many small manufacturers who may produce one item or a family of items. Both large and small have something in common, however: they may be offering the wrong things for sale. DI has no such worries. The competition has in effect killed itself off. What DI is asked to do is simply to supply knockoffs of proven winners, and DI does that very well. Presumably others can do the same thing and many undoubtedly do, but we are not told of them. Customers seem plentiful because DI offers them a chance for good profit on proven sellers. Suppliers are not a factor. Freeman says that he knows where to get piece goods quickly, and his suppliers cooperate. However, as fabric manufacturers began to understand the meaning of lean and mean, it made good business sense for them to require much greater advance notice for orders. If this trend were to continue, DI would be forced into earlier purchases. This would be worrisome indeed to the partners, because Freeman believes that poor decisions about fabrics can easily force one out of business. In effect, DI might be forced to think strategically.

STRATEGIC ADVANTAGE PROFILE

CORPORATE RESOURCES AND PERSONNEL. DI has in a very short time earned a favorable image, both with customers and with suppliers. The image reflects as much a good product as it does Freeman's formidable circle of acquaintances. There is no recognizable strategic management system; planning is on an ad hoc basis and appears driven wholly by external factors. DI's structure reflects both expediency and realism. Its operations do not require a more elaborate contrivance. Since the business is inherently repetitive, its policies and procedures are probably few and simple. Notwithstanding, its <u>control</u> procedures are undeniably sound. DI is in a labor-rich area; add to that the fact that garment labor tends to be stable, so DI is reasonably assured of high quality <u>employees</u>. Since <u>labor</u> is such a big determinant of success in the industry, the partners wisely adopted profit sharing in 1985. <u>Top managers</u> are well qualified, as we have noted before, and work together well as a team. Replacing Cohen would be far less a problem than replacing Freeman. DI stays close to its customers and <u>suppliers</u>; it listens well, and the quality of its relations all around enable it to be responsive, certainly a key factor in the rapidly changing tableaux of the industry. The company is adequately resourced, well run, lean, free of labor conflict, and actively seeks to avoid the mistakes which have ruined others in the industry.

<u>FINANCE AND ACCOUNTING</u>. Procedurally here the case is largely silent. There is an inhouse <u>accounting</u> effort, since there is a head bookkeeper and monthly financial statements are mentioned, and an accountant elsewhere offers advice. DI is in good financial condition. It can largely <u>finance</u> growth internally now, keeping seasonal borrowing to a minimum. Its ratios are good. Its <u>CR</u> approaches 2, and its <u>QR</u> is well over 1. <u>Gross margin</u> on sales hovers around 25%, and ROI in 1985 is 40.8%. Total assets to sales consistently declines. <u>Profit</u> after taxes has declined from 6.5% on sales in 1984 to 4.6% in 1986; this reflects a 33% increase in operating expenses incurred when profit sharing commenced in 1985. DI is in a <u>high variable cost</u> business. Once sales materialize, control of labor and material costs is critical. <u>Purchases</u> as a percent of sales have declined 10%, and <u>contract labor</u> expenses have been fairly steady at 46%, 47%, and 43%. There are no formal <u>budgeting</u> systems. Targeted sales increases are used as measures of performance. There are no adverse ratios, sales increase steadily, and DI shows increasing profitability.

<u>MARKETING AND DISTRIBUTION</u>. The case does not permit comment on DI's <u>market share</u>, but it firmly establishes that the company has found a comfortable, risk free, profitable niche which does not require <u>market research</u> or constant product innovation. DI simply follows the lead of customers who want knockoff versions of obvious winners. Freeman prefers to say, however, that DI fills a market void-private label work for multi-unit people, to use his words. DI succeeds for several reasons (Tom Peters would be proud of DI): quick <u>response</u> to a customer and the wisdom to listen carefully to the customer's desires, rather than to yield to an inner urge to push something else; exclusive <u>distribution</u> by virtue of geographical separation; good <u>quality</u> (Cohen: we like to add features) coupled with a desire to please; sensible <u>pricing</u> to customers, who appreciate the opportunity then to make an above average return on the product, and a reputation good enough that some customers buy sight unseen. That in itself is uncommon and points out an unusual closeness by DI to its customers.

<u>PRODUCTION AND OPERATIONS</u>. Production is simple. DI needs no designs, because it is in the copy business, though Freeman is wont to say he is a custom tailor. Production is geared to queries from customers. There is enough inhouse expertise in the small staff to manage a quick response. Collaterally DI

has practiced gathering fabric quickly once an order is on hand. Designs spreads fabric and cuts it. Others sew and press. The company then controls the two big elements of variable cost in the garment business, fabric and labor. DI has a tight hold on fabric, quantities, and piece goods loss. Since it deals consistently with six nonunion contractors, it has a fairly good grip on contract labor. DI does its part well, and its reputation attests that its subcontractors perform equally well. Its procedures for copying and design work and inventory control are obviously effective; low overhead suggests efficient facilities and tight control procedures.

STRATEGIC ALTERNATIVES AND CHOICE

Both partners are agreed on a strategy of expansion so there are no real alternatives. There is no need to retrench; stability would be counterproductive and a combination strategy is not indicated.

RECOMMENDED DISCUSSION QUESTIONS

1. What is Designs' current strategy? What key policies support it?

2. Upon what key skills is DI's strategy based?

3. How is the business doing?

4. Strategically has DI any actual or potential weaknesses or problems?

5. What specific alternatives are open to the partners?

6. Justify your selection of the most appropriate alternative.

7. What strategy and/or other changes would you recommend to Cohen? to Freeman?

ANALYSIS AND DISCUSSION

1. What is Designs' current strategy? What key policies support it?

The key strategic concept is to be a very adept copier of women's sportswear for multi-unit outlets quickly and cheaply. Key policies are exclusive distribution by geographic area; no sales force, hence no conflicting versions of the same story and no conflicting decisions; dealing in a recognizable product/market-middle class women seeking well made and reasonably priced style; flexible output, producing whatever is known to sell and eschewing suggested retail prices; tight inventory control with virtual just-in-time fabric delivery; subcontracting the labor intensive work. Just for fun, ask how DI manages its market research or R&D. There may be some blank looks, because it has already all been done for DI by its customers.

2. Upon what key skills is DI's strategy based?

Expect a list of strengths which may or may not be skills: low overhead, low prices, non-union sales, fast delivery, knockoff ability, a feel for the fabric market, contracts with mills and customers, closeness to customers and end markets, etc. Ask which of the partners has the resources or skills supporting these items. Students who grasp the essentials of DI's strategy may well reason that a critical skill is the ability to copy. That's true, and from this they may see production as the vital area and Cohen as the key to DI's distinctive competence. But a reading of Freeman's words on pages 57, 58, and 62 should make it clear that it is Freeman who has the most pronounced effect on what Cohen produces for whom and when. On reflection, it is clear that Freeman's ideas, connections, and knowledge are the true competence of DI. That does not diminish Cohen's role but merely serves to indicate that once the ball is rolling, good cost management is vital to success, but this is an operating concern and not a strategic concern.

3. How is the business doing?

Very well. We have listed DI's favorable ratios above under Finance. The firm is increasingly profitable with steadily rising sales and good cost control.

4. Strategically, has DI any actual or potential weaknesses or problems?

Strategic problems include pressure from fabric houses asking that DI order earlier, which runs counter to the company's very basic policy on the ruinous aspects of obsolete inventory; which strategic option to pursue, and the matter of choosing Freeman's successor should he leave suddenly. A distasteful decision on the most appropriate option might see Freeman simply walk away. He has done that in the past when events were not wholly to his liking.

5. What specific alternatives are open to the partners?

a. Stable growth - business as always, Freeman's preference.

b. "Horizontal" growth - new "nontraditional" product lines like athletic wear, Cohen's preference.

c. Vertical integration, either forward or backward.

d. Internal growth - Own labels, bigger margins, inhouse design, another Cohen preference.

e. Selling out, either long term or short term.

6. Justify your slection of the most appropriate alternative.

In the long term, both partners look to be acquired, so selling out short term is acceptable to neither, and the immediate concern is what to do now, not later. Unless Freeman goes with the sale, what really is left? Own labels requires expertise DI just may not have; any garments might be suspect from the standpoint of market susceptibility, let alone possibly putting DI into potential competition with present customers. Vertical integration has no logic, because doing so would take DI far from the business it is really in. "Horizontal" growth presents the same potential drawbacks as internal growth. Moreover, growth other than the stable growth that Freeman prefers might well cause Freeman to leave the firm. Cohen has too much to lose not to yield to Freeman.

7. What strategy and/or other changes would you recommend to Cohen? to Freeman?

For Cohen, take care not to overburden suppliers or subs, because they will want more lead time with larger orders. Keep the image of being small and don't overorder from any supplier. Keep Freeman happy. Learn as much as possible about the "outside" part of the business. For Freeman, develop ties to new subs, new suppliers, and new customers with a view to better planning. Planning may be forced on DI, so the time to start thinking is now. Long term, since both agree to be being acquired, reach an agreement on what general terms would be acceptable and grow accordingly.

ENVIRONCARE (EC)
TEACHING NOTE

TEACHING OBJECTIVES

EC depicts a small family business which decides to diversify in response to environmental pressures and opportunities. Specific objectives:

Understand the growing dimensions of the lawncare industry.

See how environmental changes can create opportunity in even the most ordinary types of business.

Understand the possible impact of the franchise concept on an industry.

Identify ways whereby a small business can effectively compete with those of greater resources.

USING THIS CASE

EC is a short, relatively simple case which can be used to advantage early in a course. It is an easy case to discuss. It can be used for an inclass exam or a short report. We have reservations about its use as a long report.

SYNOPSIS

A small family owned pest control business in Longmont, Colorado, Rocky Mountain Pest Control (RMPC), decides to expand into the tree and ornamental (shrub) spray business. Sensing growth, RMPC tries unsuccessfully to buy its largest potential competitor, Welco Spray, in nearby Greeley. Undaunted, RMPC not only decides to diversify but to form a new company, Environcare, to aid a geographic expansion into Greeley, its primary target market. Such a move faces competition from two large franchised lawn care companies. The case shows that if you can imagine it, you can achieve it.

OUTCOME

Environcare is doing well. Welco customers are turning to Environcare. Since spray service revenues are less than anticipated, EC is now planning to delve further into lawn care in Greeley.

TEACHING APPROACHES TO THIS CASE

Two possibilities suggest themselves here: on the blackboard, list the environmental threats and opportunities confronting EC and follow that with an analysis of the firm's strengths and weaknesses. This could take an entire 50 minute period. A second period could be given over to a mock meeting of EC officers to consider the analyses and decide on a course of action. Another approach is simply to go through the discussion questions and then ask what should be done.

CASE ANALYSIS

STRATEGIC MANAGEMENT ELEMENTS
MISSION, GOALS, AND OBJECTIVES

EC's <u>mission</u> is to provide exterior pest control, specifically tree and ornamental spray service, in the Northern Front Range area. Lawn care may also be provided. EC's <u>goal</u>, enunciated by its general manager, Don Smith, is $500,000 gross sales annually. Other than the expressed <u>goal</u> of growth, RMPC, EC's parent company, has only the implicit <u>goal</u> of increased profit. No <u>objectives</u> are given, although Smith hopes some day to own his own business.

STRATEGISTS

The case says nothing of strategists. However, it is not difficult to see that the owners and officers of RMPC and EC are hardworking, ethical, ambitious, shrewd, determined, not averse to risk, confident, technically qualified and socially responsible.

ENVIRONMENTAL ANALYSIS

<u>SOCIOECONOMIC SECTOR</u>. Environcare seems largely immune to the <u>economic cycle</u>. A good, large tree worth $3-4,000 merits a $35 spraying even in bad times, but the case ignores the economy. The lawn care industry, of which EC is a part, profits from growing family incomes, where two wage earners can make lawn care affordable. Given economies of scale in materials and equipment, a desire to spend leisure time other than in yard work, and mindful that professional care is the more expert, property owners are less and less reluctant to turn to the pros. Add to that an increasing regard for the environment and a heightened awareness of the possibility of toxic chemicals, and the call for <u>professional services</u> is even more understandable.

<u>TECHNOLOGICAL SECTOR</u>. New lawn care <u>products</u> constantly appear. A look at any container, however, almost guarantees eyestrain from reading the mass of fine print providing directions for use, precautions, disclaimers, etc. <u>Special handling</u> procedures, potential <u>hazards</u>, and the frequent need for specialized equipment make the average homeowner increasingly reluctant to do his own lawn care work. The consumer is thus inclined to deal with a firm which can readily cope with the special demands of new products. It is no longer enough simply to spray all with DDT and then forget it. The industry has become one of continued new product lines and new <u>techniques</u>.

<u>GOVERNMENTAL SECTOR</u>. As one would expect, environmental concerns and consumer awareness have combined to produce a much more stringent <u>regulatory</u> climate. <u>Employees</u> must be specially trained, certified, licensed and bonded. Regulation flows from both federal and state levels. The days of simply going into the (lawn) chemical dispensing business are gone forever.

INDUSTRY THREATS AND OPPORTUNITIES. Lawncare, the umbrella term for companies treating grass, trees and bushes, is a <u>rapidly growing</u> business. The casewriter notes that <u>industry</u> revenues increased almost 50% in two years. Since only 16% nationally of 50 million single-family residences have become lawncare customers, the <u>market growth rate</u> during the period of the case and beyond is forecast to be 30-35% annually. In areas of rapid growth such as the Northern Front Range, that figure may even be conservative. Most lawn care firms are small businesses, but there are giants such as Chem-Lawn, Orkin, Nitro-Green and the like.

Environcare is looking into the face of ample <u>competition,</u> principally Welco Spray and Greeley Spray Service, who have dominated the Greeley market for the last ten years. Two franchise operations, Ever-Green Lawns and Nitro-Green, have recently entered the Greeley market. There are some 15 lawn care firms in Greeley, and there is a possibility that a Denver company or another franchise operation may come to Greeley. EC has the advantage of synergistic potential in that RMPC's customers are also EC's potential customers, and Smith is well acquainted with Welco Spray's customers.

<u>Barriers to entry</u> are not high, and <u>competitors</u> can offer choices and combinations of products and services. Greeley's climatology is conducive to the proliferation of insect varieties. This means that lawn care companies must be knowledgeable of what chemicals to use and how. Smith, EC's general manager, believes that roughly a third of Greeley's residences avail themselves of lawn services; this higher than average <u>market penetration</u> underlines the growth factor in the industry, a fact seemingly borne out by Ever-Green Lawns' market research. Smith estimates that less than 10% of Greeley's homes use tree and bush spray services; nonetheless, he expects to make 75% of his sales on spraying shrubs and trees. In essence, the industry and along with it the Greeley market appear to be growing; however, the proliferation of companies indicates that this market is presently not well served.

<u>Threats</u> are obvious in the form of <u>franchise</u> lawn care companies, because these presumably have greater resources and can advertise extensively, attracting those unable or unwilling to take the time to differentiate between companies. At the same time, Nitro-Green, though well known and well advertised, is alleged to lack professional competence and may not be able to satisfy the interest generated by its advertising. It is a factor largely in lawn care (90% of its business), while Ever-Green exclusively fertilizes lawns. Although Ever-Green is competent and well resourced and advertises extensively, it is not a local firm. Welco Spray must be considered, too, since it holds 80% of the tree and shrub spraying market, but it gives the appearance of being poorly managed. If it were otherwise, would Smith have left Welco? <u>Regulators</u> may discourage or prohibit present products; this could raise the costs of doing business and discourage potential customers. Less obvious but

equally dangerous are the possibilities of ruinous <u>damage suits</u> by customers or employees, alleging personal injury from hazardous materials.

<u>Suppliers</u> are not mentioned as a factor but could become so were the industry suddenly to swing to the use of biological controls. Demand would swamp supply.

STRATEGIC ADVANTAGE PROFILE

<u>CORPORATE RESOURCES AND PERSONNEL.</u> The parent company, RMPC, enjoys a good <u>reputation</u>, because its pest control customers have asked the company to extend its services to trees and shrubs. It has built up a sizeable clientele in Boulder and Longmont, a clientele which can be instrumental in expanding EC's business. There is no mention of a <u>strategic management system</u>, but the company shows evidence of sound planning. Its track record profitwise has been good. The company is small and lean. Its <u>structure</u> is not depicted. RMPC is cautious and insures that its <u>employees</u> are licensed and bonded. Labor costs are kept low by use of part-time help.

EC is fortunate to have Don Smith. He knows the Greeley market - in fact, he is the key to the success of EC. He also knows the workings of Welco Spray, EC's chief competitor. He is technically well qualified and knows the Greeley market well. However, he has had no experience in cities outside Greeley where EC is expecting to expand. Unfortunately EC's finances would make it difficult at this time to develop a qualified replacement for Smith.

<u>FINANCE AND ACCOUNTING</u>. The case has little to say here, other than to mention that EC started on $25,000 of borrowed capital and should break even its first year. Even so its <u>capitalization</u> exceeds by $5000 the observed average cash investment for the typical lawn care business. It is apparent that its capital is limited and won't permit unprofitable operations for very long. Dollars limit the money available for advertising, perhaps making it difficult to counter or to respond to competitors' advertising.

<u>MARKETING AND DISTRIBUTION</u>. EC has done no <u>market research,</u> although Ever-Green Lawns allegedly has. EC is looking at a good potential <u>market</u> and despite evident <u>competition</u>, seems confident it can establish itself in that market. It has the advantage of RMPC's synergism as well as of Smith's knowledge of the Greeley market. Smith is well known locally, whereas the franchises are not. EC plans to <u>sell</u> on credit with liberal terms of payment possible. Its <u>pricing</u> will be individually determined and hence will offer attractive opportunities for product positioning. It plans an elaborate PR rollout via radio, newspaper, telephone, personal customer canvas, mailings and exhibit booths at home and garden shows. Its <u>promotional budget</u> percentagewise seems well above the 6.6% pro forma figure shown in Table 1, and that argues that the company knows full well that it pays to advertise, particularly when competing with franchised operations. As a further step, EC will have its employees brief customers on the advantages and limitations of its chemicals.

PRODUCTION AND OPERATIONS. Here the case is fairly conventional, stating that EC will handle both residential and commercial accounts, with no charge for weekend work. A phone bank in Longmont will actually receive calls for EC from various points. Equipment poses no limitation and appears sufficient for foreseeable market demands. While Welco has better equipment, that plus is offset by apparently poor usage. Greeley Spray Service, a lesser competitor, may be underequipped, since it has only an occasional presence in Greeley. Other competitors mentioned are lacking in modern equipment.

STRATEGIC ALTERNATIVES AND CHOICE

Omitted. RMPC has committed itself to a strategy of growth.

RECOMMENDED DISCUSSION QUESTIONS

1. Does Environcare have sufficient financial and marketing resources and capabilities to compete effectively with its larger competitors?

2. Was its 1983 offer to buy Welco a fair offer? Justify your position.

3. Should EC continue to attempt to buy Welco?

4. Are its marketing efforts adequate when contrasted to those of EverGreen Lawns and Nitro-Green?

5. How important are hometown origins in contrast to out-of-town franchise operations?

6. Should EC add lawn care to its line of business? Why or why not?

7. What steps can EC take to differentiate itself from its competitors?

DISCUSSION AND ANALYSIS

1. Does Environcare have sufficient financial and marketing resources and capabilities to compete effectively with its larger competitors?

Here Ec is certainly on a comparative shoestring budget. It can hardly begin to compete dollar-wise with the marketing efforts of its larger adversaries, and it lacks inhouse sophistication, witness its hiring of an ad agency for radio spots. It will have to market smarter, and it ought to be able to do so because it has the advantage of reputation, acquaintance, and local contacts. With limited funds, it could not operate unprofitably for long, and it could hardly expect help from RMPC.

50

2. Was its 1983 offer to buy Welco a fair offer? Justify your position.

This asks what really is a business worth. Detailed data were not available. One buys a business for one of three basic reasons: antitrust, to improve cashflow, or to gain a competitive advantage. Here antitrust is not a factor. Welco has had only one profitable year, so only the third reason could apply. That would take the form of customer lists, since its sales do not justify the amount of equipment on hand. The answer then has to be yes, the offer was fair.

3. Should EC continue to attempt to buy Welco?

No. As time goes on, the value of Welco's customer lists diminishes, since Don Smith has such a good knowledge of Welco's customers.

4. Are its marketing efforts adequate when contrasted to those of Ever-Green Lawns and Nitro-Green?

Probably not, though you may hear some good arguments to the contrary. It has limited formal marketing experience. Most of its planned activities are promotional and relate to personal sales contact. In contrast, one of the advantages of a franchise is the support of a very formal marketing effort. Nitro-Green advertises more extensively by newspaper, and Ever-Green does it all. Fortunately, only Nitro-Green sprays trees and shrubs and then just derives 10% of its revenues from doing so. Word-of-mouth would tend to favor EC because of Smith's following. You might want to ask students to identify EC's critical success factor. It has to be Smith. So much of this business depends on close, press-the-flesh contact which Smith is uniquely situated to give.

5. How important are hometown origins in contrast to out-of-town franchise operations?

Very. It's the difference between personal and impersonal, and most property owners have some personal feeling for their real estate.

6. Should EC add lawn care to its line of business? Why or why not?

Certainly not initially. EC should do what it does best, and that isn't lawns. Let others fight over that. As Smith says, "we have to learn to walk before we can run." If it becomes established in its tree and shrub spraying and customers press it to do lawn work as well, lawns might be worth considering. Also, if spray revenues do not meet expectations, EC may have no choice.

7. What steps can EC take to differentiate itself from its competitors?

There can be many answers here, and we don't pretend to know what might be best. However, Don Smith would like to look into biological approaches to pest control. No one else seems to be thinking of this. Biologicals might prove to be a fine market if this can be done cheaper than conventional means of control and opens up commercial business opportunities uniquely suited to this method (feedlots, stockyards, etc.).

PRINTECH PUBLISHING SERVICES, INC (PPS)

TEACHING NOTE

TEACHING OBJECTIVES

The efforts of a young married couple to start a desktop publishing business culminate in a crucial decision complicated by conflicting personal needs. Specific objectives:

See the effect of conflicting personal desires on executive decisions.

Understand how the needs of family and business may clash.

Witness the effect of good communication in a family owned business.

Discuss alternatives available to the principals in the case.

Examine other alternatives.

Recommend a useful course of action.

USING THIS CASE

PPS reads easily. Subject, style, and fine reporting of the interplay between the principals, Bob and Elyce, insure student interest. The case is of medium length. It is a simple case if students grasp its realities at the outset; if they do not the case becomes at least moderately difficult. We do not recommend it for an inclass exam. However, it could be used for a short report, a long report, or a final problem in lieu of the traditional final. It is really a fun case and an easy case to discuss because it is so real. It is a little too sophisticated for the early part of a course so is better used later.

SYNOPSIS

Bob and Elyce Warzeski go into the desktop publishing business more from luck and happenstance than by conscious design. Bob's LT objective is to be a university professor in geology. Laid off by a major oil compnay, Bob con't find a faculty poisition and drifts into desktop publishing. The story if the business is one of a recital of critical decisions. Although looking at a green light for the further

---

This Note reflects a prior Note by and conversations with the casewriter.

expansion of a promising business, Bob is suddenly asked to interview for faculty positions. What was so clear now looks like a bucket of mud as personal needs and business needs suddenly crunch.

OUTCOME

Bob and Elyce decided to expand PPS as rapidly as possible even while Bob interviewed for a faculty position. They ordered a reconditioned L-100, three more MacIntoshes, and an optical scanner. They had two full-time and three part-time employees. The business prospered. Bob never found a position. He found himself on the horns of a dilemma: he concluded he was likely to find a position only if he wrote scholarly articles, yet he realized PPS at 80 hours a week deprived him of the time and energy to write those articles.

TEACHING APPROACHES TO THIS CASE

Several possibilities suggest themselves. All will work, but the one which will work the best, in our opinion, depends on the instructor's evaluation of the class, be it sharp and sophisticated, pragmatic, mechanical or otherwise. One way is ask about the principals in the case - get students not only to describe them but to decide what makes them tick. Are they entrepreneurs? Of course they are, but suggest that some rationale is in order here. Do they plan well? Well enough for entrepreneurs. What's lacking? Many things of course, and you'll get either lots of answers here or else a bunch of blank stares. PPS lacks a strategic management system. All is by feel, by hunch, by someone's word. True, Elyce makes inquiries, but only with difficulty can this be called research. If things are on the way up, as they are here, it follows that one can do just about anything logical and make things go. How do interpersonal relationships fit in?

Recall that others had predicted either a failed business or a failed marriage, yet neither materialized. Ask why anyone would make such a prediction. There have to be some strengths here which might not be readily apparent. Rick wants to be fair to Elyce, ecstatic at her chance to use so much of her MBA lore. Fairness goes further than that, though. Rick is fascinated with the business, too, and both believe in its future. Elyce's concern is initially for Bob, saying that any business had to be one which could be forgotten as soon as Bob found a faculty position. Astutely, she tried to find something which would interest Bob. She wants to see him happy and fulfilled. She is most supportive of him, and even after the business prospers, she is reluctant to push for its expansion. Fairness and consideration for other partner are evident. Bob is the more confident, the detail "inside" man, while Elyce is the mover primarily, the "outside" partner who sells, interviews, inquires, etc. Both are realists, too, and understand that they have a complementary role in the success of PPS. They learn to confer understandingly on important matters, and they're fairly quick to realize the importance of communication in business, as well as in marriage. Bob looks at PPS as a holding operation until a faculty position opens up, but he is unstinting in his support of the business. Elyce sees it as the thing, since she really wants to be in business. This support yet divergence can be deadly.

If you can get the class to discourse on interpersonal relationships, turn the conversation to values. What are values? Invariant mental reference points on which one decides good or bad. Do values play a part here? Ask how. Press for rationale. Of course values play a part here, because values condition decisions. What overshadows the expansion decision pending at the end of the case? Why? What can be done? What should be done?

Another approach is to start with the problem and work backwards, going through business decisions in reverse order, questioning why and asking how the personalities of Bob and Elyce are reflected in each decision. You can point out the wisdom inherent in each decision and examine the underlying rationale . These were made with relative ease, it would seem. So what's difficult about the decision at case end? Bob wants to be a professor of geology. There's no way to change that. Argue however one likes, that fixation is part of Bob's value system. The trick then becomes to fit whatever decision to that value system. The casewriter's belief, with which we agree completely, is that a human mind with all its frailties underlies nearly every decision. Put differently, the big decisions are made on gut feel, not numbers. That's really the backbone of the case.

Still another approach is to take the three options, ask for others (better do this as a homework assignment), and then argue the virtues of each. Bob's desire has to surface sooner or later.

CASE ANALYSIS

STRATEGIC MANAGEMENT ELEMENTS:
MISSION, GOALS AND OBJECTIVES

None of these is detailed. PPS' _mission_ has to be to engage in the desktop publishing business on an expanding scale. Other than survival and profit, there seem to be no specific _goals._ The LT _objective_ is unclear: stay small, grow, diversify, and then what? - sell, absentee management, split household, you name it.

STRATEGISTS

The principals in this case are entrepreneurs, pure and simple. Just as in the case of greatness which was not sought, entrepreneurship may be thrust upon one. Both are intelligent, conscientious, hardworking, risk tolerant individuals who are not afraid to make decisions in the face of imperfect information. They are realistic, somewhat conservative, and honest with each other. That has to be a big plus, both in a family business and in the attendant marriage. We can say they are tolerant and understanding but nobody's fool. Like many entrepreneurs, extension of this initial commitment is step by step - a large company would see a market and make a considerable commitment, for instance. Bob is the more technical, the operations type, and Elyce is more at home in marketing. What makes it all go is their obvious love for and confidence in each other.

ENVIRONMENTAL ANALYSIS

SOCIOECONOMIC SECTOR. The economy is not a factor. The business cycle favors PPS, and it would appear that a downturn would have minimal effect on a business of this nature. PPS is able to capitalize on a society which will try something new, given half a reason for doing so. It is benefitting, albeit indirectly, from the information explosion, or more properly, from the fallout of the information processing revolution. Nothing beats dumb luck - right place, right time.

TECHNOLOGICAL SECTOR. PPS benefits from a huge array of info processing equipment, from computers and optical scanners to photo plate printers. Its equipment is high tech, and its product pushes the leading edge of technology. Product life cycles are short. This makes for continuing technological improvement, which usually translates into greater capability at lower cost. But improvement makes life complicated for equipment buyers. Will consumers be able to differentiate between MOD 1 and MOD 2 products and pay accordingly? Can MOD 2 costs be recovered before MOD 3 appears? Just what kinds of bells and whistles does the market really require? Equipment deliveries may be uncertain, and immediately ready-to-go gear is equally uncertain. There is pressure then on training, and not everyone available is therefore trainable. No materials shortages appear.

GOVERNMENT SECTOR. Not an immediate factor.

INDUSTRY THREATS AND OPPORTUNITIES. The industry dates from 1985 and seems well established by fall 1987. The pace of technology is incredibly swift. Desktop publishing bids fair to put a tremendous dent in the conventional typesetting business. While the process can deliver finished copy, the industry's nomenclature tends to be misleading - it implies great masses of copy through desktop machines, whereas what is more representative is the making of a product which printing presses can use. Although the industry had spread across America, it had barely touched New Orleans. Hundreds of small businesses had sprung up in larger cities, but there were only two or three in New Orleans. Ed and Elyce knew that major market share awaited those who got in early with the latest gear and worked to sell their products. They are sitting in the middle of a big opportunity with few competitors. They cannot be unmindful of the CB radio boom and bust - is there something out there which will shove aside desktops, like cellulars have almost obsoleted CB's? Barriers to entry are high; while physical presence is a huge plus, the modem puts any market in the world in range. Instant obsolescence of equipment, the modem, and market attractiveness to those who can afford to enter, are all threats. There are no apparent limitations in the supplier sector. Customers of all kinds exist on every hand. The more sophisticated the clientele, the greater the number of customers. Desktops aren't for handbills, but they are for highbrow, upbeat, polished flyers intended for a formal marketing program. Since the industry is new and its products and capabilities are not well known, the market to a large degree hinges on consumer education.

STRATEGIC ADVANTAGE PROFILE

CORPORATION RESOURCES AND PERSONNEL. PPS has no reputation to uphold, because it has yet to achieve an image. Small and amorphous, it has no real objectives, just the pleasant dreams by its owners. There is no strategic management system; decisions are made with little data and as dictated by events. Manning is sparse, and as in nearly any entrepreneurial enterprise, the hours - at least of the principals - tend to be long since they must do what under other circumstances a staff would do. Elyce and Bob have the virtues of intelligence, education, imagination and conviction. They believe in their business, in themselves, and in each other. That's hard to beat, especially when you're it. But realists they are, so when business booms, they are quite willing to hire additional help.

FINANCE AND ACCOUNTING. Fortunately PPS does not have the anxieties which beset most small businesses. A windfall inheritance and its subsequent interest payments are enough for a start. They are able to borrow, first $5000, then another $5000, and finally $30,000, which they plan to match with their own funds. One would have to say they have at least a sympathetic banker, influenced no doubt by the thought of reasonably affluent clients. Bob and Elyce are astute enough to opt for a Sub S corporation. We know little of accounting. There seems to be some sort of system, though, since Elyce is able to prepare financial projections. They look attractive; although her projections are called conservative, job pricing is known to be difficult, and the bases for the projections are unknown.

MARKETING AND DISTRIBUTION. Marketing is the key. None of the other desktoppers in New Orleans has established a strong market share, so it would appear that here the early bird gets the worm. The process is new to the city though well known nationally. This simply means that it must be sold as a process first of all. PPS is led by the promises of several large accounts, and although initial prospects look bright, startup lags when these accounts do not materialize. Fortunately PPS has the capital to keep going. Advertising and promotion are off to a slow start because Elyce is preoccupied with finishing her MBA. That passes, however, and the duo are ready to launch in July. Good product, wideopen market but problem: they don't know how to reach that market. This indicates a lack of formal market research.

Word of mouth advertising seems to help, and by midsummer Bob is able to say that PPS has considerable potential. How to price is a puzzle because prices for local typesetting are hard to come by, and precedents are difficult to unearth. The promotion problem is resolved by using the yellow pages and by instructional ads in local business journals. Once the potentialities of the process are accepted, the service sells itself. Educate first, sell second. By Fall 1987 PPS faces the happy dilemma of either expanding or turning business away. The equipment question is further complicated when the couple realize that a high resolution machine will open an entirely new <u>market</u> to them, ad agencies. <u>Product quality</u> is another facet. A top of the line machine, Elyce learns, can generate perhaps $5000 revenue per month, but who can tell the difference in resolution that more expensive machinery provides? And were Bob and Elyce ready for the national market that a modem would make possible?

<u>PRODUCTION AND OPERATIONS</u>. Early fall 1987 brings the fish-or-cut-bait question, grow or turn business away. The considerations under marketing above - determining precise consumer acceptance - affect equipment decisions. Once those decisions are made, should Printech continually upgrade? Could it afford to do so? Could it not afford to do so? <u>Facilities</u> must be considered, too. The bedroom no longer suits. Storefront locations seem attractive because they generate walk-in business. <u>Materials and equipment</u> appear readily available. So is <u>real estate</u>. The questions are, where and what? Once the questions are resolved, the matter of additional help must be addressed. The underlying question here is just how committed should Bob and Elyce become? They thought they had decided that well, but it all began to unravel when Bob was offered several faculty position interviews.

STRATEGIC ALTERNATIVES AND CHOICE

<u>Stability</u> in the face of rapidly changing technology and dynamic markets has no reward. <u>Growth</u> meets the needs of Elyce, who is in love with business, and Bob, who is also fascinated by PPS' progress. <u>Retrenchment</u> is not indicated. A combination strategy is infeasible. The choice by default is <u>growth</u>, which meets the values of management. (Also see discussion question 7 following).

RECOMMENDED DISCUSSION QUESTIONS

1. Are husband and wife entrepreneurships common enough to warrant detailed consideration of PPS?

2. Bob and Elyce face some very fundamental decisions. What complicates those decisions?

3. What key issues must be decided?

4. What fundamental question must be answered before the key issues can really be decided?

5. How does the fundamental question relate to the formation of strategy?

6. Why do the Warzeski's work well as a team?

7. What alternatives are there?

8. Which would you recommend?

9. What is the business worth?

ANALYSIS AND DISCUSSION

1 .Are husband and wife entrepreneurships common enough to warrant detailed consideration of PPS?

This will bring some puzzled looks. Few would know the answers. 85% of the proprietorships formed in the past five years are husband and wife, and the total far exceeds businesses owned by one man or by one woman. Any proprietorship can become a Sub S corporation literally in a matter of minutes, and expert legal assistance is not required.

2. Bob and Elyce face some very fundamental decisions. What complicates those decisions?

Personal needs complicate the decisions, and so do personal feelings for each other.

3. What key issues must be decided?

Location, equipment and firm size.

4. What fundamental question must be answered before the key issues can really be decided?

Basically, what does Bob want to do? His dream of joining a university faculty cannot simply be waved aside. (You may want to defer this question until you consider alternatives.)

5. How does the fundamental question relate to the formation of strategy?

Strategy has to be so formulated as to accommodate the values of the key executives, especially the CEO. That's why few strategies can truly be called optimum, and why many corporate strategies completely defy analysis.

6. Why do the Warzeski's work well as a team?

Be prepared for various answers here. Most will probably have some degree of accuracy. The couple care for each other; there is mutual respect; they

complement each other well and recognize each other's strengths and weak
nesses, and above all, they communicate well. The last is crucial to the making of
intelligent decisions.

7. What alternatives are there?

Three are given: Stay small for the sake of flexibility. This way Bob can look for
a position; once found, leaving New Orleans is a simple matter. To do so is to risk
killing the golden goose. Market share will accrue to those who grab it and go, and
that doesn't mean someone with small ideas. Moreover, what will be the stress on
this marriage if Bob looks and looks unsuccessfully for a long period of time, while
at the same time they see a growing market that really doesn't include them?

Go for it. Risky. Untested market which will absorb a lot of time and capital. This
is grabbing a tiger by the tail. Once in, you have to stay in. If the business is
successful, what then? Can the business be easily sold? Would Elyce be willing
to walk away from a booming job to the quiet life of a professor's wife in a small
town which might be devoid of opportunity? As reported, this was their choice, so
you should ask students, in view of geology position offers, what now? That's
where the real rub is.

Possibilities:

Bob teaches, Elyce stays and runs the business. Not good. They are a close team.
He is operations, she is the outside person. What would she do without him? Plug
the gap by hiring a manager to replace Bob. Would Bob feel comforted by being
replaced? Not very likely. The manager's tenure at best would be uncertain, and
anyone with any perception would sense that at the outset. Questions to counter
with here are how long should Elyce stay in New Orleans? Short time, just long
enough to sell PPS and recoup as much investment as possible? Longer, until PPS
is a real money maker and an attractive buy? How long then? No good answers
here.

Bob teaches, Elyce goes with him, and a hired manager runs the business. Elyce
supervises from a distance. Sounds better than it is. Any new business needs lots
of TLC for about five years. At a distance, one can hardly guarantee that there's
no business like your own. If quick decisions have to be made, who makes them?
The problems of distance, communication, interest, responsibility, and the resultant stress are really bigger than they seem. Some will argue that it's done all the
time, but parallels to PPS are hard to come by, and the fact that businesses are run
by remote control doesn't automatically mean that they are well run.

Hire someone who can be trained to take over PPS when or if the Warzeski's leave
town. That employee could possibly buy the business over time. Sounds OK but
if Bob's job turns to mud, he has burnt his bridges. Besides, as the casewriter points
out, the appropriate talent may be hard to find.

Stay small but work out a deal with the Baton Rouge contact for Litronix work. Put a pencil to this. Orders run 5-20 pages. Shipping costs are as much as $30 each way for next day delivery. Not much profit left at the estimated $5 per page. Besides, customers want <u>Printech</u> to do their work, else they would have gone to a different outfit at the outset. Personal service is the key to happy customers, so how does one make last minute changes to copy which is in distant hands?

<u>Go national.</u> This third alternative is no more than that. It would be very risky, match PPS with skilled competitors, and require an investment in all the latest gear. This has the virtue of mobility but could easily become a flop.

8. Which would you recommend?

Expand PPS as rapidly as possible to take advantage of opportunity. Make PPS as successful as possible by the time Bob started teaching. Then it could be decided to sell an attractive business, put in a local manager, supervise at a distance, etc. This course of action, growth, caters to the values of the principals in the case and gives each what is wanted. Its silent virtue is that if Bob's job search is unsuccessful, as it turned out to be, he hasn't blown a great opportunity and devastated Elyce. He has a growing business with potential, too, to cushion his professional disappointment.

9. What is the business worth?

The question is pertinent only if PPS were sold. Technical assets become obsolete rapidly. Values decline rapidly. What is of value then is that PPS be a going concern with a good client list. The casewriter notes that if assets may not be all that attractive, it would be wise to expand the client list fairly aggressively.

PS GOLF CAR (PGC)

TEACHING NOTE

TEACHING OBJECTIVE

The world of a small golf cart manufacturer is changing, and it is not entirely certain that the new world will have a place for PGC. Specific objectives:

See how managerial style shapes an organization.

Realize PGC's inherent limitations.

Recommend improvements in functional areas and in management.

Select an appropriate strategy.

USING THIS CASE

PGC discusses easily. Its simple product line and the personalities of Scooter, the 80% owner, and Pete, the Operations Manager, make the case easy to read and attractive to students. The case is simple so students will slow down long enough to see that PGC moves without conscious plan. If you disregard the attachments, we can call the case short. It fits well early in a course for a discussion of the interplay of values, style and organization, but it is probably better used in mid-course when students are better able to understand the significance of what they see. PGC can be used for an inclass exam, a short report, or a long report.

SYNOPSIS

PGC both makes and reconditions golf carts in the Palm Springs, California area. It holds only a 1% market share but ships nationally and internationally. It builds a good product and provides a decent income, but its internal limitations cause it in effect to limp along. Its small, tidy niche may be under assault by both US and foreign manufacturers, so the problem becomes one of what to do.

OUTCOME

PGC is doing well. 1988 sales were $10-11 million. Yamaha, for reasons unknown, did not enter the high price end of the cart business. The production facility expanded to meet demand. PGC cultivated a low profile in order not to attract larger companies to its markets.

This Note reflects a prior Note by and a conversation with one of the casewriters.

TEACHING APPROACHES TO THIS CASE

Owning one's own business is a consummation devoutly to be wished, and a successful story is that much more attractive. There are two approaches here: Ask if PGC is successful. It obviously is. Why is it successful: is it a case of good management or a superior product? Actually it's due to neither and illustrates that a little luck beats a goodly amount of planning - up to a point. Or one can go in reverse, discuss the company's management, and analyze the strategic advantage profile. Whatever the case, it should lead to the question of what now?

CASE ANALYSIS

STRATEGIC MANAGEMENT ELEMENTS: MISSION, GOALS, AND OBJECTIVES

No corporate mission is detailed. Implicitly we surmise it is to recondition and make golf carts on a limited scale. Goals likewise must be surmised as profitability, quality, and growth. A long term objective has to be survivability.

STRATEGISTS

Scooter, the 80% owner of PGC, and Pete complement each other as Mr. Outside and Mr. Inside. Scooter seems the more irascible and demanding of the two since he requires absolute quality in his product. The details are left up to Pete, the less volatile of the two, who seems to have strong interpersonal skills. Neither is a true planner, and there is a lack of agreement on direction. Pete sees fleet sales as the key to further growth, but Scooter believes the future lies in the high price market. Both are intelligent, nonetheless, ambitious, and willing to embrace new ideas. One has to admire Scooter's integrity, reflected in the fact that he is Mr. Quality Control. That hurts neither sales nor PGC's reputation. Realists, PGC has decided to drop the customizing of carts.

ENVIRONMENTAL ANALYSIS

SOCIOECONOMIC SECTOR. This is the recreational business, one quite sensitive to economic cycles. PGC's sales jump abruptly following recovery from the 1981-82 recession. As the economy continues to roll, so will PGC. Add to that its location in Palm Springs, California, a resort area catering to the very wealthy. While PGC's sales area extends far beyond Palm Springs, it does have the comfort of this fairly reliable local buffer. PGC also benefits from the greying of America, the growing popularity of golf, and the acceptance of the golf cart. More people retire earlier, live longer, enjoy good health, and love to play golf. In times past there were few public courses near population centers, and the game was largely restricted to the wealthy. Now there are thousands of public golf courses, at least 10 million golfers, and golf carts rather than walking are the thing. Resorts, "executive" residential areas, retirement centers, convention centers - all these now are built around golf courses. Essentially, PGC has a good thing going.

TECHNOLOGICAL AND GOVERNMENTAL SECTORS. <u>Technology</u> here is essentially static. <u>Product life cycles</u> are long, so technology is not a factor to be considered. Neither is <u>government</u>, except insofar as the ubiquitous OSHA rules are concerned, plus the additional regulations to be expected from EPA should PGC make its own fiberglass bodies.

INDUSTRY THREATS AND OPPORTUNITIES. PGC has only an estimated 1% of the domestic golf cart market. 1985 sales figures on page 105 list at least 10 manufacturers. PGC appears to make electric carts, where E-Z-GO, the dominant manufacturer, is not expected to enter the high price market. Yamaha looks a distinct <u>threat</u>, as do U.S. Car and Club Car. PGC's <u>competitors</u> are a cause for concern, especially Yamaha, which has the wherewithal to underprice PGC. Offsetting this, however, is the tremendous potential for golf. Another 20 million consumers will populate the 30-57 age bracket by the mid-90's, and by 2000 there are expected to be more than 7 million affluent golfers. Cart rentals are the major source of income for golf courses, and discount stores are lifting sales from on course golf and pro shops. PGC should be able to take advantage of this huge <u>opportunity</u>, provided it can stay active. <u>Materials</u> are no evident problem, but PGC has only one remote <u>supplier.</u> Certainly there can be more than one supplier in our economy. <u>Customers</u> are diverse, though two distributors take most of PGC's output. The fact that one of the two distributors is also PGC's sole supplier seems an anomaly, indeed.

STRATEGIC ADVANTAGE PROFILE

CORPORATE RESOURCES AND PERSONNEL. There isn't much here beyond a good <u>reputation</u> and two complementary managers. There is little formal <u>organization,</u> few written policies except those required by law, and only five short personnel rules. The climate is completely informal. Such organization as is, is basically functional. There is no <u>strategic management system.</u> The company's record, in the face of no strategic management system, has to be attributed to high quality <u>employees</u>. Both Pete and Scooter are well qualified, but no consideration is being given to training possible <u>replacements.</u> Pete is not an owner, hence can walk away at any time and truly cripple operations. There should be some key man insurance on both the Gold Dust Twins, considering that PGC rides on their shoulders, but we know of none.

FINANCE AND ACCOUNTING. Scooter is alleged to like to keep close tabs on the money, and he must because professional accounting and advice are instantly available, and there is an inhouse, computerized accounting effort. That's fine, provided the data be used, but we wonder if that's the case. The company is profitable, and LT debt is only $20,000. Not unlike many small companies, PGC is undercapitalized and experiences a shortage of working capital each fall. The company exists on supplier credit during October and November and draws on a bank line of credit, too. While it shows a half million dollars positive cash flow in 1985, it fences with reality. There is no contingency plan for another fire, a strike, or other interruptions to production. An unanticipated rise in production would have much the same effect, a capital shortage. There is advice to take on LT debt, but conservative management has failed to act.

MARKETING AND DISTRIBUTION. Marketing seems almost an afterthought. There are no sales people, and there is no advertising. PGC's market is indistinct and really consists of who calls in. The company has no idea of a customer profile and at best knows only where it has shipped carts. Are there other markets? PGC doesn't know and doesn't try to find out. After all, the company is busy and profitable, so why bother? The possibility of an economic downturn seems not considered, and if Yamaha enters the high price end of the market, PGC admittedly might be in trouble. However, no contingency plan seems to exist. Pete sees growth in the low price end, the product for fleet sales. But nationally? Hardly. He doesn't know if the market is national or not. Scooter sees that this would take additional sales effort, not to mention more distributors, promotion and the like. He is less ambitious - "we are not trying for a billion in sales" - but if he thinks the answer lies locally, Yamaha may surprise him.

Its 1% market share will expand in absolute terms, but it has done no market research, and no new cart models are planned. Distribution is primitive since there are only two distributors, one nearby and one in Atlanta. Deliveries are made to some 36 states other than to distributor states. The company nets only 5% on its sales, so one wonders if its pricing is realistic and if transportation costs are not only passed on but are incurred in the optimum manner, i.e., would shipping cost less than inhouse trucking? Pete's estimate of $600 shipping cost per vehicle seems very conservative.

PRODUCTION AND OPERATIONS. Carts are shipped unassembled from the Georgia supplier to Desert Hot Springs, assembled, and then trucked throughout the United States. Supply is inconsistent and usually late, causing Pete to find shipping and receiving a large concern. Consideration is being given to inhouse body manufacturing in an effort to reduce shipping costs and to provide more flexibility in scheduling. The assembly and storage building was constructed by increments, apparently reflecting a lack of planning. Facility capacity is more than 4000 carts per year, but production forecasts are well below that figure. The same facility is used to recondition carts. Reconditioning is done in the off season as a means of busying the work force and aiding cash flow between new cart seasons. PGC makes three models of carts: the Model 100, new in 1985, top of the line, which sells for $5-8,000 or more; the Model 200, new in 1984, a revision of the original Model 100 but priced $3-5,000 under it; and the Model 300, designed to compete for fleet sales and priced at less than $3,000. There is no evidence of any sophistication in how many to make of each model, so we must assume that it all depends on telephone calls. Volume thus has to vary, and production is undeniably seasonal. Although PGC uses the computer for accounting, design work and production control, it has yet to put inventory control under the computer.

STRATEGIC ALTERNATIVES

A strategy of stability is possible but ignores the possible threat from Yamaha and runs counter to the values of management. Growth suits Pete and Scooter. Retrenchment has little promise. A combination strategy can be considered.

CHOICE

A combination strategy of stability and growth, in sequence.

IMPLEMENTATION

The dollars are becoming plentiful enough that PGC can afford to be more formal in its approach to business life. There is no time like the present to put things on hold and figure out which way the company should go. The reader will recall that Pete and Scooter have divergent views. Key man insurance is needed first off, then a dose of strategic management to tie together the disparate pieces of the company. At some point a more formal structure may be needed, and certainly some redistribution of responsibilities has to be made. Scooter can hardly expect to inject personal quality control into 2-4,000 carts. His time is more critical to planning and marketing. If Pete leaves, Scooter has a first class problem, so either train a replacement and give Pete a piece of the action or better yet, give someone production scheduling and control and let someone else take the headaches of shipping and receiving and inventory control. Smooth out demand and try to reduce seasonality. One doesn't have to work harder, just smarter. Can PGC be content with one supplier and two distributors? And where really is its market, and for what? Once determined, pricing becomes more realistic. Certainly it costs more than $100 to truck a cart to Massachusetts. Would shipping be cheaper? At 5% on sales PGC isn't looking at as much as it might, so a price rise should not be precluded. Even having done that, it may prove a loser to truck small numbers of carts to far points. If PGC can sort out the details and observes that it faces no or little competition in the top of the line, then it should exploit its existing niche, market extensively, and grow to meet anticipated increased demand.

RECOMMENDED DISCUSSION QUESTIONS

1. What is PGC's greatest problem?

2. What is PGC's Achilles heel?

3. Should PGC make its own fiberglass bodies?

4. How would you rate PGC's management? What is lacking?

5. If PGC were to double its sales, should PGC's management change present operating methods? Would you recommend any organizational changes?

6. Are its marketing methods effective? its pricing?

7. How would you attack the seasonality problem? the problem of undercapitalization?

8. What alternatives has PGC?

9. What would you recommend?

ANALYSIS AND DISCUSSION

1. What is PGC's greatest problem?

This should bring out some interesting answers. Expect most to be in the functional areas, and all should have at least a shred of truth. We feel that the greatest problem is a lack of strategic management. PGC does well in spite of itself, by the grace of God rather than by any good strategic plan. In good times this frequently is the case. In bad times, the lack becomes apparent.

2. What is PGC's Achilles heel?

The one supplier and the two distributors. What happens if the supplier folds in September? in November? Pretty frail reeds to lean on here.

3. Should PGC make its own fiberglass bodies?

We don't think so. This is a judgment call. A modest investment will save a lot of transportation money, ensure flexibility, etc. But fabrication is not PGC's long suit. Assembly is. It will involve more labor, another supplier, OSHA and EPA headaches, and will be more bother than worth. Murphy's Eighth Law: Keep it simple.

4. How would you rate PGC's management? What is lacking?

What's most lacking is keyman insurance, plus any means of insuring that Pete sticks around. You can expect students to criticize lack of policy, procedure, formal structure, etc. Actually, management isn't all that bad. Skills are complementary and synergistic. PGC is lucky to be a slow mover of small size - that enables a lot of personal intervention when needed, whereas that would probably be in short supply in a larger company.

5. If PGC were to double its sales, should PGC's management change present operating methods? Would you recommend any organizational changes?

Doubling would mean more promotion and more of Scooter's time. He could hardly inspect each cart. Production control and scheduling would become instant problems. Adding two people, one for production and quality control and the other for inventory control and shipping and receiving, would not be amiss.

6. *Are its marketing methods effective? its pricing?*

Marketing hardly exists. If students say marketing is ineffective, ask what changes they would recommend. One can hardly be undercapitalized and advertise in the Golf Digest at $25,000 an ad. This area requires immediate attention. Findings here as to target market demography and geography bear heavily on distribution and promotion. Transportation costs make carts seem underpriced.

7. *How would you attack the seasonality problem? the problem of under-capitalization?*

Raising prices, shortening the time to pay receivables, equity issue, LT debt, etc., will help the undercapitalization problem. It is reasonable to expect market research to help in dampening seasonality and in evening out cash flow.

8. *What alternatives has PGC?*

We list those above under Strategic Alternatives. Students may add fleet sales or leasing. PGC isn't geared for the mass production and marketing that fleet sales would require, and it lacks the financial wherewithal for leasing.

9. *What would you recommend?*

PGC needs to sort some things out before it charges ahead. That argues for stability, or stable growth, if you will. Before the conscious decision to grow is made, a careful look at the competition is in order. If Yamaha does not materialize, PGC should be able to dominate its niche. Other things to be done are noted under Implementation.

TURNER BROADCASTING SYSTEM
(A,B,C) (TBS)

TEACHING NOTE

TEACHING OBJECTIVES

TBS depicts an entrepreneur on the loose who figures he can do anything, but can he? Specific objectives:

Understand the impact of managerial values on strategy

See highly leveraged operations in real life

Recommend a course of action

USING THIS CASE

TBS is long but not more than moderately complex. It reads like a novel, and since Ted Turner is at least well known, this story of his derring-do will capture student interest. It makes a fine discussion case which can be used early in a course when values are emphasized or in the middle of a course when functional areas are being studied and/or strategy is being chosen. It can be used for an inclass exam if periods are 60-75 minutes and scope is clearly defined. It can also be used for either a short or a long report. We found the case fascinating, and we think you will find it that way, too.

SYNOPSIS

Ted Turner started at age 24 with a billboard company $6 million in debt and short of cash. Advised to sell the firm, he sold some of the company's assets to improve its cash position, refinanced its debt, renegotiated its customer contracts, hired new sales people, and turned the company around. Believing he could do anything, the handwriting was on the wall. He bought a radio station and then beamed his TV signal via satellite. He bought losers, too-the Atlanta Braves baseball team and the Atlanta Hawks professional basketball club. Two winners followed these in the form of cable TV services, Cable News Network (CNN) and CNN headline news. Terrible Ted bought a competitor in 1983, Satellite News Channel, and folded it completely. The 1984 Cable Music Channel proved an immediate loser. In 1985 Turner made a hostile tender offer of $5.41 billion for CBS. He offered no money but the deal was like so many others - the *Wall Street Journal* declared Turner was "leveraged to the eyeballs." Ridiculous though it might have been, CBS took it seriously, bought back $960 million of its stock, and sent Turner packing. Undaunted, Turner bought MGM/UA entertainment from Kirk Kerkorian.

Turner borrowed $1.4 billion for the MGM sale, then sold the UA part back for $480 million plus half a new preferred stock issue. The preferred was to pay dividends in TBS common, commencing June, 1987; unless redeemed, the preferred dividend could eat up enough TBS common to reduce Turner's holdings in TBS to a minority. To head that off Turner sold two new classes of preferred stock to cable companies for $562 million, 37% of the company's voting stock, enough to redeem Kerkorian's preferred. While he still holds 51% of the TBS voting stock and is chairman of the board, the cable companies control the board of directors. Essentially, Turner no longer owns the company except in theory. Even so, he decided to launch another network, TNT. Its startup was announced March 29, 1989. TNT went on the air with 17 million subscribers and is now number 3 in the basic cable market. Turner plans to spend $300 million on original programming by 1992.*

CASE ANALYSIS

STRATEGIC MANAGEMENT ELEMENTS:
MISSION, GOALS, AND OBJECTIVES

None of these is specified. We infer that TBS has the goal of growth, which ties to the statement that the company "emphasizes the building of asset values." William Sanders, once TBS CFO, is quoted by the *Journal* as saying "Ted has almost never had, as his primary objective, generating earnings. His primary objective has been to build value ..." Later, no doubt with the MGM acquisition in mind, Turner was quoted by *Business Week* as saying: "I want it [TBS] to be the premier TV programming company in the world."

STRATEGISTS

Here Turner stands alone. One could describe him with any adjective and find complete justification for doing so. Turner is described as having an intuitive approach to business, combined with the tenacity of a bulldog. He is a combination of "Diamond Jim" Brady and "Bet-A-Million" Gates come back to life because it is said that every time he did something, he bet everything that he was right. Generally, he was. He has captured popular fancy as the most brazen of entrepreneurs, the underdog who always got away with whatever he tried. He is tempestuous and noted for an absolute lack of tact. He thinks big, and he seems to be always thinking. He encourages the antipodes: love him or hate him, call him a dummy or think of him as Robin Hood who will dare and do everything and lives always on the edge. He is a study in personal extremes: a hard line conservative who calls Castro "my Commie buddy," courteous yet tending to be authoritarian, brilliant but not given to listening to others. Above all, he is a competitor who competes only to win. But the acquisition of MGM just might be a case of hurt pride or wounded ego, coming as it did just after the CBS debacle.

---

*Also See *Business Week*, July 17 , 1989, pp. 98 - 106 for an update.

SOCIOECONOMIC SECTOR. Television is a social fixture, and few there are indeed who do not own at least one TV set. The average American spends hours watching television, yet he may say he doesn't have time for church. TV is the mass opiate, and consumers will pay for TV before many other things. Television has become regarded as a necessity. What else could it be that would make consumers pay $20 per month as a cable TV fee or spend thousands on a satellite dish just to be able to watch a boxing match? Television revenues support many professional teams as well as the college sports of football and basketball. $9 billion represents a lot of television advertising and is an indicator of how highly businesses view television as an advertising medium. While advertising may decline in recessions, no one shuts off a TV set.

TECHNOLOGICAL SECTOR. While the basic fundamentals were long ago settled, there are still innovations which represent something new in television technology - cable, VCR, satellites, and satellite dishes, to name the more obvious. Different forms of TV such as pay-to-view or pay TV hinge on new technology. The case does not single out any new technology as especially promising, though Ted is reportedly taken by a new technical process, colorization.

GOVERNMENTAL SECTOR. The Federal Communication Commission (p. 128, text refers) has made Ted's life more difficult (*Business Week,* May 30, 1988, p. 34). Ted's programming may be in for hard times. He won't be able to feed the same shows to local broadcasters who may have bought exclusive rights to syndicated features. This could require converting WTBS from superstation status to that of a cable-only station. Instead, as noted above under Outcome, Turner decided to go with a new network. He pointed out to cable operators that they were looking at 25 million people who could receive cable but had not. He felt that his new TNT would be attractive to them because it would include events for cable viewers only. Although other cable programmers had looked for niche markets, TNT would not. It would try to appeal to all, so it came as no surprise that TBS agreed to commit its entire MGM film library to TNT.

INDUSTRY THREATS AND OPPORTUNITIES. Suppliers are not a factor since TBS privides its own programs. Customers abound and choose between the signal they would like (cable, satellite, antenna) and that which they can afford. Competition is widespread, and the three major networks - ABC, NBC and CBS - have experienced an appreciable drop in viewers what with so many alternate sources of TV available. The case lists pay and ad-supported cable, independent stations and VCR as contributing to the drop, and the trend is to a still broader usage of outlets. Each competitor can be regarded as a <u>threat</u>--just as readily, each new alternative can be seen as an <u>opportunity</u> for the forward thinker.

STRATEGIC ADVANTAGE PROFILE

<u>CORPORATE RESOURCES AND PERSONNEL.</u> TBS has a favorable <u>image</u>, induced by its various outlets, and its CEO enjoys what some would call a dubious amount of <u>prestige</u>. Turner's executives are called highly qualified, experienced men. There just can't be a <u>strategic management system</u> because any such system could not exist in the face of Ted Turner's values. The case is otherwise silent on this sector - organization, manning, employees and employee policies escape mention.

<u>FINANCE AND ACCOUNTING.</u> TBS is highly leveraged, to put it mildly. 97% of its capital structure is long term debt. Its earnings have been negative except in 1978 and 1983; this is ostensibly associated with startup costs. It has not paid a cash dividend since 1971, nor is any foreseeable. In 1983 TBS could not pay its bills out of current operations, so WC deficits were met by short term credit lines and a slowdown in payments to suppliers. TBS has had difficulty in meeting the terms of its 1983 debt agreement, such as minimum levels of working capital. Ted Turner holds 51% of TBS voting stock, but its worth is a matter of conjecture, about $372 million on paper. At some point TBS must turn the corner, or the cable companies will achieve an outright majority of the TBS board. Should Ted decide to sell, these companies have the right of first refusal. Since it rides the ragged edge financially, it faces a most uncertain future.

<u>OPERATIONS</u>. WTBS broadcasts 24 hours a day. It provides most of its own programming. It is alleged to represent about 35% of each night's cable TV audience. CNN also broadcasts around the clock to CATV systems. It provides its own programming and obtains news for its own bureaus, each of which can provide live coverage. CNN thus has worldwide live coverage. CNN Headline News is another 24 hour news service to CATV systems. It, too, does its own programming. CNN is reported to be America's most popular cable service. Cable is thought to be increasing: 75% of U.S. households have access to cable but only 57% of these subscribe, *Business Week* reports, so there is enough headroom to make TBS Executive Vice President, Bob Wussler, call the future bright. About 50% of all homes are actually wired for cable, and that figure is expected to increase to 62% by 1990. TBS itself could face more competition if superstations proliferated, but that is a bridge yet to be crossed. If programming is indeed the key to success, then Terrible Ted may well have stolen a march on the industry with MGM's prodigious film library, plus a vertically integrated TV and motion picture company. He now has more options than ever, and TNT seems just one of them.

<u>MARKETING</u>. Ad time for TBS is sold by its own sales force. Revenues come from advertising time and are a function of the size of the viewing audience and the amount of time sold. Cable time demand is less than for ABC, NBC, and CBS because CATV audiences are smaller. WTBS revenues also include fees from

"direct response" advertising. TBS can improve its revenues and get more of the $33 billion expected to be spent for TV advertising in 1990, Bill Davison tells us, by getting better audience access and doing better programming. There might be some method after all in the madness of acquiring MGM.

STRATEGIC ALTERNATIVES AND CHOICE

We believe that <u>stability</u> is Turner's only choice since that will give him a chance to raise his efficiency, try for better access, and improve his programming. That's not Ted's way, though. <u>Growth</u> is, but without something new and exotic in the way of financing, TBS appears incapable of growth. <u>Retrenchment</u> seems without merit and would appear to throw the baby out with the bath water.

RECOMMENDED DISCUSSION QUESTIONS

1. What drives the strategy of TBS?

2. What strategy would you recommend TBS follow?

3. How likely is TBS to follow your recommendation?

4. Does Turner's attempt to buy CBS reflect current TBS strategy?

5. Was his attempt financially wise?

6. Was his acquisition of MGM-UA wise?

7. Can Turner extricate himself from the financial bind which confronts TBS?

ANALYSIS AND DISCUSSION

1. What drives the strategy of TBS?

Not common sense but Ted Turner's values. TBS has no strategy, but the values of management are growth-oriented. If, as some say, his ambition is to be the largest broadcasting company in America, or the next William Daley, he has no discernable LT strategy. This is not to discount his efforts, for he is indeed a force in broadcasting, because he did what others failed to try. He will do anything and try anything because he is Ted Turner. He just plays to win. Brute strength and awkwardness may win over skill and cunning, but the four together may be hard to beat. TBS is Ted Turner.

2. What strategy would you recommend TBS follow?

Stability, as we noted above.

3. How likely is TBS to follow your recommendation?

Not very. Turner is not given to standing still. Growth is in his blood. Faint heart ne'er won fair lady, and it won't win Ted Turner, either. It's just not on the edge where he lives.

4. Does Turner's attempt to buy CBS reflect current TBS strategy?

Surely. You may get an argument here that TBS really has no strategy. That's right, so reword the question if you must. The attempt is in line with Turner's values, track record, and desires. When Capital Cities bought ABC, Ted Turner wasn't one to play second best for long.

5. Was his attempt financially wise?

No. It cost TBS $18.2 million but did give Turner the spotlight briefly. It was a financial disaster for CBS.

6. Was his acquisition of MGM-UA wise?

You can expect a specturm of answers here. Allegedly TBS had two ways to go: increase its distribution base or buy some "software." CBS represented the first, MGM-UA the second. MGM was flush with "software" plus an unlimited capability to turn out more. But MGM itself has not been successful and needs an injection of wizardry that Turner may not be able to provide. All is not gold that glitters. Add to that another billion in debt and the loss of control of his company, and the acquisition looks suspect, to say the least. The imponderable here is just what is all that programming worth?

7. Can Turner extricate himself from the financial bind which confronts TBS? How?

Our opinion is that he cannot, but we are the first not to claim the wisdom of Solomon. Anything is possible, but not probable. Recovery looks improbable, but the efforts of Ted Turner have been dismissed before by those who should have known better. Turner's sale of preferred stock to cable TV companies (not in the case) is of dubious wisdom if one reads the *Wall Street Journal*, but is it? Would those companies kill the fatted calf? Not likely. If Turner needs more access, it would behoove them to cooperate. And since programming got a boost from MGM, Terrible Ted may be on to something as far as revenues are concerned. At the same time, he was trying (May 1988) to sell his downtown Atlanta building for $55 million, and he has other possibilities. Films don't have to be made in the Hollywood area, and many are not. Why not Georgia? Who could put a price on MGM's Culver City complex? Students may well not know that though, so ask them to come up with a workable plan. Once done, then ask how they would sell it to Ted Turner, neglecting the new TBS board. If it's a good plan, please send us a copy. Someone has suggested to us that Turner should approach Rupert Murdoch, who has the wherewithal to put together a very large communications empire. That sounds like a winner until you remember that there is room for only one captain on Turner's bridge.

PART III

TEACHING NOTES

ACCOMPANYING

CASES ON INTERNATIONAL/

MULTINATIONAL

ORGANIZATIONS

BAVARIAN MOTOR WORKS (BMW)

TEACHING NOTE

TEACHING OBJECTIVES

BMW charts the fortunes of a quality German automobile manufacturer which has landed in the yuppie market and finds that everyone is shooting at it. Specific objectives:

See the growth of a successful foreign manufacturer

Understand the pressures in a competitive world marketplace

Visualize the impact of management values on corporate strategy

Determine a course of action

USING THIS CASE

BMW is a short case no more than moderately difficult. It can be used early in a course where the aim is either to stress the part values play in formulating a strategy, to understand environmental pressures, or to see how functional strategies must mesh. It can also be used later where the aim is to examine reformulation of strategy. It is an easy case to discuss, readily holds student interest, and can be thoroughly covered in one 75 minute period. It can serve in several capacities, as an inclass exam, a short report, or a long report.

SYNOPSIS

BMW had to survive the World Wars and a Mercedes takeover bid before its survival was assured. Long on marketing and pushing performance and elegance to the middle class, BMW prospered in late 60s and early 70s. Despite its devotion to R&D and an extremely enlightened labor policy which brought BMW a better quality product at lower cost, the company found itself in a highly competitive situation in the world automotive industry. Despite its being a pioneer in the "building block concept" of automobile development, BMW now had to wonder if its policies, product line, and marketing efforts were enough to see it through its latest challenge.

OUTCOME

Unknown.

The most remunerative approach here is to ask about BMW's strengths and weaknesses, perhaps writing them on a blackboard by functional area. It appears that BMW has more than a few passing strengths. Why should it worry? The obvious answer is its competition, so the rejoinder then is to ask why and to examine what has been happening in the world automotive industry. Has BMW been asleep, has it just been coasting without seeing where it has been, or has it just been surprised? Why? What needs to be done? What strategy should BMW endeavor to follow now? One can also start from the other end by asking what strategy BMW has been following and wondering if changes are needed, why, and of what nature. The case is unsophisticated and therefore lends itself readily to a workable strategy.

CASE ANALYSIS

STRATEGIC MANAGEMENT ELEMENTS: MISSION, GOALS AND OBJECTIVES

None is spelled out. We surmise then that the BMW mission is to provide an automotive product noted for quality and performance to select, worldwide markets. Goals and objectives are not quantified and can only be guessed at as qualitative - highest quality induced by industry's best R&D.

STRATEGISTS

None is described. We see management, however, as pragmatic, conservative and careful of BMW's quality and image. There is a seeming reluctance to reexamine present policies, despite the company's great attachment to strategic planning.

ENVIRONMENTAL ANALYSIS

SOCIOECONOMIC SECTOR. While one would expect BMW's fortunes to rise and fall with the economic cycle, that seems not to be the case. Table 3 reflects steadily rising sales in DM, though not at a constant rate, and the same may be said of sales and production units of automobiles. Those figures serve to prove that BMW truly was able to capitalize on the good times of the early 1970s in such manner as to be able to continue its good fortune even in less favorable times. Its ability to prevail seems more due to social factors than to economic: it has found a niche in the middle class market, a market which appreciates quality and performance, and by limiting supply has ensured that BMW could just barely meet the needs of that market. Some would argue that what we speak of is marketing, and to that we would agree, but at the same time, we point out that the company very astutely reads the sociological signs of the times.

BMW operates worldwide, however, and however well it plans, it cannot escape the pressures of the environment. The price of oil rose abruptly in 1973. Environmentalists became vocal activists. Auto prices rose. There was great incentive for others to market worldwide, too, despite storm clouds in the horizon. The casewriters properly point out that circumstances combined to create a "much more homogeneous demand" for similar characteristics in automobiles. The inflation of the early 80s coupled with inevitably limping economies intensified international competition in the auto markets. BMW could not be immune to these environmental pressures.

GOVERNMENTAL SECTOR. Governments tend to intervene when free markets do not meet national goals or policies. A faltering auto industry spreads its miseries widely. What had been a relatively unregulated industry was now beset with protectionism. Vertically integrated companies became less so as manufacturers outsourced parts in an effort to minimize costs. Competitors joined in joint ventures to escape protectionist measures. Nontarriff barriers came to the fore, too, and posed different standards. The automobile industry worldwide commenced to look at a much more complex, far more competitive environment. If one exported 60% of one's production, as did BMW, there was cause for concern.

TECHNOLOGICAL AND R&D SECTOR. The auto industry worldwide has competed to a greater or less degree on the basis of engineering and performance. This is certainly true of BMW. This betokens commitment to R&D and a neverending stream of incremental improvements, if not actual breakthroughs, like the rotary engine, emission suppressor, nonskid brakes, fuel injection, and the like. More complex systems mean more chances for human error. This places a greater premium on quality control and argues for initial minimization of error by automation and the use of robots. Substitute materials - plastics for steel - have become a part of nearly every downsizing decision. Add to that the ever present cost dimension, and it is easy to see why manufacturers push technology and R&D as hard as they do. BMW is no exception.

INDUSTRY THREATS AND OPPORTUNITIES. Suppliers are not a factor in this case, but competitors are, as we noted above. While the barriers to entry may be high, the rewards for a successful competitor are great. Communication (every native a pocket portable) fuels the tide of rising expectations, so emerging economies have decided on domestic production. This raises the level of competition as markets formerly available shrink or disappear. Production itself has become globalized - transmissions made in one country join engines from another for assembly in a third. Japanese production is a fearsome factor in the equation. Competitive threats and governmental constraints seem to far outnumber opportunities unless one already is established in a market and is able to exploit that foothold, as is BMW.

STRATEGIC ALTERNATIVES. Stability implies incremental improvements and business as usual in a dynamic environment. Growth looks at new markets, new segments of familiar markets, or completely new products in new markets. Retrenchment implies cutting back or withdrawing in the face of competition. A combination strategy can be considered.

<u>STRATEGIC CHOICE</u>. Stability must be declined, since it has no long term promise. Retrenchment similarly cannot be accepted unless retrenchment means only the abandonment of restrictive policies. Growth alone can meet increased competition. A <u>combination</u> of <u>retrenchment</u> and <u>growth</u> seems optimum.

<u>IMPLEMENTATION</u>. BMW is really in the middle of the yuppie market, a market of sufficient affluence and size to attract every other automobile manufacturer. BMW, however, has squatter's rights by virtue of winning its position and understanding its market. It must exploit that position by opening more dealerships in the biggest market of all, the USA. BMW should be where the action is: if more yuppie jobs and greater population numbers are forecast for Fort Myers, Florida, then BMW should be ready to welcome that growth. Since its market demographics are graduated, it should seek out the younger adult who enjoys early affluence. This is the buyer who will or can be induced to trade up. Lead from strength again. Just as it moved its products into a higher priced market in the early 80s and did well, BMW can also focus on the upper end of its product line, since the number of high income households continues to grow. BMW can exploit its image with those who want quality, differentiated by technology, and are not reluctant to pay for it.

The company needs to rethink its policies, like the 20% limitation, which virtually cancels out a better advertising effort and simply yields the market to competitors without a struggle. Review the warranty policy for private imports - this seems self defeating, too. Extend the model lines in the US. Why should they be limited? You have to cover a broader spectrum if you expect to blanket out the competition. Parts should not be a problem, nor a limiting factor. Shelve the dislike for the joint venture and license local manufacture of parts, if it is not economical to airlift parts which are held in short supply. Certainly JVs in the Far East for parts make sense, and so might JVs for assembly elsewhere (Latin America, Middle East, South Asia) if that's the only way to enter a restricted market.

A broader line means a wider customer base, and BMW must go to this if it is to meet Japanese competition head on. The company must still push its image here, especially for first time buyers, stress service, emphasize performance, and advertise more heavily at both ends of its market spectrum. A long look at price competition may be necessary in the 300 series, simply to bar a secure Japanese foothold. As America ages, the older buyer is of more and more importance and wealth and deserves special attention, to say the least. What BMW does successfully in defending its niche in the US market should translate to other markets as well. BMW has a distinctive competence in quality, design and innovation - and that's not all bad, because it is long in what Tom Peters terms the only three truly distinctive skill packages: a focus on total customer satisfaction, continuous innovation, and a belief that its people can put it all together. These, he holds, are the only effective sources of true, long term competitive advantage.

BMW can increase its share in selected markets by trading on customer satisfaction and fine market research. It can hold its market share at the high end by improving distribution and service. It can maintain its position in all markets by emphasizing its image and performance, setting itself up as a leader in technology, and that would be true. It can also build slowly or rapidly elsewhere by emphasizing the same things - quality, design, service and performance (or leadership in technology).

STRATEGIC ADVANTAGE PROFILE

CORPORATE RESOURCES AND PERSONNEL. Here BMW shines. Its image is faultless. Its organization is not described, other than to point to its 26 member supervisory board, certainly a concession to labor, and its smaller companion management board. BMW's employees make the company stand out. They are well trained, well informed, loyal, conscientious and dedicated and make possible the quality and performance for which BMW is noted. The strategic management system operates well and is also found in each subsidiary. The system is supported by a global com net, which makes for a highly efficient management information system. Top management has an excellent track record, hence must be regarded as superior. Personnel relations policies - compensation, development, education, involvement - seem outstanding and are an undeniable factor in productive efficiency.

FINANCE AND ACCOUNTING. We know little of the systems here, and probably in the face of each corporate success they are relatively unimportant. BMW's sales (Table 3) have grown at a 7% annual compound rate, and its net income has increased at a 18% annual compound rate. Shareholder's equity as a percentage of fixed assets has increased steadily, and the dividend stream 1975-84 is uninterrupted. The 1984 annual report reports steady financial improvement. The only disquieting note is the large controlling interest in BMW which the Quandt family holds. The family is quite active on the supervisory board, a presence which decreases the flexibility in decision making. Be that as it may, BMW has the financial strength to underwrite any endeavor.

MARKETING AND DISTRIBUTION. Mark up another strong suit for BMW. The company seems always to be marketing oriented, targeting the growing middle class, rationing scarcity, trading on a well won image of quality. It knows its target market well: Table 2 shows an effective market research capability. Its product line reaches every segment of the middle class market. Its foreign subsidiaries, using a franchised dealer system, enable BMW to provide an excellent parts and service system. Its pricing is competitive, and despite fluctuating exchange rates which might make possible lower prices, company policy does not permit price competition. We have insufficient information to judge the effectiveness of the sales force or its advertising or promotional efforts, other than the statement that both have continued to "reinforce" BMW's image. Aftersales service does not extend the warranty to privately imported cars, and we wonder just how wise that policy is. The distributor net falls mainly in Europe, North America,

Australia, and Japan. We wonder if that location is optimum, just as we wonder about BMW's limiting of a subsidiary to distributing no more than 20% of BMW's production.

R&D AND ENGINEERING. Score another for BMW. It is noted for its R&D and has always advertised its engineering and performance. It seems an industry leader, for instance in the area of emission control. It builds new facilities not to increase capacity but to further product quality as well as production technology. Rather than body styles, a senior BMW official says BMW will seek differentiation on the basis of "technology and the functional use of electronics."

RECOMMENDED DISCUSSION QUESTIONS

1. What are BMW's outstanding strengths and weaknesses?

2. In what manner do its strengths complement each other?

3. How do you account for its weaknesses?

4. How does the international auto industry threaten BMW, or does it?

5. The case states that the number of models sold abroad "was somewhat restricted," yet more than 60% of BMW's production is exported. How can you reconcile the two?

6. Why not extend a warranty to privately imported BMW cars?

7. How should BMW respond to the threats to its market niche?

ANALYSIS AND DISCUSSION

1. What are BMW's outstanding strengths and weaknesses?

Basically BMW's strengths lie in engineering and marketing, in product quality and service, in images and performance. Students may also cite the quality of its labor, strong finances, a fine managerial and planning system, and they would be right. But BMW's image predominates, and that comes from fine engineering and canny marketing. Weaknesses are something else. They seem undetectable. What we have in mind is managerial inflexibility which seems to say, once a policy, always a policy.

2. In what manner do its strengths complement each other?

We put this question here to give the instructor a chance to point out how functional strategies must complement each other because strategy is a seamless garment. Engineering has produced an image, magnified and traded on by marketing. Production has not flooded the market, since BMW has limited production, thus adding to an exclusive image, and so on.

3. How do you account for its weaknesses?

This is not a restatement of Question 1. This question serves to reinforce the idea that the values of management may defy analysis and serve as sources of weakness. BMW, for example, rejects joint ventures out of hand, when joint ventures may be the only way to tap an otherwise closed market. We believe, too, that these values combine to make one more a captive of the past than a suitor of the future, and that change becomes harder to forecast and to see.

4. How does the international auto industry threaten BMW, or does it?

It does, most certainly, by raising the level of competition and making traditional markets so much more competitive. BMW is no exception. The answer here is obvious, to be sure. Our aim is simply to get the student to appreciate and to discuss the effects of competition, once competition becomes worldwide. There simply are no safe places to hide. Some may say that BMW was sleeping at the switch and that competition did not appear out of the night. True, and we believe that BMW should have done a better job in forecasting the obvious.

5. The case states that the number of models sold abroad "was somewhat restricted," yet more than 60% of BMW's production is exported. How can you reconcile the two?

We have no good answer and can only surmise that "somewhat restricted" applies to a narrow spectrum of models.

6. Why not extend a warranty to privately imported BMW cars?

There is no good answer here other than that not extending warranty protection to imported cars is a sop to foreign subsidiaries. Whether really justified is yet another matter. We believe it short sighted, in view of the relatively limited number of vehicles involved. Why not convert that buyer to a lifelong BMW devotee? If servicing demands are higher, take steps at the outset to deflect such demands.

7. How should BMW respond to the threats to its market niche?

See our remarks under Implementation.

CITICORP-BRITISH NATIONAL LIFE ASSURANCE (BNLA)

TEACHING NOTE

TEACHING OBJECTIVES

As Citicorp enters the life insurance industry by acquiring the UK's BNLA, it realizes that some changes are in order. Specific objectives:

Understand some of the reasons for Citicorp's globalization.

Witness its acquisition process.

Become acquainted with the life insurance industry in Great Britain.

Decide upon a business level strategy.

USING THIS CASE

BNLA may be long but is not as formidable as it looks. It is of no more than moderate difficulty. It lends itself readily to discussion. It can be used as a vehicle for pointing out some of the problems in acquisitions. It can also be used as an example of the need to reformulate strategy. It is suitable for either a short or a long report. We do not recommend it as a final problem.

SYNOPSIS

When Citicorp decided to become a global financial services enterprise, it came to believe that it would not be a truly effective financial services organization unless it provided insurance. Such an expansion was possible only overseas. Since Great Britain demonstrated a relatively large market for life insurance, Citicorp began a search in the UK for a suitable acquisition. BNLA filled the bill but showed that immediate changes were in order.

OUTCOME

Smith and Jones were immediately replaced. BNLA's revenues tripled in 18 months.

TEACHING APPROACHES TO THIS CASE

The desired outcome is a new business strategy for BNLA. We believe that that is best achieved by leading students through Citicorp's strategy and

---

This Note is based on a prior Note furnished by the casewriters.

decision to buy BNLA. Why BNLA? The answers to that question may be difficult to find until students really understand Citicorp's acquisition criteria. Having done that, the instructor is ready to ask what now, reminding the class that Ira Rimerman has marked an evident need for changes. There is great opportunity for number crunching here, but students should be reminded that Citicorp has already made a decision, numbers notwithstanding.

CASE ANALYSIS

STRATEGIC MANAGEMENT ELEMENTS: MISSION, GOALS AND OBJECTIVES

Citicorp's mission is to provide global financial services from its U.S. base. Its objective is to continue to build "the world's leading financial services organization" by creating value for its stakeholders (Exhibit 4). Its goals are to enter the information and insurance businesses, to be the world's largest low cost provider of financial service, and to achieve the specific goals listed on page 154.

STRATEGISTS

We are told little directly of Citicorp's strategists, but we learn much indirectly. The organization has the ability to read the marketplace and to react accordingly to take advantage of opportunity. It has a strategic plan which features the consumer as key in its strategy. Its values are published for all to see (Exhibit 5), and its flat structure is calculated to encourage innovation.

ENVIRONMENTAL ANALYSIS

SOCIOECONOMIC SECTOR. Communications and the information explosion have made the world much smaller, and the doings of one are the doings of all. This cannot be more true than in the global economy, when national economies have become incredibly interdependent. Don't believe it? Try to imagine what a drop of 1000 points on the Tokyo Exchange (now at 33000+) would do to Wall Street. With the linking of economies, rapid transportation, and instant communication, the financial world provides an attractive setting in which a shrewd organization like Citibank can expand globally. Most societies have become international in thought if not in act and thus have been conditioned to multinational organizations.

Citibank's attraction to the UK could not have been unexpected. The UK economy, sixth largest in the world, was under Conservative leadership. This meant less governmental regulation of business as Margaret Thatcher privatized more and more government enterprises. By 1985 the UK exercised less control over domestic/international financial activity than any other developed country. Its economy was moving to a service orientation, the government was politically stable, and inflation was well in hand. One must also add a common language, a common heritage, and rather similar customs as further factors influencing Citibank's outlook.

<u>TECHNOLOGICAL SECTOR</u>. Citibank's expansion into the information business reflects its conviction that information has value, and like money, has time value. Hence, early information can be advantageous, so its packaging and global distribution by electronic measures can be profitable. Citibank's intent to provide worldwide financial data is easy to understand. So, too, is its fascination with the credit card. Marrying it to the ATM and homebanking promises a billion dollar business by the 1990s.

<u>GOVERNMENT SECTOR</u>. Citibank used the bank holding company as a device to expand globally. Both federal law and Federal Reserve regulations generally barred banks from life insurance underwriting. However, the Fed found nothing objectionable to Citibank's expanding into life insurance in the UK. No major changes in the UK's regulatory environment nor in its political system were expected. Despite finding the world's most stringent regulation of life insurance in the UK, Citibank nonetheless judged the overrule regulatory climate not to be unfavorable.

<u>INDUSTRY THREATS AND OPPORTUNITIES</u>. Citibank has long been noted for provident action in response to developing trends. As international lending slowed, Citibank foresaw the need to develop indigenous capital markets. The Fed's ruling led it to consider expanding into life insurance and why not? Insurance services in 1985 made up 40% of all financial services. Citibank had the advantage of synergism, transferring expertise and proven products from market to market, so it could usually deal from a position of superior knowledge. It saw that the UK life market, seventh in the world, was growing in size and product flexibility. <u>Opportunity</u> further appeared in the fact that UK life customers were relatively underinsured, and more than half the adult population completely lacked coverage. Banks were leading the expansion into underwriting, and it was believed that banks in the future would be able to actively sell insurance to their customers. Given its desires for low cost service within a synergistic framework, Citicorp could hardly lose in outpacing the cumbersome and expensive ways of selling insurance in the UK. All signs were GO. All Citibank needed was a domestic insurance company. A suspect appeared in the form of BNLA.

Some <u>threats</u> were immediately evident. BNLA was a pygmy among giants. The Thatcher government carried with it the probabilities of further deregulation, and legislation to equalize competitive market roles had already been enacted. There had to be more players in the game - for instance, building societies - and the trend was to selling insurance as we know that activity in the US, rather than passively furnishing insurance as a service. At the same time, this passivity seemed to produce a rather negative consumer image of life insurance - something intangible, inflexible once purchased, and just "a mass of small print."

CORPORATE RESOURCES AND PERSONNEL. Citibank has everything going for it. It is known worldwide, and that name opens many otherwise closed doors. It is deep in talent and has a peerless strategic management system. It is not above taking calculated risk and encourages innovation. Its pockets are deep enough to support long term objectives. It consistently does most things well because of superb leadership, good planning and effective personnel policies. Exhibits 4 and 5 are examples of the latter, and Exhibit 7 demonstrates its high degree of internal satisfaction.

FINANCE AND ACCOUNTING. This aspect of Citicorp (Exhibits 1 and 2) can only be addressed in superlatives. Its ROE is consistently around 15% and its ROA is so high (60%+) that it must be embarrassing. Its performance profile has put it within the top 30 companies in the world. The performance of BNLA is in direct contrast to Citicorp's continuing success.

MARKETING. Citicorp has done its homework well and identified BNLA as its insurance horse in the UK race. The bank's history is one of exploiting opportunities effectively, and BNLA seems made to order. The insurance market is large, growing, being deregulated, and in a state of transition. Citicorp can market, and it is to its advantage that insurance has been "offered" by "professionals" as a service, rather than sold in the manner to which we are accustomed. It is said that "we (Citicorp) have to find new ways of doing things," and that's the game plan. Marketing is everything in this new game, especially if you're as small in a relative sense as is BNLA. Citicorp has to change some old perceptions, but it has in its favor the fact that consumers view a bank-owned insurance company positively.

There is no doubt that Citicorp will capitalize on the latter. Its interoffice memo (Exhibit 21) speaks of using BNLA and Citicorp's existing customer base synergistically, furnishing BNLA with sales prospects from the UK customer list. Just how that is done will bear dramatically on BNLA's success. Indeed, here marketing is everything, because BNLA has no sales organization. It has some marketing personnel, but its sales force is qualitatively poor, seemingly untrained, poorly compensated, and has a 95% rollover rate. It is hardly conceivable that Citicorp was ignorant of all this. Presuming it was, why then buy a moribund horse? We can't be sure but reasons like cheap, little goodwill to pay for, company small enough to support a learn-as-you-go operation, and Citicorp's belief that nothing is truly risk free, come to mind. BNLA may outwardly look like a dog, but to the talent of Citicorp it must represent no more than a challenge.

PRODUCTION AND OPERATIONS. Here we know little of BNLA, and nearly all of that is unfavorable. Exhibit 7 has to be a study in dismay - poor communications, unclear goals, lack of managerial accountability, poor planning, poor personnel utilization, etc. Citicorp could hardly make a mistake here because they've already all been made. Despite a supply of administrators, financial reporting was at a minimum, no formal activity reporting system existed, and EXCO was not informed of organizational problems.

STRATEGIC ALTERNATIVES AND CHOICE

There are no alternatives. BNLA was bought to further a strategy of <u>expansion.</u>

IMPLEMENTATION

Remedial action must be taken in nearly every area. Whoever takes over faces a Rubicon in corporate culture - just how much can be grafted on to BNLA, or in John Lin's words "... decide how to integrate the business, ... fully ..., keep it at arm's length distance, or somewhere in between , and how...."

BNLA's management must go - Smith and Jones are bunions on the heels of progress. The sales force needs an overhaul, and the marketers need to go to work. Communication must become the accepted thing, not a one time happening. A management information system just has to be - Citicorp's *modus operandi* is not fueled by silence. Exhibit 7 is a prescription for other actions which can and should be taken.

RECOMMENDED DISCUSSION QUESTIONS

1. How does BNLA fit into Citicorp's strategy?

2. Why acquire BNLA?

3. What are BNLA's strengths? weaknesses?

4. What is(are) key in Citicorp's acquisition of BNLA?

5. What changes would you recommend to Mr. Cohen?

ANALYSIS AND DISCUSSION

1. How does BNLA fit into Citicorp's strategy?

If Citicorp truly wants to be an effective financial service organization, it must get into insurance. The UK economy and insurance industry are both attractive. BNLA is a life insurance organization, hence plugs the gap that Citicorp cannot fill at home under present law. At this point we believe the instructor should require a few words be spoken about Citicorp's strategy, that it decides carefully what it wants to be, plans that accomplishment, and is generally successful. Here it wants to expand worldwide to be the lowest provider of the entire financial services line.

2. Why acquire BNLA?

BNLA is small, which means Citicorp won't have a behemoth on its hands. Better to learn the business in a small way, if possible. BNLA is cheap, because it has been unsuccessful. BNLA looks like a basket case, and Citicorp has the wherewithal to turn such an organization around. If Citicorp can do so, as it believes it can, it has bought great potential at fire sale prices and can exploit the synergism it sees.

3. What are BNLA's strengths? weaknesses?

BNLA has no strengths unless one recalls that it is in the popular linked life business. Its weaknesses are legion-in marketing, managing, controlling, communicating and planning. It is because it seems so poor that its price is so reasonable.

4. What is(are) key in Citicorp's acquisition of BNLA?

You can get various answers here. We believe that the blending of corporate culture here will take a masterpiece of doing because of the vast Citicorp-EXCO difference. The boss has to address this promptly and effectively if BNLA is to get away from the dock anytime soon. Having done that, BNLA's marketing effort has to be the next action item. The industry is in a state of transition, but it is still true that the early bird gets the worm.

5. What changes would you recommend to Mr. Cohen?

See our remarks under Implementation above. BNLA put desks in Citibank Saving lobbies. A direct mail campaign using Citicorp's customer lists was begun. Smith and Jones were fired immediately. The direct sales force was revamped, retrained, and fairly compensated. A responsible financial reporting system was installed that could accurately report costs. Communication was also refurbished, and BNLA became a classic turnaround.

ELECTROLUX CORPORATION (A) (EC)

TEACHING NOTE

TEACHING OBJECTIVES

EC follows Homer Moeller, Electrolux VP of Manufacturing, as he considers what must be done and how in a major restructuring of the company's manufacturing. Specific objectives:

Understand the role of manufacturing in industry restructuring

See the complexity of the manufacturing process

Evaluate EC's new manufacturing strategy

USING THIS CASE

EC works best in the latter stages of a course because its sophistication makes it too difficult for the student still trying to sort out the component parts of strategy. It is of medium length and contains more than enough data to be an excellent case for discussion. It deals with manufacturing, not an undergraduate subject and seldom a graduate subject, so it can be very challenging. A short report, provided the parameters are quite specific, or a long report can be used with equal advantage here. The case differs from the conventional in that it deals with an announced functional strategy and invites its evaluation only - generally we ask students to formulate a corporate strategy and somewhat less frequently a functional strategy. We generally ask for implementation in gross terms, while here implementation is laid out in detail for comment.

SYNOPSIS

Electrolux, a leader in the vacuum cleaner business, found that its market had changed. Its short run survival seemed probable, but its long term survival and future growth were in doubt. When Steve McMillan became Electrolux CEO in 1983, he felt that he saw an opportunity for manufacturing to help the company, but he wasn't sure how. Competitive pressures argued for a low cost machine which manufacturing seemed unable to deliver. A study by McKinsey & Co. indicated cost savings from consolidation but said that EC needed to investigate a series of fundamental changes that went to the heart of the manufacturing effort. The job of restructuring EC's manufacturing fell to

---

This Note reflects class notes furnished by Steven Wheelwright, one of the casewriters.

Homer Moeller, then the automation genius for GE's dishwasher line. The case relates his concerns, actions, and questions in implementing McMillan's strategy.

TEACHING APPROACHES TO THIS CASE

EC provides an opportunity to look at an oldline business facing new market trends and competitive pressures which call into question its manufacturing operations. Its situation has arisen hundreds of times in this age of industrial restructuring. The case lays out the approach to restructuring manufacturing and demonstrates that the whole organization has to be involved. With that in mind, ask why EC is in trouble. That should be easy to identify. Why the emphasis on restructuring manufacturing? That can readily be ascertained. What problems must be addressed in this restructuring? The list can be quite long. We suggest that you write them on the blackboard and then discuss the proposed strategy as relates to meeting these problems. You should expect some fumbling since it would be the unusual grad student, not to mention undergraduate, who is in any way familiar with a factor floor. The aim is not to make any experts in manufacturing but to expose students to the complexity of what is too often a neglected operation.

CASE ANALYSIS

STRATEGIC MANAGEMENT ELEMENTS: MISSION, GOALS AND OBJECTIVES

No mission is stated, so we assume it to be the production of high quality floor care equipment, primarily for the home. Goals are not quantified, although a strategic goal is to bring into being a larger and more productive sales force. An implicit objective for EC has to be that of survival and long term growth. The case also identifies two driving objectives for manufacturing, product quality and sales force support, further objectives plus the strategic approaches thereto (Table 12), and some time lines (Table 9) for implementing changes.

STRATEGISTS

Not directly described. The new CEO, McMillan, is perceptive and has a keen sense of mission. He understands what must be done and expresses that in general terms. Presented with specifics by the McKinsey study, he appears to readily understand the risks involved. It is he who hires Moeller, a genius on the factory floor.

SOCIOECONOMIC SECTOR. Electrolux is a recognized name of quality which prides itself on durability and value. Its premium price should make it responsive to the economic cycle, but it appears instead to be affected more by social factors. Inflation and the desire for careers outside the home produce two income families who present EC with a brand new ballgame. "House cleaning day" is almost passe. The woman of the house just isn't there, either to clean or to listen to a sales pitch. Moreover, the pressure of tight schedules demands the quick cleanups that a lightweight, upright model can handle.

While the economic cycle was seemingly not a factor, other economic factors figured in manufacturing costs. Oil prices rose, and so did manufacturing costs. In search of lower costs in processes and in labor, companies built new, lower cost facilities and/or sourced components overseas. While inflation rose, companies were protected from the effects of higher costs simply by raising the price to the consumer. When inflation fell, companies could no longer pass along increased costs in the form of higher prices. The specter of noncompetitive costs confronted EC, and the prognosis was all but cheery.

GOVERNMENTAL SECTOR. Not an apparent factor in this case.

TECHNOLOGICAL SECTOR. Building on their success in consumer electronics, Japanese firms appeared as competitors in the vacuum cleaner industry. Their cost-competitive products created additional pressure on EC's market. The means for EC to reduce costs on the factory floor are at hand - just-in-time materials supply, automation, robotics, automated materials handling, and computer controlled lines, to name a few. EC does not have these, and its management and facilities are not configured for their installation.

R&D AND ENGINEERING SECTOR. Here we know little other than that new product development has been limited. There has to be some capability, however, since EC has developed a proprietary motor and modified its products as new materials appeared (plastic for metal). New product development is reported to be sometimes initiated by sales but usually handled entirely by engineering.

INDUSTRY THREATS AND OPPORTUNITIES. Long a market leader, EC has fallen on evil times from the threats of changing market demographics, innovative distribution channels, and low cost competition. Its opportunities are limited unless it can find a way to become more competitive. The market is still there for the quality of Electrolux but only if the company mends its ways.

STRATEGIC ADVANTAGE PROFILE

CORPORATE RESOURCES AND PERSONNEL. Electrolux has a prestigious reputation and an image of quality and value. It is resting on its laurels, however, since its organization makes for inefficiencies, and the corporate climate does not encourage change. It does not appear to have a strategic management system prior to McMillan. Its staff support systems seem inadequate, and a management information system appears nonexistent. EC stays in business primarily because of its high quality employees who produce a quality product without the benefit of a formal QC system.

FINANCE AND ACCOUNTING. The case is silent here, and <u>finance</u> is not a factor. We know only that EC was expected to gross about $400 million in FY85. Its parent, Sara Lee, expected corporate revenues of $8 billion and net income of $200 million for the same period. Financing capital improvements for EC, after $200 million for the entire corporation, seems assured. The <u>accounting system</u> is generally inadequate for product costs, materials control, and inventory control.

MARKETING AND DISTRIBUTION. EC sells direct to consumers through a <u>quality sales force</u> which lives on commission and boasts that it can sell anything. While EC's <u>market share</u> is unknown, we judge it to be considerable but diminishing. A <u>market research</u> capability does exist but we are told that new product development has usually been handled by engineering, with no sign that the product responds to market needs. The <u>product line</u> is reasonably inclusive but its main products seem to be approaching the mature phase of the <u>product life cycle.</u> Quality is the driving force in production, an attribute reflected in widespread consumer satisfaction with its canister vacuum cleaner. <u>Pricing</u> puts EC in the premium bracket, but that is to its disadvantage since more efficient competition is underpricing it. Moreover, market demographics have indicated the need for an upright cleaner, but EC has not mustered an effective response.

The direct sales force is an important component of EC's marketing strategy. However, as related above in the socioeconomic sector, two income families make <u>direct selling</u> difficult because there is no one at home to receive sales calls and even less so for demonstrations. EC again is on the outside looking in at a less expensive sales mode, since its competitors have wisely switched <u>distribution</u> to retail channels. Discount and department stores have responded by extending store hours for consumers who prefer to shop after work or on weekends.

PRODUCTION AND OPERATIONS MANAGEMENT. EC has the capacity to meet present market demands but its inefficient <u>facilities</u> and scattered production efforts make it a higher cost producer than its competitors. The entire manufacturing function needs overhaul badly from a standpoint of <u>efficiency</u> and <u>effectiveness.</u> Inventory control, materials handling, scheduling, equipment and personnel, while meeting present needs, cannot conceivably meet future needs. EC is <u>vertically integrated</u> as a matter of choice not related to economics. McMillan notes that the problems of high costs, excess capacity and duplication are found on both sides of the border.

R&D AND ENGINEERING. The case does not mention this activity directly, but there is some evidence of expertise in product and component design as well as in materials improvement.

STRATEGIC ALTERNATIVES

<u>Stability</u> means more of the same with only incremental improvement. <u>Growth</u> is possible via new products and new prices. <u>Retrenchment</u> promises lower costs. A <u>combination</u> strategy looks attractive.

CHOICE

Stability must be rejected since it does not address present problems. A strategy of growth meets the values of management and promises to make EC competitive again. Retrenchment is a must. A combination strategy of retrenchment and growth is the most logical choice.

IMPLEMENTATION

As related in case.

RECOMMENDED DISCUSSION QUESTIONS

1. What most prompts the decision to overhaul manufacturing?

2. What above all else drives manufacturing? Why?

3. What great anomaly exists in manufacturing? Why? What would you recommend? What does Homer propose?

4. Why is EC so vertically integrated? Is that degree of vertical integration necessary? Justify your answer.

5. To what might one attribute the low rate of equipment utilization at Old Greenwich (OG)? its large WIP inventory?

6. Why did McMillan call in a management consulting firm?

7. How does the new manufacturing strategy differ from the old?

8. Which of these differences is(are) likely to be most challenging to Moeller and his organization?

9. What criteria would you suggest for evaluating the new strategy and its implementation?

10. Will this strategy put EC ahead of its competitors or just keep EC from being so far behind?

11. Where is the immediate payoff in dollar savings?

12. Are there holes in the strategy? Where?

13. Was McMillan's approach appropriate to the situation?

14. What recommendations would you make to Moeller regarding refinement of the new strategy, its detailing and its pursuit?

ANALYSIS AND DISCUSSION

1.What most prompts the decision to overhaul manufacturing?

It has to be costs. EC's marketing is expensive, but to dispense with its sales force would be to completely change the company's culture and would probably irreparably damage its image. The inefficiency of its manufacturing also puts it at a competitive disadvantage in product costs. As inflation declines, it becomes impossible to conceal higher costs with rising prices. Manufacturing as configured just cannot deliver a competitively priced new product.

2.What above all else drives manufacturing? Why?

Quality. Since EC is a direct sales organization, the product has to work where it is unboxed. Product reliability has to be 100%. Manufacturing is thus subject to critical scrutiny from its sales force as well as its customers.

3.What great anomaly exists in manufacturing? Why? What would you recommend? What does Homer propose?

Quality is the driving force, yet there is little in the way of quality control in the plants. EC instead relies on its workforce to insure quality standards. Since people are human, there should at least be final testing of the product. Homer is not about to leave things to chance - Table 11 describes his quality assurance plans.

4.Why is EC so vertically integrated? Is that degree of vertical integration necessary? Justify your answer.

EC is vertically integrated in order to insure quality. Its 90% inhouse manufacture of components cannot be justified except in the case of proprietary components like the motor. Canisters for example can be made by others and probably more inexpensively. Vendors can be held to strict specifications. Outsourcing puts a premium on quality control then.

5.To what might one attribute the low rate of equipment utilization at Old Greenwich (OG)? its large WIP inventory?

The equipment seems underutilized because it exists only for occasional use. It ought to be possible to peg the span of spare parts and to source them from vendors. The swollen WIP inventory indicates poor scheduling and poorer inventory control.

6.Why did McMillan call in a management consulting firm?

This relieves onboard personnel of any onus to support the established order. A consultant can be objective and insistent, whereas those on the EC payroll would tend to be selfserving and subjective.

7. How does the new manufacturing strategy differ from the old?

	OLD	NEW
Capacity	Duplication, excess facilities High costs	Little or less duplication Medium costs
Facilities	Unfocused, nonrational flow National focus, OG parent	Product focus, rational flow US and Canada combined Bristol parent
Vertical integration	High NE vendors only	Motors only ??
Process technology	Old equipment, manual, inflexible	Automated (Phase II) flexible
Quality	Vague, people dependent	Conformance, process dependent
Work force	High pay, old, mix of skills	Medium pay, new skills, major new approach (Bristol)
New product	Engineering under manufacturing, slow development, at parent plant	Faster pace, location?
Materials control	WIP based, inefficient, old system	Complete redo, new layouts and systems
Infra-structure	Canada and US separate OG as parent	Single organization Hq as head of manu-facturing

8. Which of these differences is(are) likely to be most challenging to Moeller and his organization?

Changing Bristol to the parent plant, doing everything at once, building a team that can pull it off, getting support during phaseout of Old Greenwich.

9. What criteria would you suggest for evaluating the new strategy and its implementation?

a. What is the degree of change, and what are the risks?

b. What's the fit with the market, competition, and business strategy?

c. Is it doable - can it really be implemented?

d. Does it provide a significant, sustainable competitive advantage?

e. Is it complete?

f. What is the impact in payoff and benefits?

10. Will this strategy put EC ahead of its competitors or just keep EC from being so far behind?

It should in its initial phases at least keep EC from being so far behind. Phases II and III with automation should put it ahead of its competitors since EC is coming with new products based on market research and produced in state-of-the-art plants.

11. Where is the immediate payoff in dollar savings?

All in labor. Table 7 provides the $11 million input to Table 5. The Old Greenwich site can be sold for $8-10 million. These sums are almost enough to cover one time expenses of $13.3 million (Table 6) and the $7.3 million capital investment proposed in Exhibit 3.

12. Are there holes in the strategy? Where?

Possibly. Consider the major changes needed at Bristol. Where should new product development be located, and what should be the role of the parent plant? Where is the necessary management team?

13. Was McMillan's approach appropriate to the situation?

We would consider it so. He realized that Old Greenwich couldn't be fixed, adopted a "fix it all at once" approach, brought in outside consultants to do the strategy, and found an outside champion to implement that strategy.

14. What recommendations would you make to Moeller regarding refinement of the new strategy, its detailing and its pursuit?

a. Fill in the holes noted in 12 above. Exhibit 7 shows that Bristol needs prompt attention and probably new management.

b. Concentrate time and attention on strengthening the manufacturing management team. The quality of management is key to the new strategy.

c. Decide how to minimize the key risks cited by McMillan. Programs developed are in Tables 10 and 11 and Exhibit 6.

d. Insure that plant managements have compete programs to translate general plans into specific actions.

e. Set up means to track and control implementation. This means a PERT chart which should reflect Table 9, and a project team which watches all actions. The team must be alert to indications that phases are lagging, and it must be able to recommend contingent responses like adding resources, slowing the pace, etc.

f. Decide how best to work with McMillan and Johnson, VP sales and probable #2 man.

g. Structure the line organization around the issues noted such as an Old Greenwich transition team, Bristol buildup team, advanced manufacturing technology, etc.

h. Manage the process rather than manage the details.

GENERAL MOTORS OF CANADA

TEACHING NOTE

This Note does not follow the format of the Notes which accompany other cases in this manual. The case was written primarily for use as a basis of discussion, not to illustrate the handling of an administrative situation.

TEACHING OBJECTIVES

To acquaint students with some of the challenges of international marketing and with some of the varied aspects of large export sales.

To compare aid with export financing and parallel financing.

To witness negotiations in a different cultural setting.

USING THIS CASE

The case is intended primarily for discussion but has limitless possibilities, especially for a long report. It probably plays better late in a course when students have become more attuned to the need for accommodation and are more apt to understand the nuances of cultures. The underlying issues are relatively simple, once identified, and can be discussed at length. The case serves to teach that sometimes there are no good answers - some answers are just better than others. It stresses negotiation - and you might want to point out that we negotiate constantly. This just happens to be in a different place. It also serves to acquaint students with Egypt, certainly a force to be reckoned with in the Middle East, and it offers an occasion to delimit the Middle East and speak of some of its problems. For those who profess no interest, suggest they try driving a car without oil from the Middle East.

SYNOPSIS

The case involves the sale of locomotives in three separate contracts by General Motors of Canada, Diesel Division (GM Diesel), to the Egyptian Railway Organization (ERO) between 1977 and 1981. In the early 1970s GM Diesel was put on its own in worldwide sales and marketing. The case reports the developments of GM Diesel's international marketing effort. The firm is favored because transportation is a Canadian export strength, and a 1977 World Bank study recommended ERO standardize its equipment. As luck would have it, ERO decided to make GM the chosen instrument because most of its stock was already

---

This note is based on a prior Note and conversations with the casewriters.

GM. Ergo, Egypt is a good customer, and GM Diesel is able to sell 65 locomotives in 1978 with the aid of EDC financing. The chairman of ERO later expressed interest in another 92 locomotives, then in another 51 (total 143), provided financing could be agreed upon.

OUTCOME

Financing negotiations were signed in June 1981. Egypt paid 9% interest on the loan. The final 1\2% was apportioned as follows: interest fee $1.63 million; commitment fee $135,000; and administration fee $200,000. GM Diesel covered some, EDC some, and Nimos some, but the details of the breakdown were and are touchy and have never been discussed. The GM Diesel Sales Manager retired in 1983 even though his company had its most profitable year ever in 1982. Egypt continued to buy Henschel locos, and when USAID lifted its requirement for competitive bidding, that brought EMD back into competition. CIDA has no more funds allocated for locomotives in Egypt but believes that parallel financing was a good idea.

TEACHING APPROACHES

Perhaps some research would not be amiss before fielding this one in class. The case follows Egypt from 1952 to Sadat and Camp David. Why does Camp David bear mention? Most students won't know, a few will guess, and fewer still will recognize it as a US peace initiative in the Middle East. This is the time to point out that US interests in the Middle East are peace and stability, noble objectives, but ones which have not been achieved in this area for 2000 years. The US is no stranger to the Middle East: a young republic fought its first foreign war in the Middle East, to the cry of millions for defense but not a cent for tribute. One William Eaton's march through the Egyptian desert has been immortalized in the words of the Marine Corps Hymn... "from the halls of Montezuma to the shores of Tripoli...." The U.S. established its first foreign consulate and owned its first foreign property in the Middle East, conducted naval patrols in the Mediterranean in the 1800s, and founded schools in the Middle East before it did in Montana.

US interests are longstanding then, and when Britain opted out in 1948 following the creation of Israel, the US entered the vacuum. An emerging Egypt spelled trouble as Egypt attempted to revitalize the old Arab League. While Egypt lost its wars against Israel in 1952, 1967 and 1973, its partial success in the 1973 war started to realign the power structure in the Middle East. We looked on Sadat as an instrument of peace, hence the emphasis on Camp David. A lasting peace argued for a strong Egypt, one not struggling for subsistence but one subscribing to the goal of industrialization.

Hungry people are restive people, and US interests are those of peace and stability. It seemed wise at the time - and still is - to help Egypt industrialize. US aid money was spent prolifically in the Middle East, and any help from any friendly quarter was more than welcome. Egypt's railroad net needed extensive repair after its deterioration in the 1967-73 interwar period, and it needed upgrading and expansion if Egypt were to have any hope of industrialization.

How did Canada come to Egypt? The presence of GM in Canada, its Diesel Division, was fortuitious. With GM U.S. operating at capacity, it was expedient common sense to launch GM Diesel (Canada) into the international market by delegating it complete responsibility for international marketing. Why? Well, GM Diesel's major export at the time was locomotives. Not unnaturally GM Diesel asked for a study of the export potential of its locomotives. Ask students the significance of the study. Most will point to the identification of potential customers and products. Some may mention the recommendations made concerning changes which ought to be made to insure worldwide competitiveness in international marketing. Ask if there were any thought of turnkey, barter, or local assembly. We couldn't find any and conclude that the requirement for Canadian content made those alternatives look unreal. The more astute will cite turnkey projects by name, but they won't be able to discuss Canadian or American content because those figures are nebulous at best. Make sure students understand what "Canadian content" implies. The U.S. has similar requirements. Reduced to simplest terms, the phrase means that items of aid should insofar as possible be purchased locally in preference to fattening economies abroad. The study also addressed the education of the local agent and general sales manager. Should they be required to visit the home office annually? Why? Is it worth the expense?

What did the study determine to be critical in marketing locomotives? Price, mix, delivery and financing. Why is financing regarded as the key? Has price no meaning? How about delivery times? How does the requirement for Canadian content affect financing? Well, it shouldn't, but it does, and this demonstrates the necessity for united policy. CIDA will not finance without 2/3 Canadian content. Wise? Unwise? What's more important - a 2/3 content lost sale, or a 1/2 content sale? This might be a good time to see if students really understand offset agreements. There will be those who will protest that this is a class in business strategy, not international trade. Agree with them - but then ask if the governmental sector of the environment is ever a factor of consideration in formulating business strategy.

If financing is the key constraint, what has GM Diesel done to shore up this point? All that one can point to is compliance with content to aid CIDA financing. What else could have been done, since the problem was flagged? Apparently nothing was, and the problem surfaced again as an impasse in 1981. It would have been better had there been better linkage in government policies EDC-CIDA. Students must be reminded that a lack of linkage is not a Canadian monopoly. Washington is famous for pursuing diametrically opposing policies. Certainly CIDA had to be aware of EMD's ineligibility for AID financing, but the case does not mention the effect of that ineligibility on CIDA. We have no way of knowing, and perhaps it was done, but that would have been the time to review governmental policies.

CIDA financed where EMD could not. Should CIDA have foreseen any future demands for similar financing? The answer is clear in retrospect of course, but bear in mind that financing was recognized as the key constraint. Enter EDC, whose motives seem different. Ask students to read the stated philosophies of both and then to compare them. EDC appears as an export facilitator with a short range financing interest, as opposed to CIDA's longer range interest in economic development. The same situation exists in the Lower 48, and students should be asked to name US organizations with contrasting motives. The questions are the same: where and who reconciles differing interests and under what circumstances? EDC filled in where CIDA could not; the terms were not nearly as favorable. GM Henschel is in the background, ready to step in if GM Diesel falters.

When ERO wanted to buy more locomotives, financing - not price - again became a problem. Egypt now knew of a growing foreign exchange problem, so its demand for CIDA funding could not have been a surprise. This should have been anticipated. Parallel financing was arranged after the Honorable Ed Lumley intervened. CIDA's money was readily accepted, but then the problem. Both CIDA and EDC could agree that parallel financing would help them serve their respective constituencies. CIDA saw that the tradeoff between limited funds and better terms, like 0/10/50 money mixed with EAC's, stretched funds and provided a lower effective interest rate, and it discussed the aid-trade mix problem. EDC seemed not to appreciate CIDA's position. The resultant need for separate contracts caused problems in Egypt and elsewhere when negotiators became blind to all but the EDC financing rate. Little else seemed to matter. A common ground was imperative but lacking.

Egypt presented a united front and was prepared to wait out GM Diesel. No one budged. Ask students what now? You should get a variety of answers. Now ask if all positions are real, or are there alternatives? Whom does time favor? Assumedly Egypt, since the longer negotiations drag over an agreed price, the more GM stands to lose by inflation or by simply doing nothing. Locos are built to order and since they present a variety of scheduling problems, delay impacts on GM Diesel's performance. GM Diesel has a chase demand strategy - no orders, no work - so the division either shuts down with high restart costs or slows down as inflation eats margins. Students will not know all this, but most can easily be developed by questioning.

Egypt has a valid point, that the last contract was 9%, and 9 1/2% would cause a lack of face. This position seems real and emphasizes the impact of different culture on perceptions. The Egyptians are willing to talk at length under conditions which a westerner finds untenable. Cultural differences again do not favor westerners because we tend to have a short term outlook. While the sellers may press for decision, they face a bureaucracy which may be all but impenetrable. Values differ; language can become a problem when it is discovered that key words have not been adequately conveyed, and even gestures can become points of contention.

Is the Egyptian argument valid that such a large buy should merit a better interest rate? Is the Canadian response, that the potential for greater loss argues against a lower rate, an acceptable reply? The Egyptian economy does face a foreign exchange shortage. While there is always some potential for loss, it cannot be forgotten that Egypt is the recipient of aid from many quarters and can hardly fail to pay its bills without calling into question its ability to manage its affairs. Egypt has a face problem, compounded by a governmental problem of foreign exchange; it will probably not yield. It has an ace in the hole in the form of GM Henschel, and there is little to stop it from playing that card. EDC must be aware of that. ERO has raised the stakes by indicating it might buy 143 locomotives, provided arrangements could be reached.

EDC could hardly afford to lose so large a contract, though the case is imprecise in stating any monetary loss. EDC was also bothered by the precedents that reducing the interest rate would set, since it had other fish to fry. ERO fixed on the interest rate and was adamant that price reductions could not be used to offset the rate increase. Besides, there were other things that ERO wanted to negotiate separately. Students should - with a little help - have gotten this far.

GM Diesel was at wit's end. EDC and the Central Bank of Egypt were at top dead center, beset with external pressures. The problem is easy to solve if one only knows who is behind what position and who has the power to approve. Here students expect you to pull a rabbit out of the hat and furnish an absolutely ingenious solution that would do credit to Perry Mason. We will never know what happened, but we surmise that the local representative played a key role in events. Resolution was much to his advantage. An Egyptian graduate of MIT unable to bridge the gap? How could he face GM Diesel in Canada? What would his other clients think? How much face could he afford to lose? He knew ERO and its people like no one else, and he worked for GM. Who would know the centers of power better and understand what would move each, if only a little?

Egypt has changed its priorities for CIDA aid, about $25 million per year, to agriculture, food, human resource development and energy, but not transportation. Canadian content remains a touchy issue with EDC. At the time the case was written (April 1983) GM Diesel was in the process of negotiating sales to Egypt of semi-armored vehicles as well as locomotives. CIDA has funds for locos in Egypt and has since allocated $5 million toward a training project for servicing and railway maintenance but doubts that GM Diesel will be awarded the contract because it is not seen as "Canadian enough."

KRAFT, INC.

TEACHING NOTE

TEACHING OBJECTIVES

In the scramble for the top of the food processing industry, the management of Kraft has to insure both optimum organization and product mix. Specific objectives:

Become familiar with the food processing industry.

Appreciate the effects of the environment on the industry.

Understand the strategy of one of the industry's leaders, Kraft.

Evaluate management's implementation of Kraft's strategy.

USING THIS CASE

Kraft is well written, easy to read, and well organized. The case should be easy to discuss, because everyone knows a little about the subject of food. The case is of medium length and no more than moderate difficulty. It does not lend itself to a good inclass exam but does fit well as a short report, long report, or final problem. Its emphasis on environmental analysis and implementation suggest its use later in a course.

SYNOPSIS

In 1980, Kraft, an old line company under National Dairy, merged to form Dart & Kraft. Its strategy was to concentrate on high quality, basically consumer-oriented businesses through controlled diversification. Though sales and profits both rose in 1985, the company split in 1986 into Kraft and Dart (later Premark International). The split apparently was to make Kraft more attractive to Wall Street and thus to enhance shareholder value.

OUTCOME

The case points out (p. 217) the 1985 food company mergers. In late 1988, Philip Morris tendered for Kraft at $90 per share, a 50% premium on the market price, but Kraft countered that anything less than $110 per share was inadequate. Philip Morris paid almost $12 billion for Kraft in December 1988.

This Note is based on a previous Note by and conversations with the casewriter.

TEACHING APPROACHES TO THIS CASE

Kraft, of course, has been overtaken by events. One can march quietly through the discussion questions. Another is to review our comments under the last discussion question. Students can review events since the split of Dart and Kraft and decide whether Miles' descriptions of Kraft's strengths and weaknesses were valid. The case is unusual in that we usually ask students to ferret out strengths, weaknesses, and strategies. Here these are given, so attention must be turned first to verifying their validity, and then having done so, to see if these were factors in the broad strategies Miles listed.

CASE ANALYSIS

STRATEGIC MANAGEMENT ELEMENTS: MISSION, GOALS AND OBJECTIVES

Kraft's <u>mission</u> is to be the world's leading food company. Its <u>goals</u> are never numerically stated, though Kraft will compete whenever returns are "at or above corporate targets." Other goals, or perhaps it is more accurate to say corporate culture, refer to customers, competitors, employees, channels of distribution, and business style (Exhibit 1). <u>Objectives</u> are not given. However, Kraft's statement of mission seems to reflect objectives as qualifiers to that mission: to outrank competition in a balance of factors such as rate of growth in sales and operating income, ROI, innovation, outstanding people and product quality, etc.

STRATEGISTS

None is described directly. Kraft's CEO, Miles, is demonstrably forthright, open, knowledgeable and decisive. Controlled diversification requires discriminating strategic judgment. Since Miles outlined broad strategies, someone has to be thinking. Kraft says its business style will be noted for planning and superior analysis, and it lists business plans as a meter of greatness. Since industry growth is virtually static, growth in domestic market shares will have to be at the expense of competitors. Kraft's attraction to strategic management is instantly understandable, and so are its five year plans at plant level.

ENVIRONMENTAL ANALYSIS

<u>SOCIOECONOMIC SECTOR</u>. Food, a basic commodity, is largely unaffected by the economic cycle, so the economy was not a factor during the time of the case. Since the food market tends to grow with the population, the low growth of the industry reflects fairly flat per capita consumption trends. More and more the customer is king, so as tastes change, one either innovates to survive or buys into the latest trend. Half the products on grocers' shelves weren't there five years ago. As DPI increases, customers demand and receive higher quality and greater variety. That is important because the Dart & Kraft answer via acquisition was to attempt to maintain that mix of high quality consumer goods. Two wage earners meant more DPI but less time to prepare food. That generated a need for healthier foods, more convenience in preparation, and more meals away from home, for all of which consumers were willing to pay. Not blessed with a greater

market share created by the rising consumption of a growing population, a company had to follow Tom Peters' litany of customer, quality, and service.

INDUSTRY THREATS AND OPPORTUNITIES. While Kraft is second only to General Foods, that fact serves merely to sharpen competition and makes the scramble for opportunities even harder. Faced with increasing competition and enjoying little recent success in developing new products, Kraft has done well with the acquisitions which reinforce market trends: With super premium ice cream growing in popularity, buy Frusen Gladje; buy an Italian cheese company as Italian cheese becomes more popular; with the decline of whole milk consumption, and with more meals away from home, buy into food distributors to capitalize on the greater percentage of restaurant meals; push the lighter versions of cheese, dressings, toppings and ice milk for the calorie counting consumer; frozen entrees are the answer for those with less time to prepare food at home.

There is no want of supplies, and customers abound. Success lies in being the first to capitalize on emerging buyer segments, such as ethnic foods. Demography matters, too. Products have been downsized to reflect the trend to smaller family units, but relatively little attention has been paid to the needs of an aging population. The industry cannot escape doing so, because that's where the action (and the money) is going to be. Geographic factors seem shortlived - cajun cooking emerged as a possible entrant in the ethnic food line, but now cajun food seems as geographic as grits, hominy, and blackeyed peas.

GOVERNMENT AND TECHNOLOGY SECTOR. Technology has little mention, but in the product-process competition, food companies must make perpetual inquiry into food machinery technology in an effort to move further down the long run average cost curve. Was rape seed (canola oil) a likely entrant into the low cholesterol bulk oil field? As consumption patterns shift and consumer desires change, the industry itself has to see major internal change. The casewriter points out that Kraft's sales reps used portable terminals to insure next-day service; further, in another effort to lower costs, that Kraft developed a computerized restaurant management system. Government is not an unusual factor, though the case notes that the Justice Department seems to almost forget the Sherman Act in permitting horizontal concentric acquisitions.

STRATEGIC ADVANTAGE PROFILE

RESOURCES AND PERSONNEL. Kraft has virtually unlimited resources by virtue of being one of the four largest food companies in the world. It is simply prestigious. Its image is one of quality and efficiency. Its reputation for producing and promoting branded foods is a major strength. Its organization by principal product lines is effective, given its sales and profits. Its strategic management system reaches down to plant level but raises a question of strategic fit: how do dishes, home appliances and cooking equipment contribute to Kraft's mission? The synergy is not obvious.

FINANCE AND ACCOUNTING. We know little other than the actual figures. Miles states that Kraft has the financial resources to support new initiatives anywhere. The retail food business is a cash cow for stars like Duracell. Scale economies and operating efficiencies through recent acquisitions have fattened the bottomline. Lower commodity prices and pending favorable tax legislation can also add to the bottom line. Sales and profits have climbed steadily, especially when ROE and ROA are compared with industry averages.

MARKETING. Kraft domestically is second only to General Foods. Kraft is either a leader or a major figure in nearly all major categories of its cognizance. It has the industry's nod for best quality. Its customer relations are excellent. Only P&G can match its sales force for skill and effectiveness. Kraft intends to push the growth of existing brands with a still larger sales force, better communication, and more timely decision making. It intends to price competitively. It will publicize any manners of product improvement, so fierce is its competition. It intends to drop and has dropped commodities where returns have become unacceptable. In 1984 Kraft was in the top 20 spenders in advertising. In sum, marketing is a huge plus, however one views it.

PRODUCTION AND OPERATIONS MANAGEMENT. Seemingly not a factor in the case.

R&D AND ENGINEERING. Miles listed a Kraft weakness as failure to develop any significant new products. He felt Kraft was too conservative. Although its announced business style spoke of innovation and risk acceptance, Miles said the company needed more challenges. The only R&D described is limited to packaging or equipment innovation pointed at greater efficiency. Efficiency is to be admired, but much more badly needed is an R&D element which leads in high value-added product development. *Business Week* (20 February 1987) reported that Kraft's bigger problem was one of image, of a firm too slow to react to the rapid environmental changes going on around it.

STRATEGIC ALTERNATIVES

Stability, fine for greater efficiency, will leave Kraft further behind. A strategy of expansion will enable it to keep pace with its peers. Retrenchment is indicated since Kraft wants "to pursue expense and asset minimizations in all areas." A combination strategy looks promising.

CHOICE

A combination strategy of retrenchment and growth.

RECOMMENDED DISCUSSION QUESTIONS

1. How well is Kraft capitalizing on the strengths identified by its CEO?

2. How well has it strengthened the internal weaknesses he also identified?

3. Do those strengths and weaknesses impinge on Miles' five broad strategies?

4. Comment on Kraft's financial strengths and weaknesses 1982-86.

5. Is the 1986 breakup of Dart & Kraft more likely to help or to hinder Kraft in pursuing its avowed mission of becoming the world's leading food company?

ANALYSIS AND DISCUSSION

1. How well is Kraft capitalizing on the strengths identified by its CEO?

a. Kraft competed in the growth markets by retrenching in fluid milk and emphasizing other dairy products. It moved up in premium ice cream, Light n' Lively cottage cheese and ice milk, super-premium ice cream, and yogurt.

b. Kraft is clearly moving toward identifiable brand names. It is advertising these brands, though it is outspent here by PG and Beatrice, its major competitors.

c. Doubling its retail sales force must indicate management's commitment to further improve already excellent customer relations.

d. Kraft's financial statements evidence tremendous financial strength, and Kraft can, does, and will operate anywhere. Exhibit 11 shows that 23% of its profit came from its sales abroad.

2. How well has its strengthened the internal weaknesses he also identified?

Here one might say not too well. Its Breyers products did well, but Breyers was an acquisition. The split of Dart & Kraft might do something toward dispelling the curse of conservatism. Competition will pose more than enough challenges, but it remains to be seen whether Kraft's responses will be couched in an innovative forecasting of environmental factors or will be reflected in the acquisition of established lines. The Street apparently guessed the latter, reading Kraft's stock price following the breakup (Exhibit 8).

3. Do those strengths and weaknesses impinge on Miles' five broad strategies?

There can be many answers here, but justifications may come hard. If the company is too conservative, will pursuing asset minimization add to that feeling? Will a lack of new products hamper the efforts foreseen by a "more active new business development effort?" Will organizational vitality alone be the best answer to increasing competition? What else should be encouraged?

4. Comment on Kraft's financial strengths and weaknesses 1982-86.

The number crunchers will love this one. Send them to the Compustat Tapes to find corresponding industry average ratios. The casewriter points out that 1986 industry averages come from a different collection of companies, necessitated by the breakup. Pertinent findings: CR halved from 1982-86 (2.02-1.08), and with QR.55 in 1986, liquidity has fallen abruptly. With Kraft's assets, is that critical? Times interest earned (11 in 1986 v 6.39 in 1982) has risen even though the debt/asset ratio climbed from .36 in 1982 to .53 in 1988. The firm manages its debt well. Its industry turnover was steady at 7 in 1955 and 1986 but far below the industry average of 25 in 1985. Profitability is strong since both ROA and ROE generally exceed industry averages.

5. Is the 1986 breakup of Dart & Kraft more likely to help or to hinder Kraft in pursuing its avowed mission of becoming the world's leading company?

This is a good discussion question which will evoke the antipodes. Evaluate the breakup based on the contents of the case, then look at Kraft's performance after the breakup and compare. Since management had no sure means of knowing performance after October 1986, our surmise is that the breakup was more likely to help Kraft. In effect, what it did was to drop excess baggage, perhaps as a reflection of Miles' desire for vitality and minimization, become lean and mean, and work the figures. Premark got the slow growers and the hardware. Richman would be free to concentrate on food (and kept fast selling Duracell which is distributed in supermarkets) and thus to look to his operating profit. Perhaps he did too well, attracting Phillip Morris as he did. Premark is listed on the NYSE at 38 as of this writing, just below its 1989 high of 39 5/8.

OZARK GLASS COMPANY (OGC)

TEACHING NOTE

TEACHING OBJECTIVES

OGC is a small manufacturer of stained glass which does well enough in export sales to win the Presidential "E" award but is faced with the question of what to do in Act II. Specific objectives:

See the expansion of a small business into international markets.

Understand how the decision to enter foreign business makes structural changes necessary.

Analyze the company's strategy for continued growth abroad.

Suggest alternative strategies.

USING THIS CASE

OGC is suitable for an inclass exam or a short report. Its brevity probably would not permit a long report without the addition of other requirements. It is short, easy to comprehend, and reads smoothly. For reasons like that, plus the fact that it is a success story in an unusual business, the case should hold student interest well. It is a good ice breaker for the early part of a course, or it can be used in midcourse when alternatives are considered. It is a good opener for later international cases.

SYNOPSIS

Ozark Glass was founded in 1974 as an antique shop simply to provide a hobby for its owners. It expanded rapidly by franchising and then opened its own glass plant. Its sales rose hundred fold in eight years, and 35% of its sales were abroad. It opened initially in Asia but withdrew from that market in favor of the European market. OGC believes that franchising is the key to long term international market growth. Fluctuating currency exchange rates have cut into OGC's export sales margins. While the firm is optimistic about sales in Europe, it is hesitant to do other than franchise.

OUTCOME

Ozark Glass is alive and well today and quite profitable.

This Note is based on a prior Note by and conversation with the casewriter.

The most sensible approach is to ask if OGC is successful. The "E" award says that it most certainly is, certainly in the international sales field, and Exhibit 1 shows a 100% increase in gross sales. Why has OGC been successful? You might want to split the question into domestic and foreign markets. It has found a niche in the do-it-yourself market and recognized that franchising can be renumerative. The boom in domestic sales is enough to require OGC to open its own glass making facility, and that facility has grown to be the third largest in the U.S. Its advertising in U.S. trade publications attracted inquiries from overseas readers. Ask students how one enters overseas markets. There are only three basic ways - export, ownership and licensing - and all others are simply variations of these. What should OGC follow? What did it follow? Does company size affect the means of market penetration? Did OGC choose the optimum way? It has done well abroad. Can it continue to do well? If continued growth is desired, what should it do now?

CASE ANALYSIS

STRATEGIC MANAGEMENT ELEMENTS: MISSION, GOALS AND OBJECTIVES

No <u>mission</u> is stated, so we surmise OGC's mission must be to provide stained glass to franchisers and wholesalers, both foreign and domestic. Other than the implicit <u>goals</u> of profit, occupation and growth, no goals are stated, and there is no quantification. There are no stated <u>objectives</u>.

STRATEGISTS

The principals are not described directly. We know only that OGC was started as a hobby. That leads us to believe that Dr. Connor and his wife are alert, energetic, daring, ambitious, hardworking, painstaking, perceptive, and not risk averse but extremely cautious.

ENVIRONMENTAL ANALYSIS

<u>SOCIOECONOMIC SECTOR</u>. Stained glass is a hobby item here and is bought out of disposable income. Its price is so low that it can hardly be affected by the economic cycle, general business conditions, or inflation. It profits from the trend to do-it-yourself, and if you can't do, learn how in one of those many adult classes which appear from time to time. Stained glass is relatively new, attractive, and capitalizes on the urge to do something different and creative.

<u>GOVERNMENTAL AND TECHNOLOGICAL SECTOR</u>. Not a factor in this case.

<u>INDUSTRY THREATS AND OPPORTUNITIES</u>. OGC faces little in the way of <u>threats</u>. U.S. facilities are few (15), and OGC is the third largest glass producer in the U.S. The domestic demand is great enough that OGC is able to franchise shortly after opening. While OGC did open an Asian market, it lost that market to a domestic <u>competitor</u> who underpriced OGC. Due to ease of entry, one would

expect competitors to abound, but none seem to materialize. OGC has never identified buyer segments - it just answers the mail. Europe is seen as a great opportunity, as is South America. There is a lack of either European or American competition in Europe, and the same appears to hold true in Latin America.

STRATEGIC ADVANTAGE PROFILE

RESOURCES AND PERSONNEL. We know nothing of the principals except what we have entered under Strategists. OGC enjoys a good reputation, particularly because of the quality of its glass and because of its handson attitude toward its clients. The organizational structure is undefined - in fact, overseas markets are attended by the President, Vice President, and national sales manager. Succession seems unconsidered. Overlapping responsibilities seem not to have affected sales. There is no detectable strategic management system, no record of objectives, and no mention of employees or personnel relations. OGC seems like many small companies then.

FINANCE AND ACCOUNTING. Not mentioned. We note that OGC has no systematic way of dealing with currency fluctuations in international markets, however.

MARKETING AND DISTRIBUTION. Ozark Glass had done little market research and spends about 1% of sales on advertising. The company relies almost completely on inquiries from the ads it places in trade journals. It does generate some sales from trade shows in Europe and in Latin America. Despite its laid back attitude, it knows that no domestic competitor has international sales exceeding 5% of gross sales. The company emphasizes quality control in its product. This seems to have paid off, especially in Europe where customers had had an erroneous impression of the quality of American glass. The company's unusual response to overseas queries - letters and telephone calls, personal sales visits to possible clients, and a willingness to work with customers via telex and watts lines in all aspects of stained glass - has been a big factor in the growth of foreign sales. The company uses a freight forwarder for international shipments. It expects to continue to use sales agents to find business in remote areas. Its cost plus pricing brings it higher margins from franchise sales, and its access to inexpensive suppliers enables it to underprice European competitors even after shipping. Its carefree approach to marketing is perhaps what one would expect in a small company, but even so it appears to succeed almost in spite of itself.

PRODUCTION AND OPERATIONS MANAGEMENT. OGC believes it has sufficient glass manufacturing capacity, though its plant can be expanded should that become necessary. We have noted that the cost of its raw materials enables it to underprice competitors. Whether facilities are efficient, inventory control is effective, and machinery is effective/ efficient, we do not know. There is no mention whatsoever of R&D.

There are no alternatives since OGC has committed itself to a strategy of growth, especially abroad.

RECOMMENDED DISCUSSION QUESTIONS

1. What are the critical elements of OGC's export strategy that led it to become so successful?

2. Can the company continue its present rate of growth in international sales, given its current marketing philosophy?

3. What weaknesses, if any, do you see in its export strategies?

4. Evaluate the stability of its export strategy.

5. Why did OGC abandon its Far Eastern market so abruptly? Should it have done so?

6. How can or should the company respond to future competition in other markets?

7. Should OGC switch to joint ventures or licensing as a means of international market expansion? What possible consequences should be considered?

8. Is there an answer to fluctuating exchange rates?

ANALYSIS AND DISCUSSION

1. What are the critical elements of OGC's export strategy that led it to become so successful?

OGC's aggressive pursuit of every sales lead-letter, call, personal visit, and personalized service-sold OGC as much as it sold OGC's product. Since it was targeting the hobby market, it had no competition and was quick to capitalize on this niche.

2. Can the company continue its present rate of growth in international sales, given its current marketing philosophy?

Probably not. Word of mouth is fine advertising, but it has its limitations abroad, just as does circulation of U.S. trade publications. This may have gotten OGC off the launch pad, but it seems a very frail support on which to lean for LT growth.

3.What weaknesses, if any, do you see in its export strategies?

This is almost another way of asking Question 2. It has no formal set of export objectives and no apparently concerted plans of action. It lacks true market research and spends sparsely on advertising. There is no reason why it can't get more mileage out of its ad dollars if it will only get a line on potential clients. Moreover, OGC sees franchising as the best way to LT market growth. If that be true, its use of agents betrays a lack of steady aim and an unsureness of foreign markets.

4.Evaluate the stability of its export strategy.

Without a more rational approach, the stability of its LT strategy is questionable. What would it do if local competitors blossomed?

5.Why did OGC abandon its Far Eastern market so abruptly? Should it have done so?

There is no good answer here. OGC made no effort to compete directly. Perhaps, given its depth of management, the Far East wasn't worth a fight, given the attractiveness of the European market. When you are spread thin, you can cover only so many bases. The reason(s) for the cost differential could have been investigated. Did its competitor provide glass of equivalent quality? Did its service compare? There are others parts to a buying decision besides price, but OGC seems to have written them off.

6.How can or should the company respond to future competition in other markets?

The obvious answer here is, it depends on the circumstances. Of course it does, so OGC should pause long enough to write a strategic plan which can be used to counter inevitable future competition. Otherwise, it may find it has done the wrong thing too late.

7.Should OGC switch to joint ventures or licensing as a means of international market expansion? What possible consequences should be considered?

The answer here has to be, why not? The attraction of franchising is not detailed. True, franchising is the way of life in the USA, but it is not the only way of life in overseas markets. OGC seems transfixed by the higher profit margin it realizes on glass sales to its franchisees. It may well be that someone abroad can produce glass almost as good at a lower cost, given shipping, insurance, breakage and inventory financing. Then what? Franchisees are not necessarily "tied" to OGC as a prime supplier, so that attraction may vanish. OGC still profits from franchise fees, however.

It could as well profit from licensing fees. Licenses can be written very rigidly and probably provide OGC an equivalent return. Whereas OGC owes a franchisee continuing management advice, it has no such obligation to a licensee, nor is it usual to require the licensor to assume any after-sale service responsibility. Moreover, a franchise may require some OGC investment, whereas a license would not. OGC reportedly is worried about quality control in its licensees; the point is well taken, but QC can be made a term of license - if licensee samples do not meet specifications, OGC has it by the throat, and there are numerous alternatives here.

The same is true in a joint venture, where OGC as a matter of contract could control quality. A joint venture (JV) may be the only means of doing business in some countries, so a JV cannot be dismissed out of hand. OGC might have to be a 49% owner, but that's a business decision which is made every day. A JV may require some investment, but then, too, so might a franchise. OGC seems a bit shortsighted when it comes to forms of business abroad.

8. Is there an answer to fluctuating exchange rates?

Of course. Hire a financial specialist, if only on a part-time basis. Many banks provide advice and will be glad to hedge currency futures. Losses here are inexcusable.

PART IV

TEACHING NOTES

ACCOMPANYING

CASES ON MANUFACTURING

ORGANIZATIONS

APPLE COMPUTER, INC. - MACINTOSH (A) (ACM)

TEACHING NOTE

TEACHING OBJECTIVES

ACM focuses on the introduction and establishment of a manufacturing technology (new to the company) which raises several major issues. Specific objectives:

See the interface between marketing and product design

Understand advanced manufacturing technologies

Appreciate the role of Macintosh in Apple's long term positioning

USING THIS CASE

Since the case was written for a course in manufacturing strategy, we judge it will be difficult for those who have no manufacturing background. It probably fits best in the latter part of a course. ACM discusses well and is best addressed as a long report or a final problem in lieu of the traditional final exam.

SYNOPSIS

Although Apple Computer was at the head of the PC pack by 1981 and expected almost $1 billion in sales for the FY ending September 1983, it was clear that Apple's product line was aging. Considering that and the industry's projected growth rates, Apple developed the Macintosh for the middle to lower end of the high volume segment. Steve Jobs saw Macintosh as a vehicle for a new manufacturing strategy, a strategy which was to prepare Apple for future competitive challenges. That strategy involves going from conventional build to automated build. Doing so raises some issues which require recommendations from Matt Carter.

OUTCOME

Apple split Macintosh automation into three stages. The plant started up in December 1983 but the case-described automated build did not appear until fall, 1984. Apple scrapped several million dollars of the materials handling system in mid-1984 because the overhead conveyors were difficult to handle, and with increasing volume, the Macintosh group was anxious to install higher speed equipment than originally planned.

This Note is based on a prior Note by Steven C. Wheelwright.

Much of the phasing of automation and manufacturing technology was dictated by the need to put Macintosh on the market as close as possible to the publicized rollout date. That date was postponed several times. Macintosh finally appeared in January, 1984. Apple, mindful of past mistakes, wanted to make sure the production system worked well and could meet the initial surge in demand, rather than to announce too early and find itself in deep trouble.

The Mac factory was built at Fremont, California, about 30 miles from Apple Hq at Cupertino. By summer 1984 the plant operated near its design capacity of 40,000 units per month and plans were afoot to double that by year's end. Another team was working on the next generation plant (hopefully Phase 2, noted on Exhibit 1, attached to this note). The basic strategy for that plant was to level the Fremont plant, just as NCR did with its original plant in Ohio, so that all would understand that the Fremont plant was not the end position. Arrangements were even made with the IRS to close the doors in 18 months, making the next generation plant all that more urgent.

We direct the instructor's attention to "Automated Apple," p. 80, <u>Discover</u>, September 1984, and to "Mac Factory," p. 130, <u>Softtalk</u>, February 1984, for a detailed description of the Macintosh facility.

TEACHING APPROACHES TO THIS CASE

The casewriter suggests breaking a class into five parts, commencing with asking students to contrast the two processes of conventional build and automated build. The aim is to recognize the major parts of the two processes and how they differ. Contrasting the two involves students in some of the specifics of the automated build, what it is and what it isn't. What's difficult and what's easy in each, what makes each attractive, and what are some of the limitations?

Next, deal with the five issues facing Matt Carter: location, parallel build, the extent of automation, the degree of vertical integration, and the production ramp (build-up in volume). This carries into organizational issues of where manufacturing should report and of the appropriate interface between design and manufacturing. Automation, it might be noted, serves as a "forcing mechanism" for better integrating design and manufacturing. That is, the tolerances to which circuit boards must be designed are different and closer if boards are to be made with automated equipment than if they are to be made for hand insertion. The proposed automatic material transfer means that vendors will have to respond to different tolerances and specifications on components, of course, and also on the packaging which brings components to the plant.

Third, consider competitive analysis and what it is that has energized Apple to go so far in Macintosh manufacturing. This should be done before students become bogged down in resolving the issues facing Carter. It turns out that most will lack resolution until the competitive environment and Apple's intentions have all been addressed. Once it is recognized that Apple is just scratching the surface, the matter of where manufacturing fits becomes clearer as one considers the next five years. Exhibit I (attached) puts Apple's conventional build in the traditional column, its Macintosh in Phase I and its competitors, IBM and Japanese, in Phase III.

Fourth, look at the risks to Apple with regard to Macintosh strategy and the challenges it faces.

Lastly, recite the outcome (publications will be immensely helpful here).

CASE ANALYSIS

STRATEGIC MANAGEMENT ELEMENTS: MISSION, GOALS AND OBJECTIVES

Mission is not stated but can be inferred to be the manufacture and distribution of personal computers. No goals are provided, other than that of producing 48,000 units by 31 December 1983. An objective of the Macintosh product is to prepare for future competitive challenges (IBM and Japan).

STRATEGISTS

None is described. Steve Jobs of course is the entrepreneur. Matt Carter, Manager of Production Engineering, is shown as a reflective, orderly thinker who can see both the forest and its trees.

ENVIRONMENTAL ANALYSIS

SOCIOECONOMIC SECTOR. The PC has become an accepted way of life. The man on the street, the home, and the school, in addition to businesses, now can own a PC. The industry sold 1.5 million units in 1982. The economy was not a factor in the case, but in 1983 the recession was a worry at Apple, and its manufacturing activity was concerned about the future. Social factors were not mentioned.

GOVERNMENTAL SECTOR. Not an apparent factor in this case.

TECHNOLOGY SECTOR. Machines make possible Macintosh's automated build. The plant can assemble a Mac every 27 seconds, to the tune of 1.2 million units per year. For instance, materials are handled by mechanical hands from the time they arrive at the plant. Just-in-time delivery prevails and is supported by computerized control of inventory. A computer-controlled crane selects a box of electronic parts from among thousands of boxes and puts the box on a conveyor belt that carries it to an assembly line. One device, a sequencer, lays out parts in the order in which they will be used, and automatic component inserters plug those parts into a circuit board. Other machines assemble logic boards, and so on.

118

<u>INDUSTRY THREATS AND OPPORTUNITIES</u>. Apple's <u>threats</u> appear to be chiefly from IBM, its main competitor, and Steve Jobs sees Japanese computers as a major threat in three or four years. The PC market projects growth rates of 100%+ a year, so there are ample <u>opportunities</u> for the company, provided it can replace the aging Apple series with a new product line. <u>Suppliers</u> are plentiful and pose no limitations to the Mac project.

STRATEGIC ADVANTAGE PROFILE

<u>CORPORATE RESOURCES AND PERSONNEL</u>. Apple has an impressive corporate <u>image</u> in the PC world. Its organizational <u>structure</u> is by product line and then by functional area, but the organizational placement of Macintosh has yet to be determined. The corporate <u>climate</u> favors product development over manufacturing. Apple has a <u>strategic management system</u> (not mentioned in case) which has enabled it to consistently meet sales objectives and to share the PC lead with IBM in 1983. It has high quality <u>employees</u>, and its <u>top management</u> is superb. Systemwise, Apple lacks nothing.

<u>FINANCE AND ACCOUNTING</u>. Except for an exhibit (Exhibit 1 <u>in</u> the case) which shows three years' income and balance sheets, we are told only that Apple had "substantial cash reserves." Income and EPS have risen more than 400%. Financial ratios are so favorable as to be a matter of embarrassment. There is no LT debt. The picture here is one of robust financial health.

<u>MARKETING AND DISTRIBUTION</u>. Apple, as aforesaid, by 1983 shared half of the PC market with IBM. Its history since 1977 has been one of risk, innovation, and an awareness of the consumer. Not mentioned in the case is an effective <u>market research</u> system. Apple's <u>advertising</u> has established Apple as being for the common man (what is made common or more humble than an apple?) and evoked positive feelings on the part of the customer. Its <u>pricing</u> strategy has been unbelievably effective: Apple makes money on its hardware and treats software as almost a free good, the opposite of other computer manufacturers. Apple <u>distributes</u> through a network of 950 independent retail computer stores (as of January 1981) and 1300 retail stores scattered around the world and served by independent distributors. Apple cultivates its <u>dealers</u> by training them well, giving them better margins than any other company, listening to their suggestions, and not competing with them through a company sales force.

Aware that the Apple line was aging, Apple brought out Lisa, the high end office product, and Macintosh for the middle to low end, high volume segment, both intended to represent a completely new generation of PCs. Arguing that the key to expanding the PC market lay in making a machine that was much, much more user friendly, Macintosh was so constructed as to greatly decrease the initial learning time for a new user. By 1985 Mac was seen as the heart of Apple's product line.

<u>PRODUCTION AND OPERATIONS MANAGEMENT</u>. Apple has been in the black since Day 1 by dint of <u>outsourcing</u> components and acting only as a <u>final</u>

assembler. It pays its suppliers in 60 days yet demands payment for products in 30 days. Since it has no investment in vertical integration nor in facilities therefor and pays little interest since it has no LT debt, Apple's costs compare favorably with its competitors. Its facilities are efficient enough to accommodate effective conventional building in Texas, California (3 locations), Ireland, and Singapore. Processes are primarily manual, labor intensive operations, so a satellite facility of 30,000 SF and 70 employees produces 450-500 units a day. Outsourcing requires expert scheduling and absolute quality control; its cost advantage in labor is somewhat offset by an inventory turnover of only 5-7 times a year, so long is the materials pipeline. Jobs is aware that Apple must become a manufacturing company, as he puts it. What this means is that he sees a great future challenge from the competition and believes that Mac is the good shepherd for putting into place the kind of manufacturing strategy Apple will need to stay with future competition.

R&D AND ENGINEERING. While the case omits specific mention here, we know that Apple is replete with basic research capability, excellent product design and engineering, and openminded in the matter of process design. It attracts trained and experienced personnel, hires what it cannot otherwise recruit, and provides a work environment suited to innovation and creativity.

STRATEGIC ALTERNATIVES AND CHOICE

There are no alternatives. Apple has opted for a strategy of growth.

RECOMMENDED DISCUSSION QUESTIONS

1. Characterize and contrast conventional build vs. automated build in the areas of processes, labor requirements, information flows, type of equipment, type of plant capabilities, control of plant, plant focus, unit assembly, and the role of vendors.

2. Is the Macintosh factory programmed for state-of-the-art technology?

3. What is easy in each process? What is difficult? What characteristics make each attractive? Where do limitations appear?

4. Where should the Macintosh plant be located and how should it relate to the rest of Apple?

5. What should be the extent and duration of parallel build activity?

6. How far and how fast should the production process move toward automation?

7. To what extent should on-site vertical integration be considered?

8. What buildup in volume can reasonably be expected?

9. How does automation serve as a "forcing mechanism" for better integrating design and manufacturing?

10. Who are Apple's competitors, and what are their capabilities?

11. How do they use manufacturing technology? Is Apple trying to catch, to imitate, or to lead them?

12. Why is Apple considering investment in advanced manufacturing technologies?

13. Considering your answers to Questions 4-8, what financial return and changes in cost structure do you expect?

14. What are the risks of the plan to Apple? Which (is) are significant, and what can be done to minimize it(them)?

15. What fundamental problem underlies the issues and questions confronting Apple in coming up with an automated build strategy?

16. What do you consider to be the toughest single task facing Apple in its contemplated strategy?

17. What should be Apple's concern in its longterm positioning and what is Mac's role in that positioning?

18. How successful do you think Apple will be in executing its proposed strategy? Why?

ANALYSIS AND DISCUSSION

1. Characterize and contrast conventional build vs. automated build in the areas of processes, labor requirements, information flows, type of equipment, type of plant capabilities, control of plant, plant focus, unit assembly, and the role of vendors.

	CONVENTIONAL BUILD	AUTOMATED BUILD
Processes	Primarily manual	Primarily machine
Labor required	Intensive	Little
Type equipment	Simple	Complex
Information flows	Minimal importance	Great importance
Plant capabilities	Greater (flexibility)	Lesser (programmed)
Control of plant	Manual	Machine
Plant focus	Narrow	Wide

	CONVENTIONAL BUILD	AUTOMATED BUILD
Unit assembly	Slow, manual, limited	Rapid, manual and automated, high
Role of vendors	Great	Greater
Information flows	Manual	Machine

2. Is the Macintosh factory programmed for state-of-the-art technology?

No. It's only new to Apple, and it is generally new to the electronics equipment industry. Joe Graziano points out that the Japanese have been using similar equipment for five years or more, so the technology is not really new and has been widely used abroad and in other industries.

3. What is easy in each process? What is difficult? What characteristics make each attractive? Where do limitations appear?

Change is _easy_ or at least easier in the conventional build because processes are primarily manual, equipment is relatively simple, and worker training is minimal. Design is easy, too, because manufacturing is not committed to close tolerances and changing a process is neither costly nor complicated. Labor is easier in the other - there's less of it, it is more skilled, and it's more apt to stick around - and repetitive tasks are done by machine, relieving monotony. _Difficult_: conventional-assembly because it is slow, manual precision work; automated - design, because tolerances are infinitely closer. _Attractive_: conventional-flexibility; automated-cost advantages. _Limitations_: conventional-output, since it is for the greater part manual; automated-flexibility or information flows (toss up) because changing conventional processes is far more simple and much less costly. There are other possible answers, of course, depending on one's perceptions. There are good points and bad points in each method. Students should know this and thus understand that while automation is fine, it may not be the answer to all prayers.

4. Where should the Macintosh plant be located and how should it relate to the rest of Apple?

This is one of the issues Carter has to address. The case lays out the pro's and con's in some detail, so we will not duplicate. The plant should be located near Apple's corporate headquarters. As Jobs said, he believes in putting all his eggs in one basket and then watching the basket carefully. If the Mac project is really the precursor of the future, then there is too much at stake to remote the project from top management. A home site places the plant near the design engineers and allows them continual interaction with those designing the process; to have it otherwise would be to displace a number of high powered brains who very well might have no liking whatsoever for another location. Here, too, is the best spot if heads have to be knocked together. Since Macintosh is a division, the manufacturing function should report to that division. There is no good case for its reporting elsewhere. Dallas does report to the Operations Division, but since

Dallas facilities will not be used if the site is placed other than at Dallas, there is no valid rationale for remoting manufacturing to Dallas' supervision.

5. What should be the extent and duration of parallel build activity?

This is a sticky wicket for Carter since there are unknowns and unknown unknowns. Exhibit 4 displays the parallel build figures. A question to be asked is, can Dallas build 6000 units a month conventionally? We presume it can. What will that do to the Apple II production? We don't know. Some impact is inevitable, but we can't sacrifice the Apple II market. This puts Carter between a rock and a hard place, because Macintosh has the company's future written all over it. Dallas may call for temporary expansion or double shifting - Dallas must contribute to Mac but continue to serve Apple II. How sure are we that automated build will commence in August? What if it slips (it did, until December 1983)? If it does, Dallas will be supplying all units until the Mac plant comes on line. A bird in hand is worth two in the bush. Introduction has been slipped to July. Jobs didn't like that, but is that date set in concrete? If the sale schedule of Exhibit 4 is correct, Dallas alone can't or couldn't meet demand. If a key concern is having adequate product available at rollout, Dallas has a big part to play. Carter should pump for Dallas' assumed maximum output of 6000 units, no matter what misgivings he has, and Dallas should continue that production until the Mac plant gives assurance that it is operating at design capacity. Targeting 48,000 units by December 1983 is fine but makes the July rollout date dubious without absolute assurance that the Mac plant will be off and running in August. Carter can't guarantee that because he can't pull all the levers by himself. He has to tell Jobs that as distasteful as it is, the "stretch" is too big a chance to take. A later date would be to Apple's benefit - better to produce and then promise than to promise and not be able to produce.

6. How far and how fast should the production process move toward automation?

The three phases of the Mac build plan are described as resting on appropriate basic premises. There is no rationale to quarrel with its timing. Two years for the completion of Phase I seems fair. Exhibit 2 (attached to this note) breaks out the Phases. Only 1A was in effect when the plant went on line in December, 1983. 1B materialized in the fall of 1984.

7. To what extent should on-site vertical integration be considered?

To the maximum extent possible, and maximum of course depends on what processes are built into the plant. Apple heretofore has outsourced for reasons of cost and only assembles and tests in-house. It is hard to quarrel with success, but automated build has to do more than merely assemble and test, else it is a big disappointment. If it is to reduce errors, inventories and costs while improving product quality, Apple should endeavor to plan maximum on-site vertical integration.

8. What buildup in volume can reasonably be expected?

There is no good answer here, so Carter is rightly concerned. He has no magic wand and no crystal ball. Manufacturing should not be expected to make up the ground others have lost. To pretend that manufacturing can do so is to betray a woeful ignorance of and indifference to that function. The conventional build figures for Dallas are probably correct. The automated build figure are a shot in the dark. In the belief that Murphy's Law works overtime in the higher tech fields, it seems wiser not to anticipate automated build until fall, 1983 - say, October. That should see 40,000 units on hand by December 31, 1983. That figure is enough to meet anticipated sales, if the sales forecast in Exhibit 4 is to be believed. That of course contemplated the July introduction, but to go for July is to bare Apple's management to a great deal of criticism. Jobs will have to swallow again, but it is that or fail miserably to meet the market.

9. How does automation serve as a "forcing mechanism" for better integrating design and manufacturing?

If automation is to see automatic insertion equipment used to make circuit boards, tolerances and specs are quite different, for example, than if boards were to be built manually. If automation is to succeed then, design and manufacturing must work much more closely.

10. Who are Apple's competitors, and what are their capabilities?

Certainly IBM today and the Japanese on down the road. Both are extremely capable, judging from their track records.

11. How do they use manufacturing technology? Is Apple trying to catch, to imitate, or to lead them?

Both are quite advanced in their use of manufacturing technology. Robotics and automation are old hat to them. Apple then isn't about to lead or to catch them. The casewriter says that Apple is just "fighting to get in the ball park," only "scratching the surface," which means that Apple has a long, long way to go if it is to meet the objective of preparing for future competitive challenges.

12. Why is Apple considering investment in advanced manufacturing technologies?

Basically, to survive. If Apple sees a Mac market of 1 million units a year, it can't hope to service that market with conventional build. Others will fill the gap, and Apple will be looking at a black hole - the Apple series is aging, and its star performer for the future has gotten lost in the shuffle. Moreover, automation is cheaper (Table 2). This means better margins for Apple and more maneuvering room if competition necessitates price reductions.

13.Considering your answers to Questions 4-8, what financial return and changes in cost structure do you expect?

Again, there are unknowns, such as costs for the conventional build in Dallas, plus whatever damage is done to Apple production there. We choose to disregard these because they are unknown, but certainly they would be known to Matt Carter. The Phase I costs are about $20 million, a figure erased by the savings generated by four months of capacity production (40,000 units per month). Apple will be $135 million a year better off in reduced costs, if the market will really absorb 1 million units a year. Slipping the introduction date will darken the FY83 figures of Table 3 a little bit, and the figures for FY84 won't be as good. We didn't do the numbers, but in the great overall scheme of things, the slippage isn't all that catastrophic, and Carter must say so to Jobs. Further slippage "was considered unacceptable," but it also looks inevitable. FY84 results won't be hurt all that much. Besides, the Mac plant could run two shifts a day, were that to be necessary, and could easily make up any shortfall.

14.What are the risks of the plan to Apple? Which are significant, and what can be done to minimize it(them)?

Things like moving too rapidly with the auto build plan, making sure it doesn't gum up the timing or the execution of the Macintosh, and recasting the company's corporate culture to one which gives manufacturing a key role in the company. Each is significant, but the last is especially so. Carter sees it as the most fundamental factor in the company's long term success. We pose no answer to minimizing the risks associated with recasting, because there is no good answer. Students should be required to grapple with this one, though, if for no other reason than to appreciate the difficulties in restructuring corporate thought.

15.What fundamental problem underlies the issues and questions confronting Apple in coming up with an automated build strategy?

Carter nailed this one at the outset. The Mac project is to make Apple a first class manufacturing firm. Carter supports the idea wholeheartedly, but management hasn't thought its way through the implications of just what becoming a crack manufacturing firm entails. There are too many loose ends, and no one has seemingly sat down and thought his way through the entire problem. Everyone apparently believes, but there is a gap between believing and becoming actively involved.

16.What do you consider to be the toughest single task facing Apple in its contemplated strategy?

This goes back to Question 14. Changing the role and status of manufacturing in the company is the single toughest task Apple faces.

17.What should be Apple's concern in its long term positioning and what is Mac's role in that positioning?

Apple has to look to the nature of its competitive advantage in the future and how best to pursue that advantage. Macintosh is both a product and a process development step along the road. Jobs and company have to be concerned about the further steps, how well those can and should be defined at this time, and how to get the company to share in the idea of what this step by Macintosh is really all about.

18.How successful do you think Apple will be in executing its proposed strategy? Why?

This should get some fervent replies. Can a freeform outfit like Apple really harness itself to a more regimented life, or if not regimented, a more directed method of operation? Can a leopard change its spots? We believe Apple will be highly successful. In effect, Jobs is betting his company on the Mac strategy. Jobs doesn't have a record of losing, or at least losing big, so it is doubtful that this is where he will start.

EXHIBIT 1 - APPLE MACINTOSH STRATEGY

	TRADITIONAL	PHASE I	PHASE II	PHASE III
Product Design	Features	Features/ Cost	Tolerances/ Cost	Performance/ Cost
Process Technology	Labor/tech intensive	Auto. test & transfer	Auto. Mfg.	Integrated/ capabilities
Design/Mfg. Link	Sequential	Loose	Parallel	Interactive

EXHIBIT 2 - APPLE-MACINTOSH UPDATE

A -   Split Technology Development (Automation)

Phase 1A - Electrical test, partial material handling, partial auto-insertion

Phase 1B - Completion of material handling and auto-insertion

Phase 2A - Remainder of PCB tasks and final packaging

Phase 2B - Assembly tasks

Phase 3 - Surface-mounted IC's

NB: Extracted in toto from casewriter's teaching note.

BEER AND WINE INDUSTRIES: BARTLES & JAYMES (B&J)

TEACHING NOTE

TEACHING OBJECTIVES

Propelled by its corporate parent, the Ernest & Julio Gallo Winery, B&J has scrambled to the top of the wine cooler industry. Its job now is to determine how to stay there. Specific objectives:

Become acquainted with the wine and wine cooler industries

See the development of a new product

Understand the reasons for B&J's success

Decide on (a) future course of action(s)

USING THIS CASE

Students are quite familiar with wine, wine coolers and beer, so student interest in the case should be high. The case affords a chance to compare Gallo with other vintners and to observe the pressures on the industry which gave rise to the wine cooler. The case is short, uncomplicated, reads well, and tracks easily. It is simple to discuss and is moderately difficult at the most. It probably fits best in mid-course or later when students are better able to understand the big picture in its entirety. B&J could be used as an inclass exam case but seems better suited to either a short report or a long report.

SYNOPSIS

Gallo Winery had been in business 50 years, graduating from being the producer of a skid row favorite to a respected maker of fine table wines. Not known for inventiveness nor for new product engineering, Gallo displayed an unerring nose for opportunity when the wine cooler emerged. Gallo brought out Bartles & Jaymes after watching wine and beer sales slide for several years in the face of environmental pressures. Although Gallo's good old boys did not appear until 1984, it took only two years for B&J to lead the cooler race. The how is a product of Gallo's expertise in advertising and distribution, bolstered immeasurably by the vertical integration of the parent company. While the case trails off into an interesting discussion of major competitors (there were some 40 producers of 154 brands in mid 1986), the major question facing B&J is what now.

Seagram's market share in early 1988 exceeded B&J's, gaining the top spot by producing a variety of cooler flavors. Consumers responded positively, and those with less diversity of products lost market share. We confidently expect Gallo to produce another line of coolers, but not produced by Gallo and probably not by Frank and Ed.

TEACHING APPROACHES TO THIS CASE

For openers, ask how many are familiar with wine coolers. What brands? When did coolers first show up locally? How about nationally? It should be obvious that coolers have a certain migratory time from the West coast to other areas. If B&J didn't appear until 1984 then, how has it done so well in so short a time? Apparently migratory time isn't always a factor in growth, or is it? What did B&J have that others didn't have? Some competitive advantage(s), which should be described in some detail. How did these advantages (advertising and distribution) come about? This can lead to a discussion of Gallo's vertical integration - what it is, and why it is. Does the environment play a part in B&J's success? It does, of course, but wouldn't it help others equally, too? Not necessarily. At this point the instructor can pull together values, environment and enterprise to show that Gallo is just doing what it does best -leading from strength, sticking to basics, and watching its customers. Others may try to do the same, but they just don't quite have the touch that Gallo has.

CASE ANALYSIS

STRATEGIC MANAGEMENT ELEMENTS: MISSION, GOALS, AND OBJECTIVES

None is specifically addressed. We judge mission to be furnishing a complete line of wine products across the entire market spectrum. Its goal here is to lead the wine cooler industry. Its apparent objective is a "constant striving for perfection in every aspect" of its business.

STRATEGISTS

Here are the Mr. Inside and Mr. Outside of wine industry. Both have had 50 years experience in all aspects of the industry. At 77, Julio, the manufacturer, is described as the more easy going, a farmer at heart, at home in the fields and very close to the details of production. The marketeer, Ernest, 88, contrasts as a demanding, driving, blunt, intense and secretive businessman, not inclined to share either power or control, who makes all the final decisions. Able executives throughout the firm make no decisions and sometimes are ignorant of the details of company operations. It is understandable that Ernest would insist on such secrecy because knowledge is power, and power he will not share.

ENVIRONMENTAL ANALYSIS

SOCIOECONOMIC SECTOR. B&J must be fairly immune to the economic cycle, since its customers seem to be those who will always be able to afford the smaller things in life, come what may. Social factors far outweigh economic factors in the world of alcohol - money seems no great obstacle to becoming an alcoholic. Beer has been a fixture on the drinking scene since the Pilgrims landed. The origins of wine are lost in history. After Prohibition the public taste first ran to the heavier bourbons, then to the lighter rums and vodkas and flavored drinks. Beer consumption rose, but wine began to creep into consumers' hands after 1945. Beer consumption increased, and wine even more so proportionately.

Public thinking began to reshape itself in the late 1970s when alcohol began to seem less a friend than an enemy. Sales of both wine and beer tailed off. The fitness craze and the nutrition jag put the health conscious public further away from alcoholic beverages. Wine sales, even of table wines, fell in the early 1980s, and both wine and beer industries found themselves apparently looking at the flat curves of market maturity. To a group used to constantly increasing sales in the face of intense competition, there was an obvious challenge here unless one were inclined to accept the inevitable. There was no such acceptance. The hunt for alternatives was on.

GOVERNMENTAL SECTOR. The alcoholic beverage industries are heavily taxed and intensely regulated. The case mentions no specific regulatory measures but does point out that pressure from society finds its way into regulation: the legal drinking age has been raised in many states, sellers face possible damage suits from inebriated consumers or their victims, the campaign against drunken driving is firmly imbedded in the statutes, and so on.

INDUSTRY THREATS AND OPPORTUNITIES. Suppliers have little power in either the wine or beer industries; indeed, many manufacturers, Gallo included, are vertically integrated. Competition is intense in both industries. High barriers to entry seem to restrict competition from breweries and wineries which contemplate the wine cooler industry, but the coolers must always anticipate a change of mind on the part of those who decide coolers are not a passing fad but are here to stay. Gallo leads the wine market by such a degree that entry barriers to the cooler industry could hardly have even been considered. Advertising and distribution greatly raised the costs of competing, but Gallo could shrug those off.

The path of the cooler industry faces threats common to the alcoholic beverage groups as a whole: Alcohol has a negative image. The public is much more aware of the evils of drink. The fitness campaign has turned potential consumers away from the empty calories of alcohol. Soft drink sales are steadily increasing. Raising the legal drinking age has cut the number of young adults who might otherwise be consumers. It is no longer considered "cool" to drink, and there is not only intense public pressure against consumption, especially by minors, but a growing realization that alcoholism is much more widespread than once thought, which means its social costs deserve more careful consideration. Alcohol will never disappear, but its future is somewhat less bright than before.

The advent of the wine cooler was a typical Californiaism. What started almost as a fad, something different, became an overnight success. Coolers presented an opportunity to rescue fortunes in the young adult group of consumers, 21-34 in age, representative of the present pluralistic society. The cooler came to look like the answer to the declining sales in beer and wine: the cooler seemed to be "wine for the common man," more kick for the beer drinker, less for the wine drinker, and an attraction for those who might prefer wine but had been awed by apparent smugness of the wine elite. Coolers looked healthier; they tasted good, and they required no special handling. Margins were more attractive than beer or wine, since capital requirements were so low. The cooler was the thirst quencher which lacked a bad image and appeared to capitalize on its relative low alcohol content. 3 proof is innocuous - it's like a stronger beer but without the detractions of beer like taste, calories, appearance, social acceptance, etc.

Gallo started late with Bartles & Jaymes. California Coolers initially led because it was first to market. By 1986 its success had attracted the world's largest winery (Gallo), brewery (Anheuser-Busch), and distillery (Seagram's). The top seven coolers controlled about 90% of the market, so Gallo was facing formidable competition from the outset. The case describes its success but leaves open the question of the future.

STRATEGIC ADVANTAGE PROFILE

CORPORATE RESOURCES AND PERSONNEL. Gallo has a fine image as a maker of quality table wines. It has attempted to distance itself from the pop wine, brown bag, high kick image it earned as a producer of low quality, bulk wines. Creation of the B&J cooler subsidiary was a calculated effort to capitalize on public perception of a different image without detracting from a well-earned gold medal prestige in quality table wines.

Organizational structure is not described but must be effective. Corporate climate is one of secrecy and dominance by Ernest Gallo. If sales representatives rate a 300 page training manual, we judge that internal operations are laid down in infinite detail and closely supervised. Gallo is vertically integrated with divisions that represent near every step in the manufacture of wine. The fact that it owns many of its own distributors is highly significant; that Gallo realizes the signal importance of distributors is illustrated by a later rescinded FTC order, which ordered Gallo not to tie its independent distributors. There is no open evidence of a strategic management system, but Gallo's preeminent position argues that it plans very well indeed and has the internal systems to provide whatever is needed. Gallo is nonunion, but there is little mention of employees. We suspect that Gallo is bright enough to be paternalistic, however - do it our way, and you can stay a long time. Vintners seem to attract that kind of person. Seems fair enough. With Gallo succession is a possible problem. There is no clear heir apparent in Ernest's sons, but Julio's son and son-in-law are possibilities.

<u>FINANCE AND ACCOUNTING</u>. Gallo is privately held, so we know appalling little here. Its 1988 sales were estimated at $1 billion and profits at $50 million. Seagram's, second largest winery, is a contrast in losing money on its table wines with $300 revenues in 1985.

<u>MARKETING AND DISTRIBUTION</u>. Here we know more, since this is Gallo's strong suit. The brothers know the industry, so not much gets by them. They know a good thing when they see it. They are expert enough to improve on an accepted product and then to present it as their own. Seeing cooler success and desiring growth, they followed others into the cooler market. The question then had to be how to do it. One leads from strength, in this case marketing and distribution, where Gallo is vertically integrated.

The case notes that success lay in proper positioning and demanded good taste at a good price. <u>Differentiation</u> could come in different flavors, packaging or advertising. Gallo chose a 12 ounce bottle similar to the Michelob beer bottle, aimed at a more sophisticated consumer than did its competitors, and went all out on advertising. Gallo couldn't run the risk of a blurred image, so its subsidiary distanced itself from the parent with its homely characters of Bartles and Jaymes. Gallo's <u>packaging</u> had a built-in acceptance. It understood the more sophisticated consumer, because after all the table wine set is not the youthful beach set. The choice of two homespun characters is a brilliant understanding that if one can capitalize on the nostalgia phase, one can do well. In an increasingly sophisticated world of fast buck artists and con men, who could be more believable than Frank and Ed? They wouldn't put you on; besides, if you've always been a beer drinker, you can identify with the good old boys - and maybe they're pushing something you ought to try. <u>Advertising</u> was one thing.

<u>Distribution</u> was another. Controlling its own distributors and leaning on those it didn't, Gallo could make it clear that the job went further than just taking orders and making deliveries. Ernest Gallo is said to have hand picked who should be on board and then planned everything down to the last detail. He also encouraged distributors to hire a separate sales force, and why not? He had produced a very detailed 300 page training manual for just such people. And Gallo distributed B&J through its own wine distributorships, as opposed to its competitors who ran coolers through beer distributors. But coolers are more like wine than beer, say what you like, and if you don't want beer, why look for a wine cooler amongst the beer? Gallo saw that, even if others wanted to believe the contrary. Since <u>prices</u> are fairly uniform, <u>image</u> is important. Gallo trades on that and achieves a <u>differentiation</u> that would otherwise be difficult to achieve.

<u>Marketing</u> here is the key to success. The product is not complicated and perhaps is not even patented. Gallo makes one cooler, a wine cooler, of one flavor and one proof in one container. The variables are few. Just do what you do well, and that's what Gallo does, without muddying the waters. It has left little to chance. With a typical thoroughness, Gallo has covered all the bases.

PRODUCTION AND OPERATIONS MANAGEMENT. Gallo is vertically integrated. This means it can assure itself of quality supplies in the desired quantity. It can produce for less because it does not have to pay profits to its wholly owned suppliers. It is able to dictate all schedules, sitings, capacities, and facilities. It has a greater degree of control than does any other vintner, and it capitalizes on that control.

R&D AND ENGINEERING. Not a factor in this case.

STRATEGIC ALTERNATIVES AND CHOICE

Stability is not in keeping with the values of management. Retrenchment offers nothing. A combination strategy is not possible. Growth alone meets the values of management and market.

RECOMMENDED DISCUSSION QUESTIONS

1. How does one account for the relatively sudden popularity of wine coolers?

2. When did B&J enter the wine cooler industry?

3. Why has it been so successful?

4. Why did Gallo distance B&J from Gallo?

5. What does Gallo have that others in the industry lack?

6. Is vertical integration of advantage to Gallo? Why is Gallo vertically integrated?

7. What should Gallo do now to stay on top?

ANALYSIS AND DISCUSSION

1. How does one account for the relatively sudden popularity of wine coolers?

Coolers were a fortuitous circumstance. They could have been ignored at any other time and probably would not have seen the light of day. It was a matter of sheer luck that coolers appeared when the beer and wine industries badly needed a new champion. Coolers had potential, and someone seized the opportunity to bring in a product with almost instant appeal.

2. When did B&J enter the wine cooler industry?

B&J entered in 1984, officially. However, since the Gallo brothers know the industry well and don't invent new products, it stands to reason that they saw this one in its infancy and carefully planned their 1984 entry. One doesn't become Number One in two years if going from a standing start.

3. Why has it been so successful?

As noted above, Gallo knows an opportunity when it sees one. If you have everything else - secrecy, facilities, marketing, resources - why not take advantage of the obvious? There is no need for market research, the product has an indicated acceptance, the technology to produce is ridiculously simple, and the machinery to bring the cooler to the consumer is already in place. It would be difficult to lose, unless B&J comes up with a real marketing glitch, and that looks unlikely.

4. Why did Gallo distance B&J from Gallo?

We touched on this above. B&J had to be distanced from Gallo because Gallo had to beware of its image. A wine cooler isn't like a table wine. To push the cooler under the Gallo aegis would cause more questions and problems than one would care to answer. It was safer, for one thing, and the boys' homely observations served to differentiate B&J from all other coolers. This was Porter's focus and differentiation at their finest.

5. What does Gallo have that others in the industry lack?

You should get many answers here. We have in mind Gallo's great competitive advantage in marketing and distribution. They are masters at marketing, as we noted above, and have the resources for the wads of advertising that are necessary to sell a new product and to keep on selling it. Experience helps, too, and Gallo positioned B&J in precisely the right place and manner. Gallo's advantage in distribution is unbeatable. It can control its own distributors and lean on the independents, getting both to adopt more active sales roles, promote special items, advertise a certain way, yield shelf space, site to best advantage in a store, etc. Those less fortunate just have expensive middlemen who may or may not promote as the manufacturer would like.

6. Is vertical integration of advantage to Gallo? Why is Gallo vertically integrated?

Absolutely. The variables in wineries are not all that many, so why not control them if you can? We reason that Ernest wanted control, so why not control everything? Gallo isn't beholden to any stockholders, so it can do what, when and if it pleases. If pricing is the key in the industry, why not the best possible handle on costs? That way pricing becomes much easier and affords much more flexibility. As the preceding question points out, owning one's own distributors is of great advantage.

7. What should Gallo do now to stay on top?

There will be various answers here. One thing for sure - B&J needs to keep up its advertising, changing it when the Frank and Ed theme begins to wear thin. New products, which means new versions? Others are introducing various flavors, or coolers with beer or spirit base, but we think that Gallo should stay as it is. If it ain't broke, don't fix it. Changing B&J would play hob with a successful ad effort, too.

New markets? Why not? Budweiser sells well in Japan, for example, and we know that the wine market is now a two way street as we export to Europe. Gallo could do this well, but it would do so without the great advantage of having its own distributors. We believe that Gallo should not change its basic formula for success - lead from strength, stick to basics, keep it simple, watch the customers.

INNER-CITY PAINT CORPORATION (IPC)

TEACHING NOTE

TEACHING OBJECTIVES

Stan Walsh, an entrepreneur in the paint business, is trying to do everything but isn't having much luck with anything as everything seems to be coming unglued. Specific objectives:

See some of the problems which plague entrepreneurs.

Analyze Walsh's situation to isolate the problem.

Witness the conflict of personal and company objectives.

Decide upon an appropriate course of action.

USING THIS CASE

IPC is short, easy to read, not too difficult to analyze, makes discussion simple, and can be used as an opening case in a course. Its brevity argues against its use for a long report. IPC could also be used in mid-course when the requirement is to decide upon a strategy.

SYNOPSIS

Stan Walsh became a paint manufacturer in Chicago, selling wall paint to small and medium sized decorating companies. It's a family business in which Stan, assisted by his mother as office manager, does everything. IPC has run into an economic slowdown and fallen into financial trouble. IPC's customers see Walsh as disorganized, financially hurt, and unable to deliver its product reliably. Stan wants to improve his reputation and find a way out of his financial problems: shall it be by computer, by consultant help or by a short term bank loan to help him pay his bills? He doesn't know, he doesn't know that he doesn't know, and he may not even be looking at the right problem.

OUTCOME

Two years after the case was written, the family sold the company, for reasons not known to the casewriters.

This Note draws on a Note furnished by the casewriters.

Students should be told before discussing IPC that direct labor costs for 5 gallons are $2.50 and for 55 gallons, $13.75. Also, that overhead costs for 5 gallons are $5 and for 55 gallons, $55. These figures are not provided in this case, but they appear in the casewriters' notes.

IPC is a fun case to discuss because all is not exactly what it seems to be, so the case is a fine vehicle for leading students new to Business Strategy, through some thought processes with which they may not be familiar. Establish what IPC does. It makes paint. Big company, little company? Small. Who put it together, and who runs it? It is not difficult to establish that IPC is an entrepreneurial undertaking started by Stanley Walsh. His mother is his office manager. Is Stan a good manager? Various answers here. Probably he isn't, because he does everything, can't delegate, trusts no one, and slows the whole operation. Why? Stan is like lots of small business people who start a business, watch it grow, and can never bring themselves to understand that roles have to be reexamined at intervals. Control, absolute control, means so much to many entrepreneurs.

Has IPC done well? Point to the sales increase. It must have been doing something right. What's all the fuss about? Some will say that IPC has a negative cash flow. OK. Why? Because IPC has to pay spot cash for materials while its customers don't pay for 30 to 60 days. Why spot cash? This will cause others to point to IPC's sullied reputation: if suppliers see IPC as unreliable, of course they want immediate payment. Customer perceptions are something not to be ignored, students must be told. Rumors are that IPC is in a financial bog, that Walsh is disorganized, etc. Result: Large companies won't order job lots for fear of nondelivery, and small companies will haggle over price and payment. Why not? They have Walsh over a barrel.

How did it all happen? IPC provided fast service at a competitive price. But as housing turned down when the economy slowed, business staggered, cash became a problem, and all of Walsh's omissions came to light. When business is on the way up, one can ignore many things and still make a good profit; however, when business slows or turns down, all the chickens come home to roost. Now is the time to ask what Walsh hasn't done. You should get all sorts of replies: he hasn't managed, he has no financial controls, no credit controls, no inventory controls, no formal marketing, no objectives, no standards, etc. What joins all this together, or should? A strategic plan produced by a strategic management system, but Walsh has no such system. Not seeing the problem, he proposes various fixes: computer, consultant, bank loan to pay bills until the economy turns around, and so on. It's axiomatic that if you don't understand the problem you have to redouble your efforts.

While this discussion is going on, someone is sure to look at Exhibit 2 and comment on the size of family salaries, something like $198,000 per year. Isn't that the problem? Well, yes and no. Reducing those salaries would certainly reduce current liabilities and perhaps negate the need for a bank loan, but that's not the whole answer. Whatever is done has to fit into an overall scheme of some kind. This points out that small family businesses or entrepreneurial ventures frequently stand short of strategic management. Action is more fun than thought. When it comes as come it must, failure is usually a big surprise. Students need to be told this need not be the case, and that no enterprise is immune to the need for a strategic management system.

CASE ANALYSIS

STRATEGIC MANAGEMENT ELEMENTS: MISSION, GOALS AND OBJECTIVES

None is stated, so we reason that IPC's <u>mission</u> is to make and market flat wall paint for small and medium sized decorators in the Chicago area. No <u>goals</u> are stated, so implicitly they must be to provide employment and to make a profit for the family. An <u>objective</u> is survival. There are no quantitative measures of any kind.

STRATEGISTS

There is little direct description of Walsh. We gather that he is like many of his counterparts: ambitious, self-centered, mistrusting, overcommitted, egotistical, seized with the idea of power, suspicious of others, hard worker, a man of action but not thought who had no prior management experience and hasn't taken the time to learn on the way.

ENVIRONMENTAL ANALYSIS

<u>SOCIOECONOMIC SECTOR</u>. IPC is sensitive to the economic cycle. The economy is turning down. Housing starts are off. Decorators want for work, and painting is postponed. IPC's business simply dries up.

<u>GOVERNMENT AND TECHNOLOGICAL SECTORS</u>. Not a factor in this case.

<u>INDUSTRY THREATS AND OPPORTUNITIES</u>. Unfortunately, threats far outweigh opportunities. IPC is a small company which prospered with competitive prices and fast service. As the economy slows, <u>competition</u> is certain to heat up. Larger companies, similarly affected by the economy, may start invading IPC's markets with competitive prices, speedier deliveries since they have no C.O.D. problems, and positive guarantees to paint contractors for large orders, if indeed there are any more such orders. If large companies will do that, small companies competing with IPC will, too.

Supplies and suppliers impose no limitations, other than pressure on IPC to pay on delivery. While IPC operates in a low rent area and thus minimizes overhead, it seems poorly situated to serve the entire Chicago area, even granting customer pickup. Its location would not be one to inspire customer confidence, and it certainly does little to allay customer perceptions about the viability of IPC.

Customers abound, provided IPC can ride out the economic slump and get its act back in order.

STRATEGIC ADVANTAGE PROFILE

CORPORATE RESOURCES AND PERSONNEL. IPC has a poor image. Its organization is not described, other than to state that most employees are part-time, and all 35 do everything. Labor is nonunion and unskilled, so labor costs appear minimal. This may be effective, but efficiency is yet another matter, where responsibility is hard to fix. (Recall that Walsh spends time answering complaints about defective paint.) There is no strategic management system, and in fact there appear to be no support systems at all other than what pass as accounting records. IPC is obviously lean, informally organized, and saw its sales boom because it delivered a competitively priced product on short notice. It succeeded in spite of itself, with brute strength and awkwardness rather than skill and cunning.

FINANCE AND ACCOUNTING. Here is trouble. If the unaudited accounting exhibits can be believed, IPC has a negative cash flow, no cash to speak of, and appears unable to pay its trade accounts. That could spell the end if creditors commence filing liens. All is disproportionate; its bad debt allowance betokens very loose credit policies, if any do indeed exist. Its CR is .92 and its QR .85. Neither figure is encouraging. The 50 day collection period is intolerable, and the approximate 5 days of inventory not only discourages any long range planning but exacerbates the C.O.D. problem.

Exhibit 2 demonstrates a gross profit ratio of almost 20%. However, when we pull out selling and administrative expenses, we find that net income all but disappears beneath the salaries of George and his mother. This cannot be. They are draining the business and unknowingly, perhaps are killing the goose with the golden egg.

IPC sells more 5 gallon cans of white paint than 50 gallon containers of colored paint. The company's lack of fiscal common sense becomes acute if someone looks closely at the numbers. Remember, students must be given the direct labor and overhead costs. It becomes apparent that IPC loses $21.35 on every 50 gallon container. Either overhead is allocated haphazardly or IPC is underpricing itself. Its salvation has been the fact that the 5 gallon can has been the best seller - and has the best gross margin. It's hard to track things because there are no inventory records.

MARKETING AND DISTRIBUTION. Walsh is sales period. He does the PR work and follows up on complaints about defective paint. It is hard to see how he alone could achieve a greater market share. He knows his market, and he knows how to reach it, but it's what follows that causes the problem. There is no market research - probably none is required - but some queries might turn up new requirements. Distribution is adequate as is.

PRODUCTION AND OPERATIONS. The warehouse manager mentally notes what is in stock but keeps no inventory records. This puts EOQ out of bounds. With no track record, it is hard to recall rush periods and to remember the best time, prices, and conditions for reordering supplies. The product is simply made, but there is an obvious quality control problem. Since a lab tests materials quality and finished paint quality, something is lacking. With constant labor rotation, we suspect the fault lies more in labor than it does in materials.

STRATEGIC ALTERNATIVES

Stability would mean more of the same. That's what got IPC to where it is. Incremental improvements would not suffice. Growth is hardly possible, given IPC's sorry financial state. Retrenchment holds promise, since there are areas where savings are possible. A combination strategy can also be considered.

CHOICE

A combination strategy of retrenchment and stability. Future growth might be feasible if IPC's problems can be sorted out and the economy improves, as undoubtedly it will.

IMPLEMENTATION

Stan must pay his trade accounts and pay them promptly, or he may be run out of business. Hard as it is, his immediate source of funds has to be family salaries. But how much and for how long? This has to come out of a strategic management process which Stan must adopt forthwith. It goes without saying that his strategic plan should be reviewed at intervals, assuming that the survival of IPC is his first consideration, and the state of his purse second.

Paying trade accounts should improve customers' perceptions, and these bear heavily on IPC's fiscal health. Without C.O.D.'s Stan has some fiscal flexibility which presently is denied him. He can and should tighten up his receivables policy, using himself as an example of a good payer. He must get the wolf away from the door and reestablish himself as a competitor if he expects to continue his own business. Along with this hard decision has to come one equally as difficult, that he is no manager. He doesn't need a consultant, he needs a business manager. They aren't hard to find, certainly not in Chicago. Stan can do what he does well, and that's sell. Some attention is needed in the warehouse - Stan has to have a reputation for quality paint, to set himself apart from others, so he must take an interest in QC, stabilizing employees, training them, and making them more efficient. This will take time and it will cost, but Stan will have the time, and the costs can be recovered in better quality work. As the economy rights itself, Stan may find it profitable to branch out from his present product line - certainly its prices need to be scrutinized - dependent on what some elemental market research discloses. Future growth is not beyond his reach if he simply learns to manage what he has. Stan reminds one of the old saying that businesses don't fail, but managers do.

RECOMMENDED DISCUSSION QUESTIONS

1. What does Walsh see as IPC's problem?

2. Is he correct? Does he understand how the problem arose?

3. What does he propose to do? Can he solve the problem in the manner(s) he describes?

4. What is IPC's basic problem?

5. What should Walsh do generally? Specifically?

6. How would you sell your recommendations to him?

ANALYSIS AND DISCUSSION

1. What does Walsh see as IPC's problem?

This doesn't come out loud and clear. Is it that IPC has a poor reputation or that it has money problems? He would like to fix both - when in doubt, redouble your effort.

2. Is he correct? Does he understand how the problem arose?

No. He knows only what he sees, and he doesn't see that very well. True, there are problem areas, but fixing those alone isn't the answer. He doesn't know the problem, hence doesn't know its origin. His impression is that the economy is poor but only for the moment.

3. What does he propose to do? Can he solve the problem in the manner(s) he describes?

He isn't sure. Buy a computer. Why not? Hire a consultant, but not a very expensive one. Borrow from a bank to pay IPC's bills. None of these will solve the problem. At best he can only plaster up a crack or two.

4. What is IPC's basic problem?

You may get several answers here, like chicken and egg. Walsh lacks a strategic management system, not one of the GE type, but a few quiet thoughts he has shared with Mom. No system, no plan, no controls, no idea of where IPC is or should be going. A good plan would have avoided the family's looting of the company - it could hardly be a good plan and do otherwise. Someone will point out excessive family salaries as the problem. Agree. OK, but are these the

140

problem, or the symptoms of a more basic problem? Here's an opportunity to point out a difference with which students seem always to have great trouble.

5.*What should Walsh do generally? Specifically?*

Generally, manage strategically. Specifically, see our remarks under Implementation.

6.*How would you sell your recommendations to him?*

With difficulty to be sure, but it comes down to a question of survival. Does he want the goose to keep laying those golden eggs or not?

NUCOR CORPORATION (NC)

TEACHING NOTE

TEACHING OBJECTIVES

Despite his unparalleled record for growth, earnings and ROE, there is concern that Ken Iverson, Nucor CEO has overreached himself by expanding when the industry is beset with overcapacity. Specific objectives:

See a recipe for success in a declining industry

Understand how management style and technology make a winner

Observe the role of unique employee relations as a determinant of success

Realize the role of costs in a basic industry

Evaluation of NC's options for the future.

USING THIS CASE

NC fits best into the latter part of a course when students are well enough acquainted with strategy to be able to appreciate the canny implementation of Iverson's strategy. The case is long, but it is written in a sprightly manner; since it tells a story of success, it holds student interest, even though steel as a subject seems deadly. The case sustains discussion well and affords ample opportunity to examine in detail some unusual subjects. Its best use is as a long report or for a final problem in lieu of the traditional final exam.

SYNOPSIS

Ken Iverson sought to rescue Nuclear Corporation of America and wound up as its CEO. Iverson opted for vertical integration and began a succession of events which produced Nucor, a steel mini-mill and joist firm that prospered even as the steel industry itself was in the throes of despair. Nucor shines like a pearl in a dustbin. It has made Wall Street happy with an ROE of over 28%. Its efficiency sets it apart - it produces a ton of steel with less than 4 man hours, a figure under Japanese mills (5) and comparable U.S. mills (6). It is a study in low costs - investment costs, labor costs, employment costs, as well as tons of steel produced per employee, 981, which ranks it second in the world. The case examines the factors which make Nucor the steel world marvel that it is.

OUTCOME

Forbes reported that Nucor acquired West German technology which will enable it to produce 2" flat rolled slabs. Score another productivity gain! This will save Nucor $50-75 per ton and hike productivity to 1200-1500 tons per employee. Could this be Nucor's entre to the automotive steel market?

TEACHING APPROACHES TO THIS CASE

Students who have read the case have no trouble concluding that NC is very, very good. For that reason we suggest starting by asking why it is as good as it is. The reasons are easy - things like vertical integration, nonunion labor, incentive plans, unique personnel relations policies, flat organization, and so on. You might want to list these on a blackboard as they are named. Then ask why NC is vertically integrated, why it employs nonunion labor, why it has a flat, thin organization, and so on. Various reasons are possible, and probably most are correct. What do they mean, what do they add up to? They all point one way - NC wants to be the lowest cost producer in the industry. Lowest cost producer - certainly words of motherhood, but why is that necessary? Students should be able to summarize the state of the steel industry, which varies from bad to worse. How else really can NC hope to compete? It does not have a niche strategy, because what it makes is in no way unique and the markets to which it sells will buy from anyone. The only basis on which NC can take on the industry is that of cost. You might want to ask how that sits with NC employees. It sits well, thank you, and they are very much aware of the company's strategy. Here is a chance to go back to the blackboard and discuss how those listed items help implement NC's strategy. What pulls it all together of course is NC's corporate culture and unusual but highly effective management style. You will have been essentially discussing NC's strengths. Has it any weaknesses? Possibly. Someone will certainly point to the duplication of effort in each division, because there is little centralization. NC is almost a one man show - Iverson seems to call all the shots. That's fine, but all men are mortal. What happens if he is incapacitated? Succession therefore may be mentioned, along with the fact there is no strategic management system and an apparent short run focus on performance. Given all this plus industry threats and opportunities, where should Iverson point NC for the future? Should NC continue to grow? How? Should it adopt a strategy of stability? Why? Was the joint venture with Koygo a wise move? Where should NC stop?

CASE ANALYSIS

STRATEGIC MANAGEMENT ELEMENTS: MISSION, GOALS AND OBJECTIVES

NC has no announced <u>mission</u>, so we take it to be the manufacture and sale of steel and steel products. These are no set <u>goals</u> except those imbedded in the incentive programs, although Iverson says he expects a 25% ROA for each division. There are no <u>objectives</u>, but growth and profitability are implicit.

The case could as well be titled "All About Iverson", because he is truly the leader in the mini-mill segment of the steel industry. He is well educated, a hard worker, bright, observant, and experienced. He strikes us as a man completely honest, absolutely free of pretense and down to earth, who practices what he preaches. He is obviously casual and informal, not given to ceremony but certainly given to people. While he can be direct, he seems to prefer to reserve judgement and to want to take refuge in compromise rather than to dictate. NC reflects his values 100%.

ENVIRONMENTAL ANALYSIS

SOCIOECONOMIC SECTOR. As a commodity good, steel is cyclical. When the economy sags, so does the steel industry because so much of its output goes to cycle-sensitive uses like autos, appliances, and construction. The economy sagged in the early 80's, and inflation became a factor. A slowing economy diminished demand and revealed the industry's overcapacity. Competition intensified. Costs were high. Cheaper inputs exacerbated the problem. Good as it was, even Nucor's attentiveness to cost couldn't keep it out of a degree of financial hot water. While most companies registered losses or closed or restructured, Nucor was able to stay in the black, but its ROE fell to 9% from 30%+. Social factors in the environment are not pertinent here except insofar as public acceptance of plastic or other substitutes for steel is concerned.

GOVERNMENTAL SECTOR. Government is a tremendous factor in the steel industry's health (or lack thereof) and operations. Steel as a basic industry is of strategic importance; the government admits that by establishing import quotas. At the same time presidents are famous for jawboning the industry for lower prices. Given its costs, high taxes, and high cost of capital, the industry has been slow to modernize. Iverson pointed at excessive regulation and unrealistic depreciation schedules as governmental factors aiding the technological deterioration of the industry. Closing plants was costly, so costly sometimes that they were still on line when overcapacity and financial prudence argued for closing. The immense amounts of capital required by environmental regulations further deferred modernization. Iverson was right in identifying government as a major factor in the industry's sickness. Obsolete plants carried higher costs. Outdated technology added to those costs. Nucor went for the smaller and cheaper mini-mill which embodied state-of-the-art technology and lower costs - mini-mill scrap, for instance, cost less than the ore old integrated plants were forced to use. Producing for less, Nucor sold for less, and its record became one of growth and profit.

TECHNOLOGICAL SECTOR. Technology is an influencing factor in this case. Older integrated mills used outmoded technology and by competitive standards, obsolete equipment. Companies either could not or would not modernize. Nucor lives by technology. Its plants are not over 20 years old, its equipment is new, and it hunts for even more modern technology. The mini-mill is smaller, cheaper, and more efficient. Its costs are lower, and Nucor competes with a strategy of cost leadership. While mini-mills can't produce sheet (steel either hot or cold rolled) or coated sheets of steel, the technology to do so will come along sooner rather than later. Technology is indeed the key to Nucor's success - and perhaps to its future as well.

INDUSTRY THREATS AND OPPORTUNITIES. Suppliers figure here - the high cost of capital or merely the lack thereof beggars companies. The supply of energy is adequate, but energy costs are up. So are labor costs, not from a shortage of supply but from an overage of union muscle; to survive, many companies were forced to renegotiate labor contracts. Iron ore costs more and generally is of lower quality. Transportation costs more, too, but deregulation has softened the impact of rising costs here. Essentially, supplies are available but cost more.

Threats arise principally from competition. The integrated mills, mini-mills, and imports are all scrambling for pieces of a smaller pie. The integrated have cut capacity as fast as possible, narrowing product lines, focusing products, and striving in every way for greater efficiency. As integrated mills modernize and adopt newer technologies, they become more of a threat because their costs are lower; while they may not compete directly with Nucor, the fact remains that they could, and should Nucor find technology that enables it to produce sheet steel, there would be a terrific fight for markets. Present technology, however, theoretically limits mini-mills to 35-40% of the market. Foreign steel, often accused of dumping, is held back because of quotas. Not even a cheaper dollar put on the brakes - foreign exporters simply cut profit margins in order to stay in U.S. markets. There are other mini-mills, too, and Iverson recognizes that the days of cutting chunks out of the market are gone. To gain market share in a shrinking market, Nucor must take something away from someone else, and that somebody will not yield willingly. Competition deserves first consideration then since it is now head-to-head, and the competitors are tougher than they used to be.

Government is a perpetual threat through tougher environmental controls, failure to renew quotas, tax laws, etc. Overcapacity continues to hang over the industry, and barriers to exit remain high. Energy prices have caused Detroit to downsize automobiles (less steel) and to substitute plastic for steel in order to reduce weight (still less steel). Other steel users are not reluctant to shift to substitutes, either.

Opportunities are more difficult to find than threats. Integrated mills are segmenting the market and using new technologies to bring out new product lines. Nucor does the same thing, as its decision to enter the steel fastener market indicates. Iverson is looking at more sophisticated products like special alloys in bars and flat rolled products, once the technology is available. Thin slab steel would put Nucor into the auto and appliance business. Iverson's interest in thin slab makes it clear he will go anywhere in the world to acquire the necessary technology, since he expects its development to be by a foreign company. Iverson also likes heavier structural steel, not yet in the ken of mini-mills, and for reasons like that he formed a joint venture in 1987 with Kogyo.

STRATEGIC ADVANTAGE PROFILE

CORPORATE RESOURCES AND PERSONNEL. Nucor has an enviable image-someone once called it the nearest thing to the perfect company. It reflects Iverson's values completely. There is no organizational chart because that's Iverson's informality. But the organization works and works well because it is flat, uncomplicated, has no technical staff, and commits little to writing. This works like a charm when an organization has good management, good people, and a common vision - in this case, the vision is of dollar signs because there are four incentive plans, and everyone understands that as the company goes, so goes their check. That's job enrichment in the pay envelope, and it works well. Iverson is a plain man and unpretentious, so he watches frills and expenses. That attitude permeates the organization and is reflected in its incredible productivity.

Nucor has no published and quantifiable objectives. That's Iverson, too. ROA by division, yes, but nothing else. The name of the game is to make money, and if you can do that as you grow, you make more money. Published objectives would be bothersome to Iverson. There is no strategic management system and no headquarters staff worthy of the name. A formal system would hogtie Iverson, just as would a large staff. His idea is to keep things simple, and it works. He develops strategy as he goes along, incrementally and carefully by watching the environment closely and listening to his people. That way he is not committed to some long term action which might or might not even eventuate. If it did not, the organization might have second thoughts. Since Iverson is direct, his style is to take things as they come and to decide after careful study. Once the decision is made the success of the project is fairly well assured. Iverson sneaks up on it, and it works. He searches constantly for new technology, so in a sense he is a large scale entrepreneur, and why not? - he plays the cards close to his vest, makes the final decisions, is dedicated to growth, and espouses a strategy that is characterized by Minzberg's "dramatic leaps" forward.

Nucor has an earnings and sales record that is the envy of the industry. But all things tail off in the long run, so there is some question as to whether Nucor can continue to do as well in the future. Top management is extremely competent - steel they know, and steel they do very well. There are a few people who function as a corporate staff, a very few. That reflects Iverson's penchant for simplicity and costs. It follows, of course, that there are no staff support systems and no MIS. Unions are unknown. Nucor's strength lies in its employees - field managers have only general direction but liberal authority to do whatever is necessary to keep the division humming as a profit center. A division manager has all the tools and minimum interference from above in using those tools as he sees fit. Both managers and line personnel have an interest in costs and productivity, an interest strongly supported by consultative management and an incredible incentive plan, described as the "foremost characteristic" of Nucor's personnel system. <u>Morale</u> is fine. Nucor takes good care of its people on payday, and its employees strive to increase productivity. It works, and that's another one of Iverson's interests.

<u>FINANCE AND ACCOUNTING.</u> Other than to attach balance sheets and income statements, the case is silent here, and perhaps it is just as well because the Tables reflect an embarrassment of riches. None of the ratios in Table 3 could cause anything but happiness. Earnings have grown 31% a year, compounded, since 1969. Working capital is abundant. ROE far exceeds the industry average, although it does show the effects of the 1982-83 recession. There is little LT debt, and Nucor has a very strong cash position. Its CR in 1986 was 2.5, and its QR was equally impressive. Five year summary (not in case) 1983-87 shows average annual increase in sales of 4.2%, of net income 20.3%, and EPS 26.9%. In essence Nucor is well off; given its reputation, it could fund any reasonable undertaking without difficulty. External funding, if needed, would seem available for the asking.

<u>MARKETING AND DISTRIBUTION.</u> The case treats marketing lightly, too, merely quoting a manager that Nucor has "the finest selling organization in the country." Iverson says Nucor isn't bad at marketing, but it's getting better. Since Nucor competes in every segment of steel or steel products, it must <u>advertise</u>. Vulcraft uses national ad campaigns, but there is little else. <u>Distribution</u> tends to regional because of transportation costs, but Nucor still advertises on-time delivery anywhere in the U.S. using its fleet of 100 trucks. Since Nucor is the low cost domestic producer, that fact must be reflected in its <u>pricing.</u>

<u>PRODUCTION AND OPERATIONS MANAGEMENT.</u> Here Nucor shines. Nucor has led the industry in mini-mill technology. Its mini-mills use an electric arc furnace, and its oldest mill dates only from 1968. Its mills are new, smaller, cheaper, more efficient and far less complex process-wise than are integrated mills. Integrated mills cost $1200-1500 per ton of capacity; Nucor's mini-mills cost less than $125. Domestic industry's energy costs per ton are $75; Nucor's are about $39. Employment costs of the seven largest integrated U.S. mills average almost $130 per ton; Nucor's costs are less than $60 per ton. Nucor can produce a ton of steel with only three production man hours, half what comparable domestic mills need. Its 981 tons produced per employee make it second in the world. No doubt about it - Nucor is cheap, and it is good.

Nucor's <u>facilities</u> and <u>equipment</u> are new and exquisitely efficient. Reviewing the comparisons above, one must conclude its <u>procedures</u> are both effective and efficient. A mini-mill uses steel scrap; there's lots of it around, and it is cheaper than iron ore. Mills are <u>strategically located</u> with reference to markets, and joist plants are sited nearby. Nucor is suitably vertically integrated; it supplies steel for its own steel products like joists and bolts, so these, too, are low cost competitors. Mini-mills cannot produce the same product line as can an integrated mill, notably sheet steel and heavy construction items, but if you believe Iverson, that capability will appear in due course. Iverson says Nucor does only two things well

- "builds plants economically, and runs them efficiently." [Steel] is "what we know how to do, and we do it well." No argument there at all.

R&D AND ENGINEERING. R&D is mentioned almost inferentially, but given Iverson's dedication to technology, some group in Nucor has to be thinking along these lines. Iverson started life as a metallurgist, and in 1984, explaining Aycock's appointment, Iverson laments being unable to put the efforts into R&D that he wanted to. Nucor spent $12 million to find out how to avoid reheating billets. That success balanced off two unsuccessful efforts to use resistance heating and induction milling. Failure doesn't bother Iverson, it seems. He expects failures, and he accepts them as a way of business, so Nucor provides a work environment suited to innovation and creativity. The company listens to its workers and uses their expertise to improve productivity. What we don't know is comparatively how much effort goes into R&D, but what we do know is that here is where Iverson needs to devote a lot of effort. Technology got Nucor where it is, and technology is what Nucor will need to stay ahead of the rest.

STRATEGIC ALTERNATIVES AND CHOICE

There is no choice. Iverson has clearly embraced a strategy of growth.

RECOMMENDED DISCUSSION QUESTIONS

1. What generic strategy does Nucor follow? Why?

2. What causes it to follow that strategy?

3. To what can be attributed its ability to do so?

4. How do Nucor's corporate culture and organization contribute to that ability?

5. If Nucor is so cost conscious, how can it permit a lack of centralization of such activities as purchasing?

6. How would you characterize Nucor's strategic management system? Would you recommend any changes?

7. There are apparent reservations about Nucor's announced joint venture with Kogyo. Are they well founded?

8. Can Nucor continue to grow with its present strategy? Why (not)?

9. What would you recommend?

ANALYSIS AND DISCUSSION

1. What generic strategy does Nucor follow? Why?

Cost leadership. Steel is basically an undifferentiated commodity. As Iverson says at the close of the case, Nucor runs plants efficiently, and Nucor does well what it knows how to do. Nucor follows this strategy because there really is no other way to go.

2.What causes it to follow that strategy?

This is not a replay of Question 1. Nucor follows a strategy of cost leadership because it is fortunate enough to be a very low cost producer. It appears not to be able to produce specialty steels, alloys, or coated sheets that might permit a focus strategy. What it makes is what everyone else makes but Nucor does a better job of it.

3.To what can be attributed its ability to do so?

Nucor is the low cost producer for many reasons, so expect to hear them all here. Its mini-mills are inherently more efficient and use more advanced technology than many of its competitors. Steel scrap is cheaper than iron ore. Energy and labor costs are much lower than in integrated mills. Ditto construction costs. Its workforce is marvelously productive, made so by good management practices, good leadership, and fine incentive systems. Overshadowing all is a supportive corporate culture.

4.How do Nucor's corporate culture and organization contribute to that ability?

Its corporate culture stresses thrift and simplicity. Everybody is in the same boat. The aim is greater efficiency, to boost productivity. There are no frills and no perks. Bare bones thrift, economy of operation, continued improvement from the floor, and worker involvement make a religion of low costs. Its organizational structure carries out the same motif. The headquarters staff is ridiculously small and basically unobtrusive. Thrift and simplicity show in the flat, unadorned structure which encourages flexibility and individual responsibility. Management is decentralized to division managers, who run profit centers and have all the tools to do so.

5.If Nucor is so cost conscious, how can it permit a lack of centralization of such activities as purchasing?

Iverson's view is to place responsibility at division level and to give the division manager what he needs to do the job. Centralization has an appeal from the standpoint of economy, but it is also true that you have to spend money to make money. Centralizing functions would mean division managers no longer had the tools for the job. Nucor headquarters would be much larger, and that would be anathema to Iverson. Bureaucracies are remote from and tend to be unresponsive to operators. Flexibility is lost. Division managers may or may not be properly supported, so it follows that they can no longer be held responsible. That would affect the profit center concept adversely, and Nucor's productivity would begin to unravel.

6. How would you characterize Nucor's strategic management system? Would you recommend any changes?

That is easy. There isn't any. One should anticipate that students will recommend that Iverson adopt such a system. Some may be uncertain. The advocates should of course be complimented, but you ought to ask how they would go about convincing Iverson of the need. That's not his style, and we would have to agree that if it ain't broke, don't fix it. Whatever the present need, Iverson seems happy with what he has. The future may be a different matter, but with Nucor's track record, one is hard pressed to speak of change.

7. There are apparent reservations about Nucor's announced joint venture with Kogyo. Are they well founded?

Not really. They are sensible, but they do Iverson little credit. He sees opportunities for "heavier structurals," to use his words. Mini-mills won't do it, since the technology is not in hand. Iverson is attracted by technology. Kogyo knows continuous casting, and Nucor can supply the management. If you don't have the capability, buy it. In this case the capability can be had through a joint venture. Iverson hasn't gone off on a tangent. There may well be overcapacity, but that doesn't translate into meeting market needs, and Iverson knows opportunity ("somewhat harder to find than [it] used to be") when he sees it.

8. Can Nucor continue to grow with its present strategy? Why (not)?

Probably not. Iverson know that the days of grabbing market share from integrated mills are over. Further gains will have to come the hard way, since competition has become so keen. When Iverson says "you've got to take something [market share] from someone else," he means it will be a head-to-head contest, either beating others or coming up with a technological breakthrough that will allow mini-mills to produce products like sheets which now are the province of integrated mills.

9. What would you recommend?

Stability is not Iverson's way, and retrenchment is not indicated. That leaves growth. Iverson ruled out conglomerate growth. Growth then comes down to new markets and/or new products. New markets, but where? Nucor is not in the business of foreign trade, and this is not the time to try to enter foreign markets. That leaves new products. To grow here, Iverson needs to push R&D and to watch technological developments closely. Anything is for sale if the price is right, so Iverson must be alert to emerging technologies which might enable Nucor to produce new products.

SPRINGFIELD REMANUFACTURING CORPORATION (SRC)

TEACHING NOTE

TEACHING OBJECTIVES

SRC, an auto parts remanufacturing outfit, in its short history has done well enough to be featured in <u>INC</u> magazine and to be the subject of a PBS television documentary. Even for so successful a corporation as this, the overnight loss of 25% of its business could be disastrous. Specific objectives:

Become acquainted with automobile remanufacturing operations

See management practices in a employee-owned firm

Understand the dangers of becoming a captive company

Appreciate the need for strategic management

Recommend an appropriate course of action

USING THIS CASE

The case is short, easy to read, and since it concerns surprising success in an unusual business, should easily keep student interest. It is of no more than moderate difficulty, hence should be relatively easy to discuss. It can be used early in a course, when one wishes to stress the need for strategic management, or in mid-course when the aim is to (re)formulate strategy. We do not recommend it for an inclass exam. It is, however, quite suitable for either a short report or a long report.

SYNOPSIS

In 1983 International Harvester sold its Springfield, Missouri diesel engine and engine component remanufacturing plant to a group of former employees. A dynamic, visionary president, a good management team, an unusual management attitude toward employees, and employee ownership of SRC spelled almost immediate success with a capital S. Sales more than doubled in three years to almost $38 million (or 400% if we go back to SRC's birth on 1 February 1983). Hard work, quality products, a unique marketing twist, and a great regard for its customers made SRC a real comer. In 1985 General Motors contracted with SRC to remanufacture V-8 diesel engines, and in 1986 half of SRC's business was with GM. In April 1987 GM cut its need for engines; to SRC this meant bye-bye to

---

This Note is based on a prior Note by and conversation with Charles Boyd, one of the casewriters.

25% of its 1987 business. The CEO is confronted with an immediate problem: he has to replace that lost business, or abruptly cut back. He doesn't want to reduce the work force, an immediate reduction in costs, but he isn't sure of his options.

OUTCOME

The CEO decided against retrenching, although 37 employees were lost to attrition. Intensified marketing efforts enabled SRC in September to project 1987 sales of $36 million. Better than that, proving every cloud can have a silver lining, SRC picked up significant new customers like Sears and Auto Shack.

TEACHING APPROACHES TO THIS CASE

Several facets of SRC make the case a bit unusual: its business is a bit out of the ordinary; its managerial approach is different, to say the least; its employees are deeply involved in its operations; SRC is to some extent a captive company, and it has chosen a relationship with OEM's that is virtually unique. It is important that students really understand what business SRC is in, so we suggest asking that question and following its answers with a request for specifics. So SRC builds or repairs engine components in the aftermarket. We feel then that SRC's relationships with OEM's should also be explored. Any description should establish that unlike most of its competitors, SRC sells to OEM's. So what? Well, this helps the OEM in its aftermarket. How? Students should be able to tick off the reasons. Sounds like it's all one-sided, for the OEM. Not at all. SRC is spared the expense of a complex distribution system. Because it virtually builds to order, it misses the expense of row on row of finished goods which have no buyer. Its efficiency in shop operations plus the expenses it doesn't have to incur, make SRC a tough combination to beat. What generic strategies pull it along? There are only three possible answers, so you should hear them all. One view is that SRC uses all three: cost, focus, and differentiation. How the last? Quality, low percent of returns, incredibly quick delivery, good warranties, and a nearness to its customers.

Even so, does all this guarantee success? It should. Its managerial practices are worth a few words, because they are decidedly not the norm. How deeply involved are employees in SRC operations? Pretty deep. Why? If one believes that all behavior is a function of consequence, ESOP plays a part here. It looks like all the lights are green. This can lead to a discussion of a captive company - what one is and does. Kellwood was for Sears. Someone will say that SRC is not truly a captive company - only 50% of its business goes to GM and not 100%. Agreed, so it's a 50% captive company. We call it this to generate discussion, otherwise it might be difficult to get students to see the con's as well as the pro's of being tied to a major company in a big way. It makes life easier, but nothing in life is free, as SRC found out. With everything going for it, how could it come up with such a problem?

Still another approach is to ask what SRC does, establish that it is successful for the following x reasons, ask what its problem is and seek recommendations. Or shortcut it all and simply ask how such a successful company could back itself into a corner.

CASE ANALYSIS

STRATEGIC MANAGEMENT ELEMENTS: MISSION, GOALS AND OBJECTIVES

The case does not directly address mission, goals, or objectives, and there is no quantification. We must infer then that SRC's mission is to repair or rebuild engine components under contract for OEM's of automobiles, trucks, and construction and agricultural equipment. Goals take the form of "better": better cooperation, better communications, better safety, better quality, better operations at lower and lower costs, better use of personnel resources, better profits, etc. Objectives are unspoken, too, so we surmise that Jack Stack, CEO, simply wants to be good, if not the best, in all aspects.

STRATEGISTS

Stack is described as charismatic and thoughtful. He is also a visionary leader who understands people and will take the time to listen. He gives the impression of a hard worker in a hurry who knows precisely what he wants and needs and will tolerate precious little deviance from his standards. He has surrounded himself with like minds. Carrigan, Production, would rather fix than buy and is admirably suited to recycling operations. Brown, HRM, looks for competitive "hungry" people who like to compete and to win. All are dedicated to quality via efficiency.

ENVIRONMENTAL ANALYSIS

SOCIOECONOMIC SECTOR. An American wouldn't be an American without his car. The American love affair with the automobile may be the ninth wonder of the world. We judge SRC, being in the aftermarket, to be largely immune from the business cycle. We do not agree that the success of the aftermarket is "highly dependent" on the rate of new car sales. Somewhat perhaps, but not highly. In bad times, new car sales slide and people do their best to keep the old bus running, rather than trade it in. As prices have risen, the average age of cars and trucks on the road has risen. This aging has dragged the auto parts aftermarket upward with it. The disillusionment of society with Detroit's products has greatly increased the number of imported cars sold to the motoring public. Some are made in the US, while many are not.

TECHNOLOGICAL AND GOVERNMENT SECTOR Not an apparent factor in the case.

INDUSTRY THREATS AND OPPORTUNITIES Both threats and opportunities abound. SRC's opportunities seem great. Aftermarket sales are expected to grow as much as 3% over the next few years as the number of vehicles in operation increases. Moreover, vehicle ages have increased, which translates to more market for SRC. SRC has only begun to look into gasoline engine rebuilding, a market which far overshadows the diesel market and grows by the day. There can well be an aftermarket for imported cars, unless versions of those cars are made in the U.S. SRC rebuilds/repairs engine components; certainly there is enough expertise to go into related items like driveshafts, brake components, and the like, provided OEM's communicate the necessary orders to SRC.

Threats exist in the form of ample competition, because the aftermarket is so vast. Do-it-yourselfers, job shops (see our earlier case, Bennett's Machine Shop), auto dealerships and auto mechanic shops (either independent or chain, like Firestone), to name a few. 1987 car and truck sales are expected to dip 5% in 1987, but that's more of an annoyance than a threat such as GM's no longer producing diesel vehicles. The casewriters point out that since SRC services such large customers, the inevitable swings in level of demand make the precise amount of plant capacity a difficult matter to judge.

STRATEGIC ADVANTAGE PROFILE

CORPORATE RESOURCES AND PERSONNEL Here one finds SRC's long suit, which is to say again that good management is everything. The company earned an enviable image in an incredibly short time. It is small but mighty. Its precise structure is not described, but its climate is.

Stack's acumen and enthusiasm are noteworthy. Stack has a reputation for snatching labor peace from probable UAW jaws. Management-employee relations are superior, and ESOP is a prime motivator. Quality circles help efficiency and productivity. Attention is focused on quality, safety, and housekeeping; data covering each are constantly updated and make employees goal-oriented. From this we infer a highly effective MIS. ESOP helps greatly since employees can relate the quality of their work to their personal income - it becomes "our company". Weekly meetings with employees go into operating income, profit, loss, etc. Stack is quoted as having said that his employees are taught finance and accounting before they are otherwise trained.

Stack calls it The Great Game of Business (not in case), which involves every employee in the details and strategy of SRC. It is as important to understand the company's performance, apparently, as it is to know one's own job. Every department operates as a small business with its own budget. All this leads to a team concept which pervades all levels. This decentralized - participative management fosters the utmost in efficiency, quality, and cost control. Personnel are selected for fit to SRC's corporate mold - "hungry" competitors - and trained well. Performance is rewarded commensurately; all this and ESOP provide lower labor costs and better, more reliable, quality products.

Rapid growth is not without some pain. There is no strategic management system, just a series of first generation one year operating plans. Management has simply not had time to catch its breath and consolidate its gains. The 1987 plan to reorganize sales and marketing and to enhance customer service died aborning when GM cut its orders back.

FINANCE AND ACCOUNTING Ratios tell us that management has done a fine job of reducing the D/E ratio (1984, 328; 1987, 2.2). CR is less than 2, and QR is quite low (.37 at best). The firm has relatively low capitalization. ST debt seems high and complicated by irregular cash flow from year to year. At the same time, management has done a masterful job of reducing SRC's initial high levels of debt, and SRC has turned a profit while other companies have not. ROI and ROE have climbed steadily. As a reflection of efficiency, inventory turnover has increased almost 300% while inventories have been reduced 60%. All in all SRC is financially sound albeit cash poor. ESOP provides a terrific incentive but could conceivably be a loose board in the future should it be necessary to raise large amounts of cash by other than bank loans.

MARKETING AND DISTRIBUTION Another big plus for SRC. There is no market research but this has not proved a hindrance since the company has had a 40% growth in annual sales each year since 1983. We are not told SRC's market share in the aftermarket, but we do know that SRC's sales increases each year of up to 40% (1985) are sensational. SRC's success here must in large be attributed to its strategy of working with the OEM rather than competing with the OEM in the aftermarket. This is eminently sensible - smart small companies don't tackle big ones head on; instead, they look for a niche. SRC has such a niche by virtue of adding value to the OEM. Sales personnel sell the sizzle before the steak, and it works. Since SRC increases OEM profitability and share of the aftermarket, it's hard to ignore SRC's logic. The company's devotion to efficiency and cost control gives it a pricing appeal that others are hard to come by. For one thing, SRC doesn't bear the expense of a distribution system when it sells to OEM's. That's an OEM problem. A return rate of less than 1%, one sixth the industry's average, rapid delivery, and a good warranty system, are all boosts to marketing. Even so, Stack saw room for improvement so his 1987 plan called for reorganizing sales and marketing and concentrating on better service to present customers, rather than seeking new ones. There is no mention of promotion or advertising.

PRODUCTION AND OPERATIONS MANAGEMENT The case does not describe facilities in detail but does state that business increased enough to require another building. Its location, 20 miles from Springfield, indicates it was standing, not built to order. This would appear to reflect the pack rat approach of Carrigan, VP Production, who leads the way in method improvement and waste reduction. One can't judge efficiency, because we have no standards, but a less than 1% return rate and vaunted warranties certainly argue for an effective operation. ESOP, participative management, making work fun, employee involvement in decision making - all this comes together in manufacturing. Little wonder that after little more than a year of operations, all this has brought SRC a designation as the "best" of those doing remanufacturing for its former parent company. Quality control and effective scheduling are evident, and constant watch is kept on safety and housekeeping. Overhead costs decreased 5% despite a 400% increase in business. We guess at some slack in the operation, however, since SRC has recently gone to rebuilding gasoline engines, but there are no signs of an upsurge in employees. This implies skilled <u>personnel</u> who are able to transition to new tasks with minimum training and little downtime.

STRATEGIC ALTERNATIVES

<u>Stability</u>, stable growth, cannot answer the loss of GM's orders. Only <u>expansion</u> can do that. <u>Retrenchment</u> seems desirable but should be only a last ditch effort because of the probable damage to fine management-employee relations. A <u>combination</u> strategy is not recommended because SRC, though it has an immediate problem, really doesn't qualify for classic turn-around strategy treatment.

CHOICE

A strategy of expansion.

IMPLEMENTATION

SRC needs to put all plans on hold except for an all out marketing effort in each of its four "cylinders". It has made a start in the remanufacturing of gasoline engines, so it is not without entre and expertise here. The size of the probable market commends it to SRC's closest attention; despite intense competition, SRC's reputation has to be worth something as a marketing device. SRC might at the same time (re)examine its efforts as a remanufacturer for imported vehicles. What else can be done immediately without extensive retooling or retraining? Put scouts out. And although GM has cut its orders, there is still a sizeable diesel truck fleet which will need more and more attention as it ages. The casewriter suggests that SRC is considering a means whereby it can sell to automobile dealerships directly. But this is not short term, and even doing so in the long term has to be considered in relation to SRC's link with OEM's. We noted above that the case omits mention of advertising, other than that done by sales personnel in the normal course of business. Since these are desperate times and require desperate measures, SRC needs a massive shot of advertising. Certainly Stack can afford that.

Once SRC turns the corner, management must realize several things: It's dangerous to put too much reliance on one customer, so a broader base is indicated. How could SRC, which does so many things right, have been brought up so short? Turning the corner will solve the immediate problem, but that tends to obscure the fact that the company has no strategic management system. Such a system does not guarantee success, but lack of a system generally means that disaster comes as a complete surprise. Operational plans of a year are not enough. The company must take time out for strategic management - that's about the only way to insure against another ghastly surprise. For starters, Stack might want to articulate the company's mission and set some quantifiable goals and objectives. SRC's quantitatively oriented employees would probably surprise with their response.

RECOMMENDED DISCUSSION QUESTIONS

1. Why has SRC been so successful?

2. Why spend so much time explaining the financial workings of SRC to its employees?

3. Why measure, graph and update cost, profit and company overhead measures?

4. To what can SRC's fine quality be attributed?

5. How does SRC obtain such exceptional cooperation from its personnel?

6. How important is it for a CEO to conceptualize and share his vision for the company with his employees? How is that best done?

7. Why has SRC adopted a togetherness with OEM's?

8. What basic error did Stack make?

9. What should he do?

ANALYSIS AND DISCUSSION

1. Why has SRC been so successful?

There are a host of reasons, so you should hear just about everything here. Principally, ESOP which gives employees a true stake in SRC's financial performance. Then Stack's style of communication and participative management, which make for a positive climate for change. Effort to help employees understand financial statements, so that they can relate their own performance to SRC's results. Last but not least, a superb marketing effort.

2. Why spend so much time explaining the financial workings of SRC to its employees?

There may be conflicting views here. Some will say that since ESOP makes employees investors, they want to be well informed about their investment. Others will say workers tend to view profit as the responsibility of top management. Most studies on ESOPs seem to straddle the fence here: ESOP employees like a high degree of control over decisions which affect their own area of responsibility but not over decisions which affect overall strategy. That's understandable. The casewriters state that ESOP employees are interested in the financial return on their investment, and several studies relate the importance of top management's telling employees of the progress of the ESOP.

3. Why measure, graph and update cost, profit and company overhead measures?

This increases feedback when one can post and compare performance between departments and overtime; it makes performance appraisals easier when goals

157

and their achievement are known; it tells people what management considers important, and it provides a means of improving anything to which a standard can be applied.

4. To what can SRC's fine quality be attributed?

Teamwork and a cooperative attitude, mutual respect, shared responsibility and participative management, setting goals and managing performance, employee interest, pride in being a member of a select organization where people are important.

5. How does SRC obtain such exceptional cooperation from its personnel?

Sharing information about how and why the company operates as it does, involving employees in decisions, putting supervisors in charge of operations outside their immediate area of responsibility (i.e., control of all costs of a certain type, rather than just those costs in the supervisor's area), putting each activity on a budget, etc. The object to be taught here is that things like cooperation don't happen just because of the pay envelope.

6. How important is it for a CEO to conceptualize and share his vision for the company with his employees? How is that best done?

Very. People like Stack and Sam Walton help provide a central focus for their companies. Each employee feels like a member of a family which has both a goal and a personality. Stack's way was to maintain personal contact, treat employees as equals, reduce status barriers, share information, provide jointly accepted goals which could be measured to judge performance, etc.

7. Why has SRC adopted a togetherness with OEM's?

This is a large piece of SRC's success. If you can't lick'em, join'em. SRC saw immediately that it was better to go with OEM's rather than against them. Why oppose a large company? Why not help the large company help itself? Turn about is fair play and far more profitable.

8. What basic error did Stack make?

Most will probably say something like becoming overly dependent on one customer, GM. True to a degree, but what would you have Stack do, turn GM down? We argue that the GM problem was a symptom of a much more fundamental problem, a lack of a strategic management system.

9. What should he do?

See our remarks under Implementation.

ZAREMBO CORPORATION (ZC)

TEACHING NOTE

TEACHING OBJECTIVES

George Wood, ZC's president, has all kinds of numbers to work with in deciding investment alternatives, but he can't be sure that the "best" numerical answer will adequately address all the issues. Specific objectives:

Become acquainted with the forest industry

Visualize the investment alternatives to ZC

Afford an opportunity for spreadsheet analysis

Understand that the best decision may not always lie in numbers

Recommend a course of action

USING THIS CASE

The case is straightforward and reads easily. It appears more formidable than it is, because the variety of alternatives and their accompanying numbers is a bit uncommon. The case is very much real world, and its nature is unusual enough that student interest seems assured. Wood, ZC's boss, has all sorts of numbers, so the case can be a real feast for those who like to crunch numbers via Lotus 1-2-3 or VisiCalc. It is easier for a finance major than say a management major, and it makes for a good review of basic numbers handling. ZC is best covered in two sessions. It would be moderately difficult to difficult for most, depending on how well students handle numbers. It affords limitless opportunity for spreadsheet analysis because so many variables like discount rate, loan rate, selling price, and costs of various types can be changed, sometimes with startling effect on NPVs. It probably fits best in the middle of a course when strategic choice is being considered. It could possibly be used later in a course, when students should have a growing awareness that the most favorable number and the values of management, the nonquantifiable factors, need not and often do not coincide. A short

---

This Note draws heavily on a fine prior Note written by Nick Tupper and Dr. Stuart Rich, Professor of Marketing and Director, Forest Industries Management Center, College of Business Administration, University of Oregon, Eugene, Oregon. The discussion of alternatives, NPV tables, and interpretation of results are quoted from their Note.

report is not indicated, nor is the use of ZC for an inclass exam. The case is better suited as a long report or a final problem.

SYNOPSIS

The Zarembo Corporation in Waterville, Alaska, almost completely Alaskan native-run, is concerned with native advancement through better living conditions. The latter would be a natural outgrowth of employment opportunities generated by local businesses. SFPC, a regional native corporation, proposes to George Wood that it be assigned Zarembo's timber cutting rights. Although the proposal is advantageous to Zarembo, George sees a number of possibilities involving ZC's timber. The case addresses those possibilities and in doing so furnishes a brief but accurate picture of the forest industry. Although George can examine the profitability of each major alternative, he realizes that he must consider other factors in arriving at the best course of action.

OUTCOME

Unknown.

TEACHING APPROACHES TO THIS CASE

A direct approach is to discuss each alternative, list its pros and cons, and examine the NPVs. This certainly has the virtues of continuity and simplicity. A more circuitous approach is to ask what SFPC's are. Do these have any meaning to ZC? They certainly should, because they embrace such laudable ends as responsible development, sound financing, and profit for ZC. If SFPC is to receive no profit, then why is Wood thinking of alternatives? The case does not make this crystal clear, but we suspect that George has something more than money in mind. In discussing what this might be, logic should suggest that he must be mindful of the nonquantifiable factors which the village board will have in mind as it pores over George's NPVs. This then can lead into a discussion of the alternatives George sees.

CASE ANALYSIS

STRATEGIC MANAGEMENT ELEMENTS: MISSION, GOALS AND OBJECTIVES

The mission of ZC is not precisely stated, but one of its primary concerns is to improve the living conditions of native Alaskans. There are no quantifiable goals, and no objectives are stated. There is enough elasticity in the mission to justify numerous goals. SFPC's objectives are something else.

STRATEGISTS

Here the case is silent. George Wood, ZC president, is not described in any detail. It is easy to believe that he is thoughtful, well educated and imaginative. Beyond that we can only speculate.

SOCIOECONOMIC SECTOR. ZC's town of Waterville appears down on its uppers. It is mainly dependent on the fishing industry. Unemployment is high. Among other things, ZC would like to create greater employment opportunities, so SFPC's proposal has to be highly welcome. We note that one of Woods' alternatives is a sawmill, which at capacity would usually employ about 60 people.

GOVERNMENT SECTOR. Government is pervasive here. ZC exists by virtue of the Alaska Native Claims Settlement Act (ANCSA). The same Act gave ZC the forest land which underlies the case.

Government also plays a regulator hand in the forest industry. A market for raw logs exists in Japan, but the US prohibits the export of federally owned timber as raw logs; this is advantageous to ZC since its timber is regarded as privately owned. For the same reason, ZC does not have to export its timber as finished lumber. The actions of other governments - Canada and Russia - are restrictive of log exports to Japan, and so are those of the states of Oregon, Washington and California. Last but not least, the Jones Act means high transportation costs for timber shipped to the U.S.

INDUSTRY THREATS AND OPPORTUNITIES. The forest industry lives and dies with the U.S. housing industry, so far as domestic timber markets are concerned. At the time of the case housing was depressed, and the U.S. lumber industry was in serious trouble. Fortunately, the export market was an opportunity and was forecast to remain so. That meant that the Alaskan export market would stay strong. Unhampered by federal and state regulation, as noted above, ZC could take full advantage of the Japanese market. Its competition was restrained by national or state regulation. China and South Korea are additional possibilities. In effect, ZC has a ready market, virtually free of any threats.

STRATEGIC ADVANTAGE PROFILE

CORPORATE RESOURCES AND PERSONNEL. Whatever it is, ZC is short of it. The corporation is small, young, inexperienced, has no depth of management, and lives wholly on ANCSA funds. There is no experience in the timber business and little or no knowledge of land use planning or land management. High area unemployment guarantees a labor supply, but none of it is skilled. Strategic management seems unknown.

FINANCE AND ACCOUNTING. ZC has some funds, extent and origin unknown. It would require external financing to pursue any of Wood's alternatives. Nothing further is known, save that George Wood has some knowledge of finance, judging by his use of NPV methods.

MARKETING AND DISTRIBUTION. Another blank. No one has a background in marketing, and distribution would be an insurmountable problem. If ZC is to sell in Japan, Wood knows that it cannot sell directly to Japanese saw mills. He must deal with a Japanese trading company, or if not that, then with a major exporter like SFPC or a log broker, both of whom deal with trading companies. The way to other markets is unclear, and the market in the lower 48 is anything but promising. On its own, ZC could hardly market to Japan.

PRODUCTION AND OPERATION. ZC has no capability here. Nearly any alternative would require starting from scratch. Equipment and bodies are the least of Woods' problems, but there is so very much more - roads, training, corporate operations, etc.

STRATEGIC ALTERNATIVES

There is no choice. ZC has adopted for a strategy of growth. The only question to be decided is how.

RECOMMENDED DISCUSSION QUESTIONS

1. What must Mr. Wood take into account when he addresses ZC's board of directors?

2. Is ZC sure of a market, should it decide to handle the operation itself? Why?

3. Which alternative promises the highest NPV, assuming 20% cost of capital and 18% financing charges? Justify.

4. What are the advantages and disadvantages of each?

5. Which should Wood recommend and why?

ANALYSIS AND DISCUSSION

1. What must Mr. Wood take into account when he addresses ZC's board of directors?

Wood must also consider company resources, corporate objectives, managerial skills, market information and profitability.

2. Is ZC sure of a market, should it decide to handle the operation itself? Why?

As sure as anything can be. Table 1 recites a long history of log exports from Alaska to Japan, and the market is growing rapidly. As a private entity, ZC is free from state and federal restrictions which might otherwise interfere with marketing logs to Japan.

3.Which alternative promises the highest NPV, assuming 20% cost of capital and 18% financing charges? Justify.

4.What are the advantages and disadvantages of each?

Alternative I
(See Exhibit I)

Harvest and sell own logs, purchase new logging equipment

Advantages:
1.High NPV = $5,819,780.
2.Independence from Seregion.
3.Get to employ 20 villagers.
4.Accounting depreciation on equipment may be at zero after ten years, but the economic life of the machines could be much longer.
5.Market demands logs now; much of the present supply base of logs (Washington) will likely dry up in the near future, leaving Alaska in good position. Japanese trading companies anxious for long-term agreement; Japanese may provide capital investment funds at lower rates.

Disadvantages:
1.No experience in: -- logging
                     -- road building
                     -- marketing logs
2.Had recently acquired cold storage facility and oil storage facility, representing their only business experience to date.
3.12,000 MBF is not a significant volume and thus Zarembo would not be in a strong position for price negotiation.
4.Lack experience in dealing with Japanese.

Alternative II
(See Exhibit II)

Harvest and sell logs; purchase used logging equipment. (Had to assume logging equipment available for same price in years 5 and 9.)

Advantages:
1.High NPV = $6,177,635.
2.Independence from Seregion.
3.Only four year investment life per cycle.
4.Maintain flexibility.
5.Less investment necessary than Alternative I, therefore less risk involved.
6.Employ 20 village people.
7.Japanese prefer logs and will be looking for a replacement in case the Washington log source dries up in the future. Japanese trading com-

panies are probably anxious for long-term log agreement and may provide capital investment funds at lower rates.

Disadvantages:
1. No experience in: -- logging
                     -- road building
                     -- marketing logs
2. Would probably need to stock inventory of machine parts, since using older machinery.
3. Accounting life is probably closer to economic life of equipment for used equipment, as opposed to new. Thus replacement is much more likely at investment book value at life end.
4. Used equipment is often purchased at auctions, hence financing would be difficult. Had to assume cash outlays. If financing is available, then this becomes a more attractive alternative.
5. Lack experience in dealing with Japanese.

Alternative III
(See Exhibit III)

Harvest own timber and process into squares, chips. Purchase new mill (purchase price includes woods operation).

Advantages:
1. Positive NPV = $2,107,513.
2. Economic life of actual mill equipment, buildings, etc. is probably much higher than accounting life indicated, thus reducing future investment if business continued.
3. Employ 60 village people.
4. Remain independent from Seregion.
5. Increase product choice flexibility--reserve right to produce what market needs are.
6. Can help provide energy supply--log fuel, chips, etc.
7. Alaskan market should expand in future. Currently about 15% of Alaska's wood product needs are being supplied by Alaskan mills (see Case Appendix D).

Disadvantages:
1. No experience in logging, road building, saw milling, timber products marketing.
2. May have enough new business to administer with fish storage and oil storage facilities.
3. Market doesn't pay as well for processed timber because Japanese prefer logs right now.
4. Future for processed timber looks competitive, with pressure on state of Washington for curbing log exports.
5. Would require much greater market effort than Alternatives I or II.

6.Lowest NPV of all alternatives.

Alternative IV
(See Exhibit IV)

Harvest own timber and process into squares, chips. Purchase used mill operation (includes woods operation).

Advantages:
    1.Positive NPV = $3,568,963.
    2.Same advantages as #3 through #7 in Alternative III.

Disadvantages:
    1.Economic life and accounting life probably close to equal, so reinvestment probably necessary in ten years.
    2.Same disadvantages as #1 through #6 in Alternative III.

Alternative V
(See Exhibit 5)

Seregion Timber Corporation proposal; assume 5% commission.

Advantages:
    1.As outlined in STC proposal.
    2.Allows Zarembo to concentrate on its current business and still enjoy highest NPV = $6,732,096. Since there is less risk involved here, it could be argued that the cost of capital should be lower - around 15%, for example. This yields an even higher NPV of $8,060,208.
    3.Flexibility of being able to terminate at whatever time it desires allows Zarembo to attempt another alternative when it is in a more financially sound position.
    4.Market will be calling for more Alaskan logs soon.

Disadvantages:
    1.Lose independence.
    2.Employ no villagers.

Alternative VI
(See Exhibit VI)

Sell stumpage @ $141/MBF

Advantages:
    1.Allows concentration on oil storage and cold storage operations.
    2.Positive NPV = $3,830,146. (Assuming a 15% cost of capital, NPV would be $4,585,760).

Disadvantages:
1.Employ no villagers.
2.Not the largest NPV.
3.Not in a position to capitalize on new market opportunities.
4.Lose title to the timber.

NPV Summary

Alternative	I	II	III
NPV @ 20%	$5,819,780	6,177,635	2,107,513
NPV @ 15%	--	--	--

Alternative	IV	V	VI
NPV @ 20%	$3,568,963	6,732,096	3,830,146
NPV @ 15%	---	8,060,208	4,585,760

5.Which should Wood recommend and why?

Looking at NPV alone, Alternative V, the proposal of Seregion Timber Corporation (STC), is the best option for Zarembo. However, since our NPV figure does not include non-quantifiable attributes as discussed earlier, we must look at other alternatives as well. We will limit these to the three alternatives with the highest NPVs. This leaves us with Alternative I, with an NPV of $5,819,780; Alternative II with an NPV of $6,177,635; and Alternative V with an NPV of $6,732,096.

The case states that one of the major concerns of the Board is to improve living conditions in Waterville, and employing villagers will help reach that goal. Thus, Alternatives I and II (purchase new/used logging equipment and harvest and sell logs) look superior to Alternative V in that each requires hiring 20 people to Alternative V's none. However, it may perhaps be possible to modify the contract that would be signed by Zarembo and STC to specify that STC has to hire its logging and road building crews from Waterville.

Alternatives I and II carry one major hurdle in common for Zarembo management. That hurdle is that both alternatives require a background in timber harvesting and marketing that apparently does not exist among the management or the workers. The marketing problem could be solved by using a broker or by signing a long-term arrangement with one of the Japanese trading companies. This, however, would be similar to the STC agreement with fewer advantages and would cut into Zarembo's profits. The trading company option limits Waterville to a set price or price schedule, and it would probably not represent top dollar. Thus, both the broker and trading company alternatives would probably reduce the NPV of Alternatives I and II. With the STC agreement, Zarembo management can get the best price and NPV, and yet this alternative requires no timber management background.

In terms of commitment or length of project, if Zarembo chooses Alternative I, it would face a 10-year investment project. This would be desirable in terms of cash flows and people employed, but with the time horizon and cost of equipment, it represents a higher risk than Alternative II. Even so, Alternative II with a four-year project life (but an NPV based on ten years) was still calculated with a 20% cost of capital just as was Alternative I. The shorter time horizon might be more agreeable to Board members worried that they might be getting in over their heads. This might partially make up for the differences in NPV between the two alternatives. The STC deal would, in effect, have no specified time horizon. Timber assignments could be made for any period that Zarembo desired, and Zarembo would be free to terminate the relationship at any time for any reason. Thus, in addition to the zero investment required, the STC alternative would mean that there would be little risk for Zarembo, and thus 15% could be used for the cost of capital. This nets an $8,060,208 NPV, which is obviously superior to that rate, and yet even when a 20% cost of capital is used, STC's NPV = $6,732,096, is still the best alternative in terms of NPV.

All of the above point to STC as being the best of Alternatives I, II, and V. However, to cover all aspects of the problem, Alternatives III and IV (build own sawmill, harvest own logs, produce and market lumber squares) are worth discussing even though they represent the lowest NPV's. The focus would be on jobs and stability created in the community with a permanent investment such as the mill represents. There would be immediate jobs created by the mill construction and 60 permanent jobs running and supplying the mill. This could add stability to a small town that depends so heavily on the fishing industry.

However, by accepting Alternative III or IV, the Zarembo management, knowing relatively little about the timber industry, could be creating a situation where the whole corporation would suffer because of being overextended and expanding too quickly into areas with which they are not familiar. This would be a deterrent to the desired stability.

Furthermore, all indications point to the fact that logs will continue to be in greatest demand, and that the supply of logs from the Pacific Northwest will likely be diminishing in the next five years due to regulation. Thus, the Pacific Northwest timber industry will need to process its logs into squares and lumber, making that market look more competitive in the future. Alaska and Zarembo Corporation should take advantage of the log demand-supply situation and leave the processing industry, which is less profitable, to the other regions.

The final point to be made regards the management of Zarembo Corporation. Mr. wood appears to be the only one deeply involved in this company. If it is true that he lacks solid support, whether through inability or unwillingness of his associates, then now is not the time for him to take on any new business, and thus the STC proposal is the best from this standpoint.

Recommendations

The foregoing analysis shows that Zarembo Corporation should accept Seregion Timber Corporation's proposal. It should attempt to integrate employment clauses into the contract in an effort to boost village employment levels.

With the high NPV and cash flows resulting from this alternative, Zarembo's management can concentrate on making the oil and fish storage operations profitable. In addition, since the STC agreement can be terminated at any time, the people of Waterville and the management of Zarembo Corporation can be training and familiarizing themselves in forest industries management. Then, alternatives not accepted at present might be re-evaluated when the company is more financially stable and knowledgeable.

ZAREMBO CORPORATION - Exhibit I

Alternative I - Harvest and Sell Own Logs - Purchase new Equipment
(See Assumptions next page)

	Year 1	Year 2	Year 3	Year 4	Year 5
Revenues	5,400,000	5,400,000	5,400,000	5,400,000	5,400,000
Cash Oper. Expenses:					
logging cost	1,680,000	1,680,000	1,680,000	1,680,000	1,680,000
road construction	750,000	750,000	750,000	750,000	750,000
administrative	120,000	120,000	120,000	120,000	120,000
Tot. Cash Oper. Expenses:	2,550,000	2,550,000	2,550,000	2,550,000	2,550,000
Plus Other Expenses:					
depreciation	150,000	127,500	108,375	92,119	87,001
interest	144,000	116,390	83,810	45,365	-
Total Expenses	2,844,000	2,793,890	2,742,185	2,687,484	2,637,001
Taxable Income	2,556,000	2,606,110	2,657,815	2,712,516	2,762,999
Tax Expense (46%)	1,175,760	1,198,811	1,222,595	1,247,757	1,270,979
Revenues	5,400,000	5,400,000	5,400,000	5,400,000	5,400,000
less: cash oper. exp.	2,550,000	2,550,000	2,550,000	2,550,000	2,550,000
tax expense	1,175,760	1,198,811	1,222,595	1,247,757	1,270,979
debt service	297,397	297,397	297,397	297,397	-
Cash outflow	4,023,157	4,046,208	4,069,992	4,095,397	3,820,979
Net cash flow	1,376,843	1,353,792	1,330,008	1,304,846	1,579,021

NPV @ 20% = $6,019,780 less $200,000 down payment = $5,819,780

It is assumed that the $200,000 down payment for the equipment in Year 1 is to be made at the very start of the year (or during "Year Zero"), rather than at the end of the year as in the case of other payments. Hence, this $200,000 is not discounted, but the whole amount is subtracted from the NPV figures for other cash outflows to get a final NPV figure.

Exhibit I - Alternative I - Assumptions

Depreciation method used on equipment = 150% declining balance first four years, straight line thereafter for a 10 year equipment life. Assume salvage value at end of 10 years = $0.

Investment required for new equipment = $800,000 financed at 18% for four years, plus $200,000 down (Total $1,000,000).

Balance	Year	Principal	Interest	Debt Service Payment
$800,000	1	$153,397	$144,000	$297,397
646,603	2	181,008	116,389	297,397
465,595	3	213,590	83,807	297,397
252,005	4	252,036	45,361	297,397

Altternative I. (Contd.) - Years 6 - 10

	Year 6	Year 7	Year 8	Year 9	Year 10
Revenues	5,400,000	5,400,000	5,400,000	5,400,000	5,400,000
Cash Oper. Expenses:					
logging cost	1,680,000	1,680,000	1,680,000	1,680,000	1,680,000
road construction	750,000	750,000	750,000	750,000	750,000
administrative	120,000	120,000	120,000	120,000	120,000
Tot. Cash Oper. Expenses:	2,550,000	2,550,000	2,550,000	2,550,000	2,550,000
Plus Other Expenses:					
depreciation	87,001	87,001	87,001	87,001	87,001
interest	-	-	-	-	-
Total Expenses	2,637,001	2,637,001	2,637,001	2,637,001	2,637,001
Taxable Income	2,762,999	2,762,999	2,762,999	2,762,999	2,762,999
Tax Expense (46%)	1,270,979	1,270,979	1,270,979	1,270,979	1,270,979
Revenues	5,400,000	5,400,000	5,400,000	5,400,000	5,400,000
less: cash oper. exp.	2,550,000	2,550,000	2,550,000	2,550,000	2,550,000
tax expense	1,270,979	1,270,979	1,270,979	1,270,979	1,270,979
debt service	-	-	-	-	-
Cash outflow	3,820,979	3,820,979	3,820,979	3,820,979	3,820,979
Net cash flow	1,579,021	1,579,021	1,579,021	1,579,021	1,579,021

ZAREMBO CORPORATION - Exhibit II

Alternative II - Harvest and Sell Own Logs - Purchase Used Equipment

Depreciation method used on equipment: 150% declining balance first two years, straight line thereafter for a four year life. Assume salvage value at end of four years = $0. Assume salvage value at end of 10th year = $150,000.

Investment required for used equipment = $250,000. Used logging equipment often bought at auctions, financing uncertain, therefore investment paid in cash. Replacement in years 4 and 8 assumed at year-end.

	Year 1	Year 2	Year 3	Year 4	Year 5
Revenues	5,400,000	5,400,000	5,400,000	5,400,000	5,400,000
Cash Oper. Expenses:					
logging cost	1,680,000	1,680,000	1,680,000	1,680,000	1,680,000
road construction	750,000	750,000	750,000	750,000	750,000
administrative	120,000	120,000	120,000	120,000	120,000
Tot. Cash Oper. Expenses:	2,550,000	2,550,000	2,550,000	2,550,000	2,550,000
Plus Other Expenses:					
depreciation	93,750	58,594	48,828	48,828	93,750
Total Expenses	2,643,750	2,608,594	2,598,828	2,598,828	2,643,750
Taxable Income	2,756,250	2,791,406	2,801,172	2,801,172	2,756,250
Tax Expense (46%)	1,267,875	1,284,046	1,288,539	1,288,539	1,267,875
Revenues	5,400,000	5,400,000	5,400,000	5,400,000	5,400,000
less: cash oper. exp.	2,550,000	2,550,000	2,550,000	2,550,000	2,550,000
tax expense	1,267,875	1,284,046	1,288,539	1,288,539	1,267,875
Cash outflow	3,817,875	3,834,046	3,838,539	3,838,539	3,817,875
Down payment	(see note below)-	-	-	250,000	-
Tot. Cash Outflow	3,817,875	3,834,046	3,838,539	4,088,539	3,817,875
plus:salvage payment					
Net cash flow	1,582,125	1,565,954	1,561,461	1,311,461	1,582,125

NPV @ 20% = $6,427,635 less $250,000 = $6,177,635

Note: It is assumed that the $250,000 down payment for equipment Year 1 is to be made at the very start of the year (or during "Year Zero"), rather than at the end of the year as in the case of other payments. Hence, this $250,000 is not discounted, but the whole amount is subtracted from the NPV figures for other cash outflows to get a final NPV figure.

Alternative II (Contd.) - Years 6 - 10

	Year 6	Year 7	Year 8	Year 9	Year 10
Revenues	5,400,000	5,400,000	5,400,000	5,400,000	5,400,000
Cash Oper. Expenses:					
logging cost	1,680,000	1,680,000	1,680,000	1,680,000	1,680,000
road construction	750,000	750,000	750,000	750,000	750,000
administrative	120,000	120,000	120,000	120,000	120,000
Tot. Cash Oper. Expenses:	2,550,000	2,550,000	2,550,000	2,550,000	2,550,000
Plus Other Expenses:					
depreciation	58,594	48,828	48,828	93,750	58,594
Total Expenses	2,608,594	2,598,828	2,598,828	2,643,750	2,608,594
Taxable Income	2,791,406	2,801,172	2,801,172	2,756,250	2,791,406
Tax Expense (46%)	1,284,046	1,288,539	1,288,539	1,267,875	1,284,046
Revenues	5,400,000	5,400,000	5,400,000	5,400,000	5,400,000
less: cash oper. exp.	2,550,000	2,550,000	2,550,000	2,550,000	2,550,000
tax expense	1,284,046	1,288,539	1,288,539	1,267,875	1,284,046
Cash outflow	3,834,046	3,838,539	4,088,539	3,817,875	3,834,046
Down payment	-	-	250,000	-	-
Tot. Cash Outflow	3,834,046	3,838,539	4,088,539	3,817,875	3,834,046
plus:salvage payment					150,000
Net cash flow	1,565,954	1,561,461	1,311,461	1,582,125	1,715,954

Alternative III - Harvest Own Timber and Process Into Squares, Chips - Purchase New Mill (Includes Woods Operation) for $4.5 million

Depreciation method used on mill and logging equipment = 150% declining balance first four years, straight line thereafter for 10-year mill and equipment life. Assume salvage value at end of 10 years = $1,000,000.

Investment required for mill and equipment = $400,000 down, plus $4,100,000 finance at 18% for 10 years (total $4.5 million).

Balance	Year	Principal	Interest	Debt Service Payment
$4,100,000	1	174,328	738,000	912,328
3,925,672	2	205,707	706,621	912,328
3,719,966	3	242,734	669,594	912,328
3,477,232	4	286,426	625,902	912,328
3,190,807	5	337,982	574,345	912,328

	Year 1	Year 2	Year 3	Year 4	Year 5
Revenues	6,156,000	6,156,000	6,156,000	6,156,000	6,156,000
Cash Oper. Expenses:					
logging cost	1,680,000	1,680,000	1,680,000	1,680,000	1,680,000
road construction	750,000	750,000	750,000	750,000	750,000
administrative	200,040	200,040	200,040	200,040	200,040
manufacturing costs	1,670,040	1,670,040	1,670,040	1,670,040	1,670,040
Tot. Cash Oper. Expenses:	4,300,080	4,300,080	4,300,080	4,300,080	4,300,080
Plus Other Expenses:					
depreciation	675,000	573,750	487,688	414,534	224,838
interest	738,000	706,621	669,594	625,902	574,345
Total Expenses	5,713,080	5,580,451	5,457,362	5,340,516	5,009,263
Taxable Income	442,920	575,549	698,638	815,484	1,056,737
Tax Expense (46%)	203,743	264,753	321,373	375,123	486,099
Revenues	6,156,000	6,156,000	6,156,000	6,156,000	6,156,000
less: cash oper. exp.	4,300,080	4,300,080	4,300,080	4,300,080	4,300,080
tax expense	203,743	264,753	321,373	375,123	486,099
debt service	912,328	912,328	912,328	912,328	912,328
Cash outflow	5,416,151	5,477,161	5,533,781	5,587,531	5,698,507
plus: salvage payment					
Total cash outflow	5,416,151	5,477,161	5,533,781	5,587,531	5,698,507
Net cash flow	739,849	678,839	622,219	568,469	457,493

NPV @ 20% = $2,507,513 less $400,000 down payment = $2,107,513

Note: It is assumed that the $400,000 down payment for mill and equipment in Year 1 is to be made at the very start of the year (or during "Year Zero"), rather than at the end of the year as in the case of other payments. Hence, this $400,000 is not discounted, but the whole amount is subtracted from the NPV figures for other cash outflows to get a final NPV figure.

Balance	Year	Principal	Interest	Debt Service Payment
$2,852,824	6	398,819	513,508	912,328
2,454,005	7	470,607	441,721	912,328
1,983,398	8	555,316	357,012	912,328
1,428,082	9	655,273	257,055	912,328
772,809	10	773,222	139,106	912,328

Alternative III (Contd.) - Years 6 - 10

	Year 6	Year 7	Year 8	Year 9	Year 10
Revenues	6,156,000	6,156,000	6,156,000	6,156,000	6,156,000
Cash Oper. Expenses:					
logging cost	1,680,000	1,680,000	1,680,000	1,680,000	1,680,000
road construction	750,000	750,000	750,000	750,000	750,000
administrative	200,040	200,040	200,040	200,040	200,040
manufacturing costs	1,670,040	1,670,040	1,670,040	1,670,040	1,670,040
Tot. Cash Oper. Expenses:	4,300,080	4,300,080	4,300,080	4,300,080	4,300,080
Plus Other Expenses:					
depreciation	224,838	224,838	224,838	224,838	224,838
interest	513,508	441,721	357,012	257,055	139,106
Total Expenses	5,038,426	4,966,639	4,881,930	4,781,973	4,664,024
Taxable Income	1,117,574	1,189,361	1,274,070	1,374,027	1,491,976
Tax Expense (46%)	514,084	547,106	586,072	632,052	686,309
Revenues	6,156,000	6,156,000	6,156,000	6,156,000	6,156,000
less: cash oper. exp.	4,300,080	4,300,080	4,300,080	4,300,080	4,300,080
tax expense	514,084	547,106	586,072	632,052	686,309
debt service	912,328	912,328	912,328	912,328	912,328
Cash outflow	5,726,492	5,759,514	5,798,480	5,844,460	5,898,717
plus: salvage payment					1,000,000
Total cash outflow	5,726,492	5,759,514	5,798,480	5,844,460	5,898,717
Net cash flow	429,508	396,486	357,520	311,540	1,257,283

Alternative IV - Harvest Own Timber and Process Into Squares, Chips - Purchase Used Mill (Includes Woods Operation) for $1 million

Depreciation method used on mill and logging equipment = 150% declining balance first four years, straight line thereafter for 10 year mill and equipment life. Assume zero salvage value. Investment required for mill and equipment = $800,000 financed at 18% for four years, plus $200,000 down (Total $1,000,000).

Balance	Year	Principal	Interest	Debt Service Payment
$800,000	1	$153,397	$144,000	$297,397
646,603	2	181,008	116,389	297,397
465,595	3	213,590	83,807	297,397
252,005	4	252,036	45,361	297,397

	Year 1	Year 2	Year 3	Year 4	Year 5
Revenues	6,156,000	6,156,000	6,156,000	6,156,000	6,156,000
Cash Oper. Expenses:					
logging cost	1,680,000	1,680,000	1,680,000	1,680,000	1,680,000
road construction	750,000	750,000	750,000	750,000	750,000
administrative	200,040	200,040	200,040	200,040	200,040
manufacturing costs	1,670,040	1,670,040	1,670,040	1,670,040	1,670,040
Tot. Cash Oper. Expenses:	4,300,080	4,300,080	4,300,080	4,300,080	4,300,080
Plus Other Expenses:					
depreciation	150,000	127,500	108,375	92,119	87,001
interest	144,000	116,389	83,807	45,361	-
Total Expenses	4,594,080	4,543,989	4,492,262	4,437,560	4,387,081
Taxable Income	1,561,920	1,612,031	1,663,738	1,718,440	1,768,919
Tax Expense (46%)	718,483	741,534	765,319	790,482	813,703
Revenues	6,156,000	6,156,000	6,156,000	6,156,000	6,156,000
less: cash oper. exp.	4,300,080	4,300,080	4,300,080	4,300,080	4,300,080
tax expense	718,483	741,534	765,319	790,482	813,703
debt service	297,397	297,397	297,397	297,397	-
Cash outflow	5,315,960	5,339,011	5,362,796	5,387,959	5,113,783
Net cash flow	840,040	816,989	793,204	768,041	1,042,217

NPV @ 20% = $3,768,963 less $200,000 down payment = $3,568,963

Note: It is assumed that the $200,000 down payment for mill and equipment in Year 1 is to be made at the very start of the year (or during "Year Zero"), rather than at the end of the year as in the case of other payments. Hence, this $200,000 is not discounted, but the whole amount is substracted from the NPV figures for other cash outflows to get a final NPV figure.

Alternative IV (Contd.) - Years 6 - 10

	Year 6	Year 7	Year 8	Year 9	Year 10
Revenues	6,156,000	6,156,000	6,156,000	6,156,000	6,156,000
Cash Oper. Expenses:					
logging cost	1,680,000	1,680,000	1,680,000	1,680,000	1,680,000
road construction	750,000	750,000	750,000	750,000	750,000
administrative	200,040	200,040	200,040	200,040	200,040
manufacturing costs	1,670,040	1,670,040	1,670,040	1,670,040	1,670,040
Tot. Cash Oper. Expenses	4,300,080	4,300,080	4,300,080	4,300,080	4,300,080
Plus Other Expenses:					
depreciation	87,001	87,001	87,001	87,001	87,001
interest	-	-	-	-	-
Total Expenses	4,387,081	4,387,081	4,387,081	4,387,081	4,387,081
Taxable Income	1,768,919	1,768,919	1,768,919	1,768,919	1,768,919
Tax Expense (46%)	813,703	813,703	813,703	813,703	813,703
Revenues	6,156,000	6,156,000	6,156,000	6,156,000	6,156,000
less: cash oper. exp.	4,300,080	4,300,080	4,300,080	4,300,080	4,300,080
tax expense	813,703	813,703	813,703	813,703	813,703
debt service	-	-	-	-	-
Cash outflow	5,113,783	5,113,783	5,113,783	5,113,783	5,113,783
Net cash flow	1,042,217	1,042,217	1,042,217	1,042,217	1,042,217

ZAREMBO CORPORATION - Exhibit V

Alternative V - Accept STC Proposal - Assume 5% Commission

* Investment required = 0

<u>Years 1 through 10</u>

Revenues		$5,400,000
Cash Operating Expenses:		
logging costs	1,386,000	
road construction	750,000	
STC commission	270,000	
administrative	<u>20,040</u>	
Total Cash Operating Expenses		2,426,040
Taxable Income		2,973,960
Tax Expense (46%)		1,368,021
Revenues		
less: cash operating expenses	2,426,040	
tax expense	<u>1,368,021</u>	
Cash outflow		<u>3,794,061</u>
Net cash flow		1,605,939

NPV @ 10% = $6,732,096
NPV @ 15% = $8,060,208

ZAREMBO CORPRATION - Exhibit VI

Alternative VI - Sell Stumpage at $141/MBF

* Investment required = 0

<u>Years 1 through 10</u>

Revenues	$1,692,000
less tax (46%)	<u>778,320</u>
Net cash flow	913,680

NPV @ 20% = $3,830,146
NPV @ 15% = $4,585,760

PART V

TEACHING NOTES

ACCOMPANYING

CASES ON SERVICE

AND NOT-FOR-PROFIT

ORGANIZATIONS

BURGER KING'S (BK) BATTLE FOR THE BURGERS

TEACHING NOTE

TEACHING OBJECTIVES

BK relates the efforts of Burger King to overtake McDonald's as the leader of America's hamburger pack. Specific objectives:

Become acquainted with the fast food industry.

See BK's various functional strategies.

Understand how those strategies fit together.

Decide whether BK can overtake McDonald's.

Recommend (an) appropriate course(s) of action.

USING THIS CASE

BK is suitable for an inclass exam of limited scope, a short report, a long report, or a final problem. It is of no more than moderate difficulty, but it has a little too much punch to use early in a course. We recommend its use in mid-course, when functional and generic strategies are being discussed, or later when reformulation is being considered. It is beautifully written, recent, and given its subject matter, easily holds student interest. It lends itself to discussion.

SYNOPSIS

BK started in 1954 and was sold to Pillsbury in 1967 for $18 million. Its founders needed that kind of backing in order to expand and increase market share. It grew rapidly via the franchise system under Donald Smith, who had been No. 3 at McDonald's. He became the first of four CEO's in three years, a progression to Jeff Campbell in 1983 following Smith's departure in 1980. While BK seems to do most things right and scores higher with many customers than does McDonald's, it seems always to run second to McDonald's. As the fast food industry matures, Campbell is faced with the necessity to run faster just to stay in the same place. The case reviews an impressive array of constantly improving functional strategies. Will these be good enough to keep BK in the No. 2 fast food slot, and what can be done to become No. 1, Campbell wonders.

This Note is based on an excellent prior Note by the casewriters.

BK is alive and well but still No. 2. Its FY87 sales of $4.5 billion represented a 60% increase over 1983 sales, compared to McDonald's $12.4 billion and 44% increase. BK meanwhile has enlarged its product line; like McDonald's, it has a special children's meal. It pushes seasonal dishes, like barbecue beef in summer. It spotlights new burger variations, like Triple Cheese, for 3-4 months and then replaces that with a newer version. It does the same thing with its pies, so there are new faces on the menu. It has also tried retitling and repackaging, changing the Whopper Jr. to Hamburger Deluxe, wrapping it rather than boxing it, and lowering its price 10¢. Last but not least, Pillsbury sold Burger King to Grand Met, a British Corporation, in early 1988. BK franchisees objected vehemently prior to the sale but to no avail. One of Grand Met's first actions was to fire BK's Madison Avenue ad agency and then to hire two more. That might help, but Grand Met has a long way to go to match McDonald's outlay on advertising (estimated $900 million in 1988).

TEACHING APPROACHES TO THIS CASE

Since BK homes in on marketing, one can examine its advertising themes one by one, ask what the competition was doing at the time, and what next transpired. Coincident functional strategies can be discussed at the same time. Another approach is to analyze the fast food industry, ask how BK has positioned itself in the industry, and relate functional strategies to that positioning. Still another approach is to require recommendations to Jeff Campbell as to how he might do better against McDonald's. Whatever the approach, students should be encouraged to read the fast food industry note which precedes the case.

CASE ANALYSIS

STRATEGIC MANAGEMENT ELEMENTS: MISSION, GOALS AND OBJECTIVES

No mission is stated, but it can easily be inferred as providing hamburgers and supporting menu items quickly and efficiently to the discriminating customer. Goals are somewhat easier to come by. CEO Campbell says in 3-4 years he wants a little more than half the number of restaurants of McDonald's, about half the market share, higher restaurant profits, higher average sales, and hopefully a better ROI for the operator. BK's 1985 goal was to raise the average domestic restaurant's sales to near $1 million to obtain a 17.4% operating profit per unit. Campbell's objective is to "change the competitive environment of the fast-food industry," a 3 to 5 year job.

STRATEGISTS

The case does not describe Jeff Campbell directly. He came up from the ranks, so he knows BK well. He is perceptive, aware of BK's problem areas, and given to decisive, imaginative action. His early focus was on quality control, efficiency, and doing what BK did best - taking care of hamburgers. He understands the value of communication with employees and franchisees, and the need for stability in senior management as well as for employee confidence in top management. He is ambitious but appears at the same time to be a realist. There is no profile of the typical franchisee, so we cannot generalize about BK's operators.

ENVIRONMENTAL ANALYSIS

SOCIOECONOMIC SECTOR. Burger King is one of the players in the fast food industry, an American institution (we believe) which has been successfully exported. Fast food implies quick service, abbreviated menu choices, limited table service, and moderate price, recognizing that the consumer wants to eat and go or take and go. The last is a reflection of a faster paced life, more DPI per household, more leisure time, greater mobility, more travelling, and perhaps less inclination to cook at home as more and more women join the workforce and have less and less time to prepare meals. Thus, fast food is perhaps more reflective of lifestyle than it is of the economic cycle. It is here to stay. While fast food is paid for at least in good part from DPI, only a recession of major dimension would hurt this industry. The recession of 1982, for instance, does not seem to be reflected in Burger King's sales. Also, many families dine as a unit at fastfood restaurants, so it could be argued that even given a recession, fast food sales would not fall out of bed. If the industry suffers, it will undoubtedly be more as a result of changing social mores.

GOVERNMENTAL SECTOR. Not an apparent factor in this case.

TECHNOLOGICAL SECTOR. Not a factor, either, although BK makes use of emerging technology as it becomes available, for example, television terminals for cooks.

INDUSTRY THREATS AND OPPORTUNITIES. Here there is a very full plate. The industry wants for neither. Its threats are exceeded only by its opportunities, which in 1988 took the form of an estimated $60 billion in sales. Fast food is a subset of the commercial food industry, so BK's competitors abound (McDonald's, Wendy's, Hardee's, etc.), not only in the burger line but in every other fast food line, because there is little consumer loyalty with which to offset much consumer whim. Add to this a range of consumer choice which ranges across eating places, full service restaurants, commercial cafeterias, bars and taverns, and what have you. Specialty stores, supermarkets, gourmet restaurants, department stores and hotels prepare take out orders or specialty dishes which can be warmed and eaten at home, along with a veritable horde of frozen dinners scheduled for microwave ovens.

There is a perception that fast food is junk food and therefore injurious to health because of its high fat content, so consumers look elsewhere. If it isn't junk food, then it is either not nutritious or too full of calories. Add to all this a coming higher minimum wage, a labor crunch, employee motivation, managerial ineptness, and possible restrictions abroad on future restaurant development and advertising, and the industry's threats grow by leaps and bounds. Even given all that plus a maturing of the industry, there is still <u>opportunity</u> for those who are close to their customers and exploit location features, item peculiarities like ethnic foods, speed of service, super quality, reasonable prices, delivery, and the like. Since the barriers to entry are low, the potential rewards to one who possesses a competitive advantage can be quite attractive. There is an obvious opportunity in the international environment, which seems far from saturated by fast food restaurants.

STRATEGIC ADVANTAGE PROFILE

<u>CORPORATE RESOURCES AND PERSONNEL</u>. Burger King has an uncertain <u>image</u> but a good reputation; while consumers say they prefer BK's food, they prefer to eat at McDonald's. A succession of CEOs generated a lack of employee confidence and rebellion amongst the franchisees. <u>Management</u> is decentralized among four major operating units, and the company is organized on a geographic basis. Division managers were given more authority, and an attempt was made to improve communications by meeting personally with employees. Campbell came up from the ranks, a possible effort to restore an impression of stability at the top. Campbell tried to rein in franchisees by stressing their following of corporate policy and required them to live within an hour's drive of their stores.

A <u>strategic management system</u> is not obvious, but a planning system certainly exists. We believe <u>corporate support systems</u> are adequate. A problem area is that of <u>labor</u> and high quality <u>employees.</u> Employee turnover is high, and the labor crunch makes recruiting difficult for those working at or near minimum wage. BK tried paying up to $4.50 an hour, well above minimum wage, and it went to elaborate lengths to improve productivity through time and motion studies. Even so there seems a lack of employee pride and motivation, factors which are really internal to any franchise.

BK has ongoing <u>training programs</u> for franchisees and managers, noting the uneven performance between company restaurants and franchisees. It developed a career ladder for senior managers and allows franchisees to establish their own incentive programs. Useful productivity suggestions earn bonuses for franchise and restaurant managers. Each store receives a monthly management assistance visit. A successful program to improve employee pride is noted, but there is no suggestion that it was copied. The crux of BK's management problem is in its <u>employees</u>, who control productivity, company image, and costs. There is no obvious solution to the problem other than through a kind of leadership which is lacking. Parttime employees during rush periods (to minimize labor costs) are not the answer.

<u>FINANCE AND ACCOUNTING</u>. Here we run into difficulties since BK's figures are reported on Pillsbury's consolidated income statement. Its 1985 goal then would translate into a $614 million profit (p. 323, $174,000 profit for 3526 stores). We don't know what 1985 profit was but *Business Week* (9 May 1988) reported BK's May 87-May 88 profits as about $59 million, down 27% from the prior year, or $80 million. This is such a comparative difference that all figures are

suspect. Low franchise fees encouraged expansion. Pillsbury's purchase of BK as a growth opportunity, of course, guaranteed strong financial backing. In an effort to sort things out, the casewriters compared Pillsbury's ratios as a surrogate for BK and concluded that the ROS of 4.1% was right on the industry average, whereas ROA, inventory turnover, and collection period were between restaurant industry averages.

MARKETING AND DISTRIBUTION. BK's story is really the story of its marketing. It competes profitably as No. 2 in the burger industry with around 18% of the market share enjoyed by the top 4 - BK, McDonald's, Hardee's, Wendy's. Its advertising budget is far below McDonald's. Perhaps for that reason, the company resorted to a series of advertising campaigns. These seemed to help growth but generated law suits as well as some turned off consumers. It has a full product line, carefully arrived at and continually but cautiously changed, apparently without any extensive market research. BK's products are well regarded by the same consumers who say they would prefer to eat at McDonald's. The company is represented in all 50 states and has more than 300 restaurants in foreign countries. Since location is a factor of sales, the company consistently tries to add new sites, often in nontraditional locations, and to increase its market penetration where it already holds metropolitan locations. The company has experimented with home delivery, apparently without conclusive results. It has a case of me-tooism, copying McDonald ideas like playgrounds, children's meals, and breakfast. We ask if BK's salad bar will disappear in favor of prepackaged salads, a la McDonald's. Its menu changes seem sensible, but it did suffer through an embarrassing supply problem when it brought out its Chicken Tenders. And its ads fell short when it featured Herb, the nerd who had never eaten at a Burger King. Its pricing strategy is acceptable, but it laid a major egg when it raised prices and McDonald's didn't.

PRODUCTION AND OPERATIONS. Here Burger King shines, or tries hard to do so. Its units are scattered over 50 states and 25 companies. 80% of those are franchised, so it has to be a continuing headache to realize that company operated units all sell more than do franchises, at least in the U.S. Units are sized to local demand and generally built to standard plans. 95% have drive-thru facilities. There may be a future for the Whopper Express, a scaled-down, bare bones operation that does its best to encourage takeout food. Site development is computerized, and design is short when done by the regional construction specialist.

Speed is a watchword. Customer waiting time has been cut by automatic drink machines, computerized french fry machines, TV terminals for cooks to avoid misunderstanding orders, relocation of the bell hose for drive-thru customers, etc. Productivity suggestions are welcomed and rewarded. Menu changes are made only after careful consideration of labor, machinery and space required versus profit and effect on other items. National distribution, supplier availability, and the price stability of any new ingredients are also considered.

Innovations introduced include the chain broiler, the addition of the drive-thru window, inside sit-down seating for once what had been only takeout food, and new menu items. The latter are helped along by an R&D center in Miami. BK is a believer in new product development because in fast food just as in consumer electronics, chains not growing will be left behind.

STRATEGIC ALTERNATIVES

There are no alternatives. The CEO has adopted growth as BK's future strategy.

IMPLEMENTATION

The CEO has indicated his areas of desired growth. More restaurants for sure, but where? The cost of prime sites is high, if any can be found. This suggests unconventional locations, which can be translated to mean any place people congregate or need a fast meal. BK has partially solved that problem by locating on military installations and by co-locating with Woolworth stores. Since McDonald's four years later decided to co-locate with Sears, perhaps BK can extend itself to the ubiquitous Wal-Mart chain. Possibilities here seem limitless. Government buildings, civic centers, stadia, college campuses, bus terminals, interstate highway rest areas (a tough nut to crack) and so on. Since 60% of the food in the typical hamburger operation is sold for off premises consumption, BK might be well advised to consider home delivery seriously. That feature caused Domino's Pizza to become quite popular and made its owner one of America's 400 wealthiest people. The Whopper Express concept seems very promising and perhaps could rescue some of BK's so- called poor locations.

More profits and better ROI are close relatives of higher sales. Sales are a factor of siting, as noted above, menus, quality service, and obvious price-value. If we consider menus, the industry note points out that diverse menus are a necessity, meaning continual differentiation, but there is a risk then of blurring BK's image. While BK experiments with new combinations and tests carefully, the process is apparently devoid of any market research which involves determining consumer wants before firing up the kitchen. Consumers want an increasing variety of high quality, healthful, good tasting food without unnecessary calories. Could BK offer waffles at breakfast, or potato pancakes? Would ethnic foods at lunch and dinner be wise? Pizza bombed for Burger King. Chicken and steak are big sellers. Would these go? It would pay to ask. At the same time, new items ideally should not require exotic new equipment, special storage requirements, or long preparation time. A new motif and more cheerful uniforms seem worthy of consideration, too.

BK appears to have made no special effort to appeal to specific market segments. True, it copied McDonald's playground and meals for kid's ideas, but it hasn't aimed any advertising at the little folks. McDonald's long ago concluded that children play a loud part in deciding where fast food is bought. Similarly, BK could make a determined play for the elderly, who are a growing part of our society and have mobility, time, and most of the DPI. What would attract them - lower prices to senior citizens? Draw a bigger crowd at breakfast with free coffee and free newspapers? And what sells best and has the best track record? Emphasize its sales.

If profit is the difference between revenue and cost, then a collateral approach. is to reduce costs. BK has a dedication to efficiency. Leadership, better and more stable management, more training, better personnel recruitment helped by still better wages, an incentive system - these wouldn't hurt productivity and employee motivation. BK certainly hasn't exhausted all the ideas from its workforce.

Attaining a market share equivalent to half that of McDonald's may be difficult, if not out of reach. More locations would help. Burger King faces an almost hopeless task in making up the unit gap between it and McDonald's. A possibility is greater emphasis on international franchising - Burger King has only a third as many units abroad as McDonald's. We should note that the Golden Arches make 20% of their profit abroad.

RECOMMENDED DISCUSSION QUESTIONS

1. List BK's strengths and weaknesses.

2. How do those weaknesses reflect on BK's achievement of its goals?

3. Identify BK's functional area strategies.

4. What overall generic strategy is BK following?

5. What contributed to BK's rapid growth in the early years and what is its aftermath? What can be done?

6. Why do those who profess to like Burger King food better eat at McDonalds?

7. What major issues confront Campbell?

8. What should Campbell do?

9. Should Campbell further diversify?

ANALYSIS AND DISCUSSION

1. List BK's strengths and weaknesses.

Strengths and weaknesses are listed in each applicable section of the SAP. Weaknesses we flag are the low morale and high turnover in senior management due to numerous CEO and strategy changes; high employee turnover, with consequent higher costs and lower productivity; franchisees on the loose, to the detriment of BK's image and standards; an almost positive disregard for children and the oldsters; a me-tooism toward McDonald's; an ad program of uncertain return; lack of a true competitive advantage after McDonald's, and an unspectacular menu.

2. How do those weaknesses reflect on BK's achievement of its goals?

There is all manner of possible responses here. What they amount to are causes for lower sales and higher costs. Campbell's dreams of better market share, higher sales, higher profits, and better ROI seem just that if he can't apply some fixes. If Campbell wants half as many units as McDonald's, adding 300 a year within his time frame will hardly do it since McDonald's builds about 500 a year. In FY87 McDonald's outnumbered BK 12000 to 4700 and declared it would build 600 stores in 1988.

3. Identify BK's functional area strategies.

See our remarks in the Strategic Advantage Profile section.

4. What overall generic strategy is BK following?

All three, really: low cost by going after the fast food section of the young consumer; focus, by catering to those in a hurry; and more than all else, differentiation by the way it prepares food and facilities to meet consumer wishes, i.e., flame broiled special orders to a drive-thru window.

5. What contributed to BK's rapid growth in the early years and what is its aftermath? What can be done?

BK grew rapidly in early years because it franchised. And it franchised much more cheaply than McDonald's and offered relatively few restrictions. The low barrier to entry did not act as an effective screening device for franchisees. The lack of restrictions has become a problem because franchisees do pretty well what they please. This makes for inconsistencies, uneven performance, lack of cooperation,and disregard of company policies. Campbell is doing what he can, but even today no one has a handle on this one. It would probably take a renegotiation of franchises, a very unlikely development.

6. Why do those who profess to like Burger King food better eat at McDonalds?

We don't know. The survey should be validated first of all and then an extensive effort be made to ascertain why. That should be Campbell's starting point if he really wants to be a comfortable No. 2. In no way can BK ever overtake McDonald's, and Campbell seems to know that.

7. What major issues confront Campbell?

Productivity, employee turnover, a better ad campaign (but how?), menu revision, franchisee relations, ways to capture the child and oldster markets, image burnishing, answers to the junk food,high fat perception, new off-premise services, finding a real competitive advantage, etc.

8. What should Campbell do?

See our remarks under Implementation. Grand Met's advertising effort is very meaningful and bears close watching. If McDonald's is the King of the french fry world - and that attracts a lot of people - need that always be the case?

9. Should Campbell further diversify?

We don't think so. He has enough problems to solve as is. He doesn't need another chain to fret over, and he would be ill advised to change the basic nature of BK. That would create a terrific image problem and put BK into an area or areas (say full service restaurants like Big Boy's) in which BK has absolutely no expertise.

MCDONALD'S CORPORATION (MC)

TEACHING NOTE

TEACHING OBJECTIVE

McDonald's has led the burger world lo, these many years but the pack is baying at its heels and the industry has matured, presenting management with the problem of knowing where to go now. Specific objectives:

See a highly successful company in action

Understand the reasons for its success

Recommend what management should do in the future

USING THIS CASE

McDonald's as a company is as familiar as the flag, so students should find this case of great interest. It lends itself to discussion, and as we point out later, can be run over a period of two days. It is of medium length, well supplied with tables, and of no more than moderate difficulty. It fits best in mid-course or later, depending on the instructor's desired emphasis, as a vehicle for examining functional strategies or later when reformulation is being discussed. It is in these ways similar to the previous case relating to Burger King. It can be used as an inclass exam, short report, long report, or final problem.

SYNOPSIS

Ray Kroc knew a good thing when he saw it, franchising his first restaurant from the McDonald brothers in 1955. He was a keen observer of the demographic changes taking place in America at that time. He hung his hat on QSC - quality, service, and cleanliness. He read the times very well and prospered. Five years later he bought out the McDonalds and started franchising. His has to be one of <u>the</u> success stories of our time. Today MC feeds more than 18 million customers per day around the world. It stands head and shoulders above its competition. It is innovative, consistent, and well managed, but it is not immune to environmental changes. Its competition is probably no more than bothersome, but it has other, larger problems on its plate which it can ignore only at its own peril. To ignore the obvious is not in character, so MC will react - but how?

This Note draws on a prior Note by the casewriters.

MC is today's picture of success. *Business Week* (9 May 1988) reported that MC's systemwide 1987 sales were up 15% to $14.3 billion, and profits were up 14% ($549 million) to $4.9 billion, brushing aside Burger King at $58.8 million and Wendy's at $4.5 million. It has added prepackaged salads (no dirty salad bar), is testing new chicken sandwiches, and has dabbled with different types of pizza. And there are more Golden Arches than ever. In a novel move, MC has also signed a licensing agreement for children's clothing with Sears.

TEACHING APPROACHES TO THIS CASE

We recommend that one read our Industry Note here and the Burger King case and its accompanying Teaching Note before reading MC. Noting similarities will be helpful, and the differences should stand out clearly. The most straightforward approach is to ask for an identification of functional strategies. Having done that, then ask how these have produced No. 1. It should emerge that MC does have a strategy and that it all fits together.

Carrying on from that, another approach is to require the justification of recommended product/market opportunities. Any justification cannot be made other than superficially if it does not make reference to present functional strategies and indicate what change(s) may be required.

More broadly, analyze the fast food industry. This could be a challenging final problem. Contrast MC's strategy to that of its major competitors.

The casewriters suggest that students identify MC's most critical problem and in a memo, identify four possible alternatives, indicate which is preferred and why, and discuss its implementation. Use the memo for class debates. Collect memos one session, select those who argued for different problems, and next session let them debate their various proposals. Sounds like fun, we think.

CASE ANALYSIS

STRATEGIC MANAGEMENT ELEMENTS: MISSION, GOAL AND OBJECTIVES

<u>Mission</u> is not spelled out but we have no hesitation in saying that it is to provide a quality hamburger and limited menu support items quickly and inexpensively at lunch and dinner and to provide a limited breakfast menu. <u>Goals and objectives</u> are not quantified. However, in 1985 the CEO set <u>goals</u> of 500 new restaurants per year, maximized sales at existing restaurants, and a greater emphasis on international expansion and profitability.

STRATEGISTS

Of these we know little. Ray Kroc, the founder, impresses us as a hard worker, a visionary yet a realist who never missed a detail. He was unbending in his devotion to QSC, so we picture him to be demanding. He was a fast learner who apparently surrounded himself with a good team. His successor, Fred Turner, was Kroc's disciple, so we assume Turner to be a chip off the old block. Hands on experience and attention to detail prevail.

ENVIRONMENTAL ANALYSIS

SOCIOECONOMIC SECTOR. Ray Kroc was a keen observer of the great passing scene. He understood the portent of a massive move to the suburbs, mobility, a casual lifestyle, and increasing number of working wives with less time and inclination to cook and a contribution to larger family DPI. Kroc capitalized on cleanliness, good tasting food served hot and fast, friendly service. Probably society pushed him along more than did the economy, though he was certainly the beneficiary of an expanding population and a growing economy. He foresaw the need for an informal atmosphere if he were to pry parents with children away from full-service restaurants. His prices were intended to reinforce the desirability of a family meal at McDonald's. As in the case of Burger King, only a massive recession could touch MC.

GOVERNMENTAL AND TECHNOLOGICAL SECTORS. Apparently not factors in this case.

INDUSTRY THREATS AND OPPORTUNITIES. MC has great buying power and therefore a good handle on its suppliers. For a long while its beef was shipped frozen from Australia in its effort to keep costs low. Threats to MC are those which confront the industry as a whole, although in its position as No. 1 MC must regard them in a slightly different light. Only an absolute cataclysm of indescribable dimension would unseat MC as No. 1 in burgers. The competition from BK, Hardee's and Wendy's together doesn't have MC's market share, and as others go about shooting themselves in the foot, it would be a mistake to worry too much. Wendy's made a ruinous attempt at breakfast, and BK smarted under a series of CEOs and marketing mistakes. These two attacked each other, and Hardee's fattened at their expense. More than the inroads of its competitors, MC has to be concerned at the threats inherent in a maturing industry saturated with competitors, stable population, changing consumer food preferences, a move toward full-service restaurants, and competition from other purveyors of food like supermarkets with delis, sit-down food operations and take out foods for home consumption, frozen meals for home microwaves abetting a trend toward more meals at home, a full blooded challenge to fast food as being junk food full of calories and fat but not nutritious, expensive unit stores, hotels, caterers, and so on. Its opportunities are perhaps less well defined. The overall commercial food service industry should approach $200 billion in 1989 and fast food outlets $65 billion. Its opportunities take the shape of retaining MC's present dimensions while trying to cater to the fickle tastes of demanding consumers who have no brand loyalty: off-premise services, a choice of type of service, more varied menus, healthful food, home delivery and capsule versions of the Golden Arches. Foreign expansion is far from dead.

CORPORATE RESOURCES AND PERSONNEL. Here MC stands deep by anybody's measure. It has an image second to none, a worldwide reputation, and international recognition of its name. It is widely involved in community affairs, notable in its Ronald McDonald houses and its support of Jerry Lewis' muscular dystrophy efforts. It encourages employee involvement as well in community affairs. MC is organized geographically, with a further split into national and international operations. A strategic management system is not mentioned, but it would be difficult to maintain that MC is a stranger to such a thing. Good planning, good management, and excellent marketing have put MC ahead of the pack. Its performance year after year is consistently good enough to leave others in the dust.

MC has a highly decentralized system of management due to its size and geographical extent. Basic policies are made by top management, but operating decisions are left with field offices. Home office specialists will respond to help calls from managers of individual restaurants who can't find the answer in MC's lengthy policy and procedures manual. MC promotes from within. Since many managers have had extensive company experience, there is a pool of managerial talent. Both CEO and COO, up from the grills, confirm that succession is no problem.

The company early recognized the importance of training. New employees are given about four weeks of OJT and are crosstrained to permit the scheduling flexibility absenteeism demands. MC's training is a factor in locating managerial talent, but like the rest of the industry, it has a high labor turnover problem. We note that one of its ways of fighting turnover has been its drive to hire senior citizens, who are ostensibly more stable.

FINANCE AND ACCOUNTING. Here is another impressive sector. Financial strength and planning are evident. Ratio analysis proves little: its CR is a weak .5, but with a collection period of about 8 days, does the CR really matter then? Its ROS is 11.2% compared to the restaurant industry's 22.5% average. Revenues for company units increased 10.5%, we note, compared to 5% per franchised unit. (MC itself operates about 50% of its restaurants.) Franchise fees keep MC healthy since they usually take 11.5% or more of a restaurant's sales. New licensees can look forward to a 14% fee. MC protects its foreign restaurants by issuing debt in local currencies. MC generally finances its operations with a relative balance between stock and LT debt. Oddly enough, Wall street has not demonstrated any great regard for MC stock, which has sold as low as 42 vs its 62 before the 1987 crash.

MARKETING AND DISTRIBUTION. Advertising and lots of it is a key factor in MC's success. $900 million (1988) buys a lot of attention. It advertises nationally in a variety of media and was the official fast food sponsor of the 1984 Olympics. Catchy TV ads focus on a specific product, like the McD.L.T. Its name has tremendous recall, and its gold arches have become gastronomical reference points. It has targeted its efforts well, to that middle class family with children that Ray Kroc discovered at the outset. It catered to the baby boom market, initiated meals for kids, sponsored Ronald McDonald houses, and was the first with playgrounds, admitting that children influence fast food choices. How many chains incorporate party rooms for children? The public has positive feelings about MC, despite frequent criticisms of its often already prepared foods.

Its pricing strategy reflects value and is competitive, putting its burgers equal to or cheaper than those of its competitors. The CEO avers that there is "considerable" research into what people want, as well as what they think McDonald's should sell. Support items are also competitively priced but have higher markups, consequently larger profits. Its operations support its marketing efforts by polishing its image. Table 3 shows that customers value a good product made available quickly in a clean, friendly atmosphere. Management and employees are equally conscious of Kroc's QSC. MC pioneered breakfasts. Much of its early progress has to be attributed to its wisdom in restaurant siting. The rest of the industry was given to saying, "Find McDonald's and then get as close as possible." Notwithstanding an advertising effort which swamps any competition and astute menu changes, MC still has to face societal changes like a shrinking market segment, and the jury is still out on its efforts to do so.

PRODUCTION AND OPERATIONS MANAGEMENT. Ray Kroc's QSC dominates this sector. Siting, noted above, is a planning factor and is changing from the suburbs to accommodate new traffic and shopping patterns. Franchising played and plays a major role in MC's growth, but management was quick to realize not only the importance of careful selection and training of franchisees, but the need for a tight string on them at all times. A voluminous manual spells out policies and procedures and is the restaurant's Bible. Periodic retraining reinforces the manual. MC protects its image with a system of operational audits, and it is not unknown for the golden arches to be taken down. The menu is uniform everywhere, as is its quality. The number of units has climbed steadily; much construction is standard, but owners are expected to help in selecting an exterior that blends in with its surroundings - be visible but don't be obnoxious. 79% of its units have drive-thru facilities which do a land office business, and interiors are designed for efficiency as well as for the possibility of future expansion.

RESEARCH AND DEVELOPMENT AND ENGINEERING. MC shows its devotion to quality by extensive testing of all new items to include taste, appearance, overall preparation, ingredients and holding requirements. Operations tests at a small number of restaurants follow taste panel refinements, then a true marketing test is run. If completely acceptable, the item becomes a permanent menu fixture. Market research provides continued inspiration for menu changes. New products sometimes lead to new equipment like clam shell grills, convection ovens, a computer controlled french fry machine, wireless headsets for drive-thru operations, light control panels, and so on. The effort is pointed toward effectiveness, efficiency, and of course the bottom line. Not all effects are a resounding success, to be sure. When the price of beef went up, MC responded with cheaper pork as McRib, but that was a dud, along with McChicken. Chicken McNuggets are a success, however.

STRATEGIC ALTERNATIVES AND CHOICE

There are no alternatives since MC is wedded to a strategy of growth.

IMPLEMENTATION

MC has the money to acquire prime sites, to add at least 500 units per year to meet Fred Turner's objectives. Some locations can be conventional, such as airports. MC fell behind Burger King in this area, surrendering sites on military installations to BK in 1984 and again lagging behind in the matter of colocation. Sears' co-locations have promise, however. Mobile food vans seem logical, and if they do, can one put an MC jr. on wheels, cook on the roll, and crack the home delivery market? Certainly there are innumerable sites for shrunken versions of the typical McDonald's using drive-thru operations exclusively, since 60% of the usual hamburger trade is sold for off-premise consumption. New menu items are indicated. MC has a priceless competitive advantage in the breakfast trade, so every effort should be made to increase that. Could that also be sold to late night customers? MC can be made habitforming. MC can also reshape its advertising to attract the adult customer, just as Wendy's and BK have done. If that's done, then MC must be able to deliver lighter, more nutritional well-balanced meals. Prepackaged salads (1987) were the low cost answer to messy salad bars. Senior citizens shouldn't be neglected - a hearty meal featuring main menu items with less fat and less sodium, or a slimline of offerings for the weight conscious? And there is still ample opportunity to put more McDonald's overseas.

RECOMMENDED DISCUSSION QUESTIONS

1. List MC's strengths and weaknesses.

2. Which functional area strategies must contribute to MC's success and why?

3. Which overall generic strategy does McDonald's follow?

4. What major problem does Turner face?

5. Are Turner's goals attainable?

6. What should he do?

ANALYSIS AND DISCUSSION

1.List MC's strengths and weaknesses.

We listed strengths in the various parts of the Strategic Advantage Profile preceding. Some weaknesses are industry - common, like high employee turnover, maturation of the fast food industry, competition from every quarter (from gas stations and convenience stores to supermarkets and specialty restaurants), rising prices with the uncomfortable options of higher prices or lower margins, an aging America, and the junk food syndrome. We look on MC's competitors as necessary evils, like Her Majesty's Loyal Opposition, as the minority in the House of Commons is often called. MC can simply overwhelm them. The factors we list are another matter.

2.Which functional area strategies must contribute to MC's success and why?

This should get all kinds of answers. You might want to split up the board into the areas we discuss under the SAP and list what you hear. Strategy is a seamless garment. No functional strategy could be erased without damage to the whole. If a winner has to be picked, it might be the truly gigantic ad effort MC contemplates. Advertising is said to sell beer. Our view is that it sells burgers, too. The question is also a lead-in to the question following. A point to be made is that good management has consistently updated those strategies - MC has not rested on its laurels ever.

3.Which overall generic strategy does McDonald follow?

We venture cost leadership. Fast food concentrates on low price, low cost, and MC's tremendous volume and marketing clout generates genuine economies of scale. Thus,lower unit costs, helped along by parttime workers with few benefits who keep labor costs down. When the company develops new items, it does so with an eye to that new equipment which can efficiently trade those products. Together, these factors enable MC to pursue a cost leadership strategy.

4.What major problem does Turner face?

This is perhaps another way to ask Question 1. We feel the major problems are a decreasing market segment, a nutritional challenge (it's junk food, etc.) a numerically decreasing workforce, rising prices, and the competition which emerges on every hand, reflecting the fact that the barriers to entry in the restaurant business are low, and the possible rewards are so attractive.

5.Are Turner's goals attainable?

Probably, though not all pertinent factors lie within Turner's purview. New units are no problem, given MC's resources. Maximizing sales is a too-elastic term. What represents the maximum? Certainly new menu items are an answer to fickle fast fooders, so MC's efforts at market research may be the answer to "maximizing" sales. Kroc's QSC is still in vogue, and MC has the ad might to keep those factors before the public. There's no substitute to leading from strength. Since these loom so high in public perception, anything to trade on that perception would be helpful. MC visualized international operations as a probable growth area, and it has been exactly that, contributing about 20% of MC's profits. This can be pursued, since none of MC's competition seems to have the answers to successfully competing in this area. Here Turner is in tall cotton indeed.

6. What should he do?

There are some obvious answers here. Menus must reflect new products. Open more units, perhaps the slimmed down drive-thru only type which produces such good returns per square foot. The industry may be mature, but there is still room for MC's in unconventional locations. If things work out with Sears, why not co-locate with another national chain? Sales may be flat in the industry, but a mammoth ad budget can't hurt sales - it hasn't so far.

Effort in that budget should be directed to the adult population, since McDonald's market segment seems to be shrinking. This requires a collateral effort by management to think a way through the nutritional challenge; that has to be done if MC is to be able to respond to the demand for "healthful" food. Another approach has to be the attraction of the elderly in America, but just how we aren't sure. Would it be special prices for seniors? Is the answer in decor or is it in a different menu? Whatever the way, the greying of America seems to have been forgotten.

Someone may suggest buying a chain of family style, sit-down restaurants like Denny's as an answer to capturing those who tend to leave fast food in search of something "better." But that's not MC's business, and the losses are not so great that attention to overlooked market segments can't make them up. We have no answer to the inroads of supermarkets, delis, and 7-Eleven's and we doubt if MC does, either. Despite the turn away from beef, we believe many specialty restaurants will last only until novelty wears off. Turner didn't express a concern for his fast food competition, and he was probably right. Let sleeping dogs lie. There are enough larger problems to wrestle with, like rising prices and a shortage of minimum wage workers, that management's work seems already cut out for it. MC can always cut prices as a means of increasing market share; that should be fearsome to the competition, which is far less able to stand the impact of reduced profits. That threat alone should cause competitors to be most circumspect in what they do. After all, why wake a sleeping lion?

DREXEL BURNHAM LAMBERT, INC. (DBL)

TEACHING NOTE

TEACHING OBJECTIVES

This case relates the incredible story of DBL, a story that shook the Street and occupied the Wall Street Journal for some time. It was a Cinderella story that seemed too good to be true, and it proved to be just that. Specific objectives:

Understand some of the forces behind the merger/acquisition wave

Realize the relationship between theory and practice, that is, between financial theory and strategy formulation and implementation

See the formulation of a niche strategy in a service industry

Appreciate the need to revise that strategy as threats to it develop

See how the CEO practices damage control while trying to preserve his firm's leading position in a profitable business

USING THIS CASE

DBL has a subtlety that better consigns it to the latter part of the course where reformulation is being considered. Reading the case is like inventorying Fairyland; certainly finance majors will love it, and so will the more thoughtful students. Others to whom the terms are unfamiliar may be unable to grasp the tremendous significance of what they read. The case itself is not all that complex, but its complete understanding may be difficult for some. We say then that it is at least moderately difficult. It can be used for a short report, a long report or a final problem. We predict its behavioral aspects will elude many.

SYNOPSIS

DBL is a privately held investment banking firm. In 1973 it was fifteen among privately owned underwriters of corporate securities and had no noticeable competitive advantage. Starting in the 1970s, however, Drexel drew on the genius of Mike Milken and became a power in the unwanted business of other investment bankers by virtue of the genius of Mike Milken and by virtue of its junk bonds, first issued in 1977. It provided contingency financing for corporate raiders and became Wall Street's most rapidly growing firm. It literally coined

---

This Note reflects a prior Note by and conversations with the casewriter.

money, but an insider trading scandal touched it. Guilt by association took over. The CEO began to fear for the future of his firm. The SEC issued a complaint in September, 1988, to which Drexel later pleaded guilty.

OUTCOME

The SEC settlement requires that Drexel pay a $650 million fine, discharge Milken, and deny him any compensation for 1988, even though Drexel denied any complicity in the allegations filed following the SEC's charges. The settlement also installed a management oversight committee. Drexel has since left the OTC market completely, ceased selling stock to individual investors, and sold off its mutual funds. DBL cut operating and administrative staffs almost in half; despite an 8% drop in revenues, the firm realized a 22% operating profit. It moved its junk bond operation to New York but still claims 70% of the junk bond market. Drexel is going into real estate buying and selling (in addition to financing) and intends to stay active in investment banking, especially international investment banking. Milken pleaded not guilty to 98 counts of securities-related racketeering and posted a $650 million bond.

TEACHING APPROACHES TO THIS CASE

There are two possible approaches, each of which should be effective. Charge someone with bringing to class the most recent developments in the DBL case. We have furnished developments through May, 1989, under Outcome above. Direct attention to developments and the case Epilogue and ask if DBL should have pleaded guilty as it did. Its rationale, reproduced on p. 363, tells why it did, but the question is, should it have done so? There will be a spectrum of answers from yes to no and many in between. Students may tend to lose sight of the fact that the case recites a *fait accompli* and that the major issue is how the CEO has to walk a tight line if he is to save his firm. In order to know when the line even exists, it will be necessary to go back over events, ask what happened and/or why, and inquire as to the significance. It becomes obvious that there may be more here than meets the eye. Invoking RICO law against Princeton/Newport sets a precedent for its possible use against DBL. The costs to DBL could have been astronomical and posed potential ruin. Is DBL the target, or does Giuliani have bigger fish to fry? Giuliani is above suspicion but not above ambition. Could Giuliani be interested in persuading Milken to deal and implicate some of his clients, as *Business Week* suggested (6 February 1989)? Giuliani's reputation already is considerable, but think of the popularity that bringing some of America's biggest names into court would generate. One with political ambitions could go far.

Justice is not the only shark circling DBL. Are there others? This brings in a discussion of the other threats to the firm. How did these threats materialize? In a general sense, because DBL was a maverick on Wall Street and beat the establishment at its own games - you can almost hear competitors saying that DBL doesn't play fair, and that's why they (DBL) won. What did DBL do? If it had been unsuccessful, there would be no case. But DBL was successful. For what reason? Is Joseph nine feet high, or does DBL read palms? None of these, of course. DBL did what others could have done but didn't. One does not laugh at the Street through the eyes of a pariah and walk away scotfree. These are big people with long memories who have the capability of great damage. DBL made them look bad and cast doubt on their values and their competency. What's the old saying? - Hell hath no fury like a woman scorned.

This should back the discussion up to junk bonds, their beginning, Milken, plus all the pros and cons and economic theories. Ask again, should DBL have agreed to the settlement? There may well be some changed opinions. Ask why the switchers changed their minds.

The other approach is a mirror image of the first. Chronicle events, asking why and discussing the importance of each and then ask what students would have done had they been Joseph. What advice would they have given and why? Rarely do we see a case with such far reaching implications, and the case is far from over.

CASE ANALYSIS

STRATEGIC MANAGEMENT ELEMENTS: MISSION, GOALS AND OBJECTIVES

We conceive of DBL's mission as providing the public with a full range of brokerage services. Its goals are not quantified; therefore, we assume them to be profit and prestige. No objective is furnished although Joseph states that he wants Drexel to remain dominant in junk bonds. Reading between the lines one guess is that DBL's wish is to be No. 1 on the Street through its prowess as an investment banker.

STRATEGISTS

Frederick Joseph, DBL CEO, is not directly described. We picture him as honest, discreet, hardworking, highly intelligent, perceptive, self confident, concerned with DBL's image, and a survivor. Mike Milken is described in various publications. He is a billionaire by virtue of his DBL $1.2 billion salary 1984-87, $550 million coming in 1987. A full page ad by 87 supporters praises his "honesty, integrity, and ethical conduct." He is also described as compassionate, generous, quiet, conservative, a private person, very bright, a creative genius all alone in his impact on America's corporate reorganization binge.

ENVIRONMENTAL ANALYSIS

SOCIOECONOMIC SECTOR. This sector dominates the case. Mergers and acquisitions marked a massive restructuring of the U.S. economy in the 1980s. Jauch writes that 1969-80 only 12 transactions of over $1 billion occurred among U.S. firms. In 1985 alone, 35 mergers of $1 billion or better took place, and an average of 11 firms per day were wholly or partially acquired. That takes money and lots of it, and that means investment banking. Stock prices rose, purportedly reflecting Adam Smith's theory that the market was undervaluing the worth of corporate physical assets. A companion theory holds that mergers will continue as long as the Q ratio is less than one.

197

We believe that the restructuring of American industry was and is more of a response to reality than to theory. We recall the conglomerate mania of the 1960's and events subsequent, such as the loss of many of America's markets and a realization that if one shouldn't buy what one can't run, it would be better to get back to basics. Asset disposition would at least be difficult in the face of a falling market, but less so in a rising market. If you believe that the emphasis unfortunately is on short term performance, then we are faced with the realization that the hardest thing in the world is to bring something new to market. It is easier and quicker to buy all that expertise and agony than it is to grow it at home, thus more impetus to buy. So lean and mean (divestment), get it while you can, and buying is cheaper than building, started a wave of mergers and acquisitions.

Drexel profited from the rising <u>economy</u> and from the demand for funds to finance the restructuring wave still in progress. DBL rose to fame and fortune with its Milken-ideal junk bond, first with small companies, then with large. It was a logical extension of its junk bond philosophy to offer financing for corporate takeovers. If T. Boone Pickens would do it that way, why not? It became a sign of the time to go with DBL. With very little money of his own plus DBL's junk bond wizardry, a corporate raider like Carl Icahn could fatten on greenmail or buy airlines like TWA using junk bonds in a leveraged buyout. Essentially, DBL was a classic example of being in the right place at the right time and with the right thing.

<u>GOVERNMENT SECTOR</u>. John Riley, writing for the *L.A. Times - Washington Post Service* quotes Alfred Chandler, a Harvard business historian, as saying that "Wall Street is always suspect." Only rarely are financiers the bad guys when times are good, so Chandler theorizes that the Milken case reflects our ambivalence about the prosperity of this decade: it may be a boom to a few, but most worry that prosperity "is a balloon over-inflated by little understood financial machinations," and it may burst any minute. DBL's junk bond activity gained Washington's attention in late 1985, a merger-mad year, and possible limits on junk bond financing were considered but never materialized.

Paul Volker at the Fed doubted the long term financial stability engendered by junk bonds, but the Fed did not intervene. The next year the SEC collared a DBL employee for selling inside information on pending mergers. The trail led to Ivan Boesky and then to DBL, since DBL was involved in some of the transactions which implicated Boesky. That triggered an SEC investigation and the complaint noted previously. Then the Justice Department intervened and notified DBL that it could become the target of criminal charges.

Other branches of government were concerned, too. Congressional attention and concern gathered over the part of junk bonds in big leveraged buyouts. Such buyouts puzzled Congress, since we tend to fear what we do not understand. *Insight* (12 June 1989) relates that Fed Chairman Alan Greenspan testified before a Senate committee on banking when a group became concerned about the possible non-payment of junk bonds if a recession were to occur. There was fear that massive defaults would put the American banking system at risk if credit structures folded like houses of cards. Greenspan was not frightened, believing that LBOs carrying junk bonds were not "inherently inimical" to the financial strength of the banks involved.

The dangers imputed to junk bonds he classed as apparently not "particularly serious." He believed that the corporate restructuring enabled by junk bonds appeared to be enhancing operational efficiency. The debate continues. Junk bonds are declared to be either a ticking economic time bomb or a wonderfully ingenious way of promoting economic growth and creating jobs. Michael Jensen, also at Harvard, regards junk bonds as "one of the most important innovations" in the history of corporate finance (*Insight*, 12 June 1989). High-yield bonds are not new, he points out, but what was new was Milken's use (and application) of the concept of junk bonds. Barry Friedberg, head of investment banking for Merrill Lynch, avers that no one did more (referring to Milken) in the last 25 years to rearrange the look of corporate finance.

Milken himself reminds of banks who called loans back in the mid-70's. Companies affected vowed never again and opted for long term money, like 20 years. He cites MCI as an example of a junk bond beneficiary which responded with growth and jobs. Many small companies were regarded as risky, hence were low-graded and consequently had no access to Wall Street's capital. However, they blossomed after they issued junk bonds. Milken is not concerned that they will not be able to repay their debt, and he regards them as the best risks on any debtor list. Admittedly, what is addressed here is economic in nature and might well be sited elsewhere, but the visibility of and the doubt surrounding junk bonds has gained - and will probably hold - more than passing governmental attention.

INDUSTRY THREATS AND OPPORTUNITIES. Threats abound. We have noted that government actions have been urged that would put limits on the use of high-yield instruments in highly leveraged transactions, transactions that made DBL's reputation. The SEC is still investigating insider trading. A Drexel trader has been jailed for perjury, so Drexel may yet hear more from the SEC. The Justice Department's 98 counts against Milken cannot be taken lightly, and a possible spillover effect on Drexel cannot be ignored. Drexel's competitors are entering the junk bond market in greater numbers, and some are introducing innovations like bridge loans. Some state legislatures have passed bills to inhibit hostile takeovers. If the market continues to rise and values corporate assets upward to where that valuation nears the replacement value of those assets, mergers may abruptly decline. At that point it may be advantageous to build new assets rather than buy, and if that happens, the need for junk bonds may almost disappear.

It never rains but what it pours. Drexel's SEC settlement required DBL to set aside $350 million in anticipation of damage suits. Milken's trial may generate a rash of suits. The settlement also required DBL to withhold Milken's 1988 compensation of $200 million, a provision challenged by Milken's attorneys as denying his right to due process. Drexel is also on probation for three years, hence like Lot's wife, must be above all sin. When Drexel settles finally with the Justice Department, it then must confront possible disciplinary action from the New York Stock Exchange.

Drexel must also be concerned with its <u>competitors</u>. DBL has no patent on junk bonds; while the Street scorned junk bonds, DBL made out like the proverbial bandit. Money talks, sometimes loudly, so some of DBL's competitors are also entering DBL's province despite DBL's preeminence. Salmon Brothers and Lazard Freres lobbied for intervention by the Fed, some indication of the depth of feeling on the Street against DBL.

Perhaps the "club," as the casewriter called it, remembered the debacles of railway bonds in the 1930's and sought to distance themselves from what looked just as dangerous. Wall Street was not remembered well by many who held these bonds. It had to be a bitter pill to see DBL, a new firm and remote from the East in Beverly Hills, succeed where others refused to tread. Despite their evident jealousy and resentment of DBL, members of the "club" decided to test the junk bond market. Milken and DBL had no corner on creativity, either. To those now disinclined to deal with Drexel, other bankers offered innovative bridge loans, a technique effective enough that Joseph at DBL considered it worth copying.

Bond prices dropped after the Boesky scandal, and some feared for the viability of the junk market. It was not surprising to learn that some of DBL's major competitors sought to capitalize on any uneasiness by approaching DBL's top accounts. Overtures like this would only make those clients even more nervous, so Joseph had to worry about a defection problem - once something like that started, it could well get out of hand.

Drexel's image isn't helpful, either. It is disliked by the "club" for its arrogance, its refusal to follow Wall Street etiquette by sharing its offerings, and the feeling that DBL perhaps had not been completely honest. Such an image does not bode well, either in the banking fraternity or among advisers who might be quite reluctant to steer clients to DBL anymore.

The <u>threat</u> is internal as well. *Business Week* (6 February 1989) reported that Drexel's settlement with the SEC caused even more internal dissension and disillusionment. Dropping the pilot, as Drexel did with Milken, deprives DBL of a reservoir of contracts and expertise. *Business Week* opines that Milken's departure might well take others with him, so personnel in the high-yield bond department have to be of particular concern to DBL. If there are major defections in senior ranks, DBL's obligation to buy their stock could imperil its vital equity base, and put it at a competitive disadvantage.

Every cloud has a silver lining though, and there are opportunities. Drexel is widely known, more so than ever, though it would have preferred to achieve fame in a different way. Much of the mystique surrounding junk bonds has disappeared; since many investment bankers now offer high yield securities, junk bonds have suddenly gained a new respectability. DBL can certainly trade on all these factors unless it completely leaves the junk bond market, but there is no indication that it will do so. DBL started its climb with small and medium sized companies. They ought to have long, favorable memories, so this store of good will could be tapped.

So long as interest rates stay low, as the Fed seems to want them, junk bonds offer high yields not available elsewhere. There have been no notable failures, and the economy declines to rollover and play dead, so the high-yield market can't look all that bad to many. And if the magic worked in America, why wouldn't it work elsewhere as well? Drexel has a long client list, and Milken's indictment has generated a wave of favorable comment both for him and for the high-yield concept. DBL should surely be able to extract some mileage from all this. And as Joseph pointed out, DBL has a major presence in other security markets, too, so it can trade on its name here, too, in furthering its abilities in these areas. Real estate, commodities, tax shelters, mortgage-backed securities - these are a long way from the furor relating to Milken.

STRATEGIC ADVANTAGE PROFILE

CORPORATE RESOURCES AND PERSONNEL. Drexel has a problem of the first order in image. It isn't a member of the "club." It is scorned and resented and now faces disciplinary action which can only put it in a bad light. It is viewed with distrust, jealousy, and antagonism. Others revel in its ill fortune. It is a maverick in a generally conforming community, a loner, and has to be generally unpopular. Its reputation for creative financing is tops and such that corporate raiders will have it high on their lists when money comes around. Its size is not a factor, but its personnel are. It has some of the brightest financial planners in the country, rewards them fabulously well, and hires the best it can find. They have been quite innovative, do what they do well, and enjoy widespread confidence. The case does not mention a strategic management system, but BDL has to be doing something right. It is eminently profitable, whatever its objectives may be. Its image gives it little influence with regulatory bodies. Its leadership is not described in the case, but we surmise that the firm is well managed, even if its personnel system hired Dennis Levine, and capably led.

FINANCE AND ACCOUNTING. BDL is privately held. None of its systems is discussed. The case estimates 1983 earnings at $250 to $300 million. 1984 revenues were over $1 billion, and stockholder equity rose from $150 million to $320 million. Its 1985 net was estimated at $450 million on total capital of $1.2 billion. 1986 profits were estimated as high as $1.5 billion, approaching its $1.7 billion capital. It seems skilled in tax planning and is able to raise capital at will.

<u>MARKETING, PRODUCTION AND R&D SECTORS.</u> Apparently not factors in this case.

STRATEGIC ALTERNATIVES

<u>Stability</u> means doing much the same thing as before, meeting the public in the same way, providing the same services, etc. DBL just can't continue as before. It would be foolhardy not to change its Rambo image, conveying a disclaimful attitude which says it is above reproach. That's not credible and would serve only to reinforce feelings of hostility against the firm. Moreover, DBL's acceptance of the SEC settlement and its guilty plea aren't very good arguments for going on as before. For one thing, the SEC isn't about to permit that.

<u>Growth</u> has to appeal to Joseph. He still wants to dominate the junk bond business. It was the Street's fastest growing investment banking firm; Joseph has not forgotten that, and it is doubtful that he will. It's hard to forget when one led the pack. Joseph's quandary is how to grow without destroying DBL: its corporate culture puts him in a box. Let's see: Junk bonds? Give them a new twist to meet those innovative bridge loans. But with all the competition, DBL will have to be Rambo again, damning its detractors and the watchers along the Potomac. To do so is like playing Russian roulette with all cylinders loaded. Joseph has enough trouble as is without stirring up more. Besides, Milken is gone. But there has to be a chance for this overseas, where Drexel's past will not follow it, and where Joseph can use whatever talents are left in DBL. This would help hurt feelings within the firm.

Emphasize the more conventional aspects of investment banking. This could hardly draw adverse criticism. Directing commensurately more effort here rather than to the high yield market will act to lower DBL's profile. Were the firm to give some ground to its competitors, and remembering that there are more players in the game now, DBL can regain some respectability. Joseph said "We're ...in the process of becoming establishment," and this will help Drexel become more acceptable. It will also tend to distract its competitors and turn aside some of their ill feelings. More players mean more money on the table, so if one believes that takeovers aren't dead, we could well see more than fewer. That would mollify DBL's competitors even more. The casewriter, we inject, does not believe that long term prospects for junk bonds are all that good in view of the rising market and the Q concept material above.

Real estate has an appeal. DBL has clients, means, and expertise in this area and lies in a go-go real estate market. Joseph probably knows that contrary to popular opinion, both Carnegie and Rockefeller made their real millions in real estate. And DBL has always been in mortgage-backed securities.

<u>Retrenchment</u> may be forced on Drexel by the terms of the SEC settlement. It need not be consciously embraced as a strategy, but it should be accepted as a foregone conclusion - something has to give. The SEC must be placated, or things could conceivably get worse. Believing that, the question is to decide what (or

who) must go, even while maintaining your innocence. Better to volunteer what you can best get along without, rather than be given something absolutely unpalatable. While sorting that out, DBL should distance itself from any financing efforts directed at hostile takeovers. Let sleeping dogs lie. Joseph is a growth man and would look on retrenchment as a bitter pill, but he literally has no choice. A combination strategy would make swallowing that pill easier.

CHOICE

A <u>combination strategy</u> of retrenchment and growth.

IMPLEMENTATION

First things first. The SEC has to be handled before all else before it becomes a rogue elephant. Retrenchment by cooperating with the SEC is a selfserving move, but is not the alternative worse? Answer its questions, offer up sacrificial lambs, but do so quickly and maintain that DBL has done no wrong. It has to be done like this; admitting guilt would wave a red flag in front of a bull and set poorly in DBL's corporate culture. Joseph can't afford that. He would probably see wholesale defections, both within and without DBL. What should he offer? We don't know, because we aren't close to the SEC. Maintaining innocence means hiring lawyers and defending oneself vigorously. Some will suggest that the SEC settlement be declined, that accepting it is abject surrender. Joseph is thus between Scylla and Charybdis. Staring at RICO, he would easily imagine the crushing of DBL.

What's DBL worth to him? Everything. Survival is paramount, so better to accept the inevitable rather than to tempt fate. Along the way, adopt a lower profile, do whatever possible to burnish the DBL image and appear contrite, whether one feels that way or not. Don't ruffle any feathers. Maintain innocence. (It is interesting to see that DBL actually spent $100 million in trying to prepare a defense.) Joseph has an unenviable line to tread. In his accepting the settlement, we have to believe that a good run is better than a bad stand. At least DBL has survived, but Joseph has to live with DBL and its corporate culture or see it shake itself to pieces. *Business Week* could conceivably have a point: Any charges filed against Milken would be in Drexel's interest because that would justify the decision to accept the settlement. Charges were filed the following year. Does Machiavelli still live?

Growth can take any or all of the forms noted above. DBL has the personnel, funds, smarts, and management ability to operate across the entire spectrum of financial services. It has been innovative in the past and can be so in the future. Joseph's concern now has to be keeping the assets of the firm intact, especially the "best guys" to whom Joseph referred. He has something for starters which few other firms can match, much less even approach, an incredibly renumerative reward system of salaries and bonuses. Milken's reported $550 million in 1985 makes one stop and think. What someone once said of ITT's Harold Geneen must apply to Frederick Joseph, "He has them by their Cadillacs." There don't seem to have been any notable defections, and we reason that DBL can buy whatever talent it needs.

RECOMMENDED DISCUSSION QUESTIONS

1. What strategy has DBL been following?

2. How has it used financial theory in formulating that strategy?

3. Given the events described in the case, just how real is the Efficient Market Hypothesis? Are financial markets efficient in the sense that the theory describes?

4. Just what has DBL done in the investment banking industry? How?

5. Are the takeovers it has facilitated good, bad or neutral for the long term health of the U. S. economy? Why or why not?

6. Was DBL wise in agreeing to the SEC settlement, since it professed innocence? Why or why not?

7. What strategy should Joseph adopt now?

ANALYSIS AND DISCUSSION

1. What strategy has DBL been following?

It's a classic niche strategy. You may hear other answers here, but they ought to lead under questioning to the fact that DBL has brashly carved out a niche. Has DBL defended that niche, you might ask? Perhaps not, but then would it be necessary to defend what others scorn? With Milken and momentum, DBL is a hard act to follow.

2. How has it used financial theory in formulating that strategy?

Adam Smith's beliefs are reflected here by the actions of the market, as is the theory of the Q ratio. If assets were fully valued, would merger and takeovers still occur? Probably, but perhaps not to the extent we have seen. Corporations would probably still be bought for the classic purposes of increasing cashflow or achieving some competitive advantage, but if assets were fully valued, suitors would be inclined to think twice. Takeovers would tend to be much more costly, as would mergers, and how could their costs be justified? Junk bonds might still figure in, but to what extent is another question.

3. Given the events described in the case, just how real is the Efficient Market Hypothesis? Are financial markets efficient in the sense that the theory describes?

The hypothesis of the Efficient Market seems valid, as discussed above in our remarks under the Socioeconomic Sector, and we consider that markets operate with reasonable efficiency. The key is "reasonable," so that might be a point to be discussed. If reasonably efficient, why do security prices tend to rise in response to tender offers? Under theory, do those offering tenders possess superior information, or is it that the hypothesis is baseless since management has misrepresented or mismanaged assets so badly that public information cannot possibly be accurate?

4.Just what has DBL done in the investment banking industry? How?

DBL has carved out a niche and stood the industry on its head. You might ask students how, at this point. Guttfreund says DBL has created an entity "completely outside the traditional banking industry." How again? Starting with Milken's ideas and creative genius in the junk bond, DBL started with smaller businesses and worked up. Success breeds success. If others wouldn't or couldn't, DBL would and did. Growth companies stymied elsewhere for financing because they were deemed poor risks turned to DBL and did not come away disappointed (*Insight*, 12 January 1989). Their success and DBL's innovative solution to an old problem attracted others higher on the corporate scale. Essentially, DBL became the leading financier in America's corporate restructuring. Students should recall that DBL sometimes didn't find it necessary to put up any cash - its "highly confident" better served instead and really became DBL's secret weapon. The Street saw a kind of innovation which set DBL apart.

5.Are the takeovers it has facilitated good, bad or neutral for the long term health of the U. S. economy? Why or why not?

See our remarks under Socioeconomic. Opinion is split, but the sky hasn't fallen yet.

6.Was DBL wise in agreeing to the SEC settlement, since it professed innocence? Why or why not?

In our opinion, yes. Joseph saved his company. Perhaps he could have done that also by battling the SEC to a standstill in court. Anyone venturing that opinion should have to prove that DBL could win its argument, and that can't be done. At least Joseph didn't think so, or did he? Some may point out DBL will not be the same without Milken. Perhaps not, but an old saying has it that graveyards are full of indispensable people. Our rationale is laid out in detail above. This question is probably the most important of all because it requires you to dwell on the anatomy of a decision that put DBL at an absolutely critical crossroad.

7.What strategy should Joseph adopt now?

See our remarks under Implementation.

JENNIE STUART MEDICAL CENTER (JSMC)

TEACHING NOTE

TEACHING NOTE

It's business as usual at JSMC, and despite its membership in a dynamic industry, there is no inclination to change, let alone any thought as to what should be changed. Specific objectives:

Observe one of many, many small town hospitals

Understand that the bottom line is not an infallible indicator of organizational health

See the need for strategic planning in healthcare operations

USING THIS CASE

JSMC is short and simple. It can be used near the beginning of a course when the objective is to list problems and pose solutions, or it can be used in mid-course where students can handle it more effectively and the objective is to stress the need for a strategy and for strategic management. The case tracks easily, so it lends itself to discussion. It can be used as the subject of an inclass exam or of a short report. We do not consider it suitable for a long report.

SYNOPSIS

JSMC is a hospital in western Kentucky at Hopkinsville, a town of 27,000. The hospital has gone through numerous expansions. Although it has an apparently healthy bottomline, there are indications that its financial success may not last forever. It has overbuilt, as have many, and it can't seem to convince its catchment area that JSMC is for real. The hospital follows the times, and the prevailing attitude is to deny a need for change. At the same time its administrator talks of adding to the hospital, and one begins to wonder if JSMC isn't just like little Topsy - it just growed.

OUTCOME

No significant changes took place in any aspect of JSMC.

TEACHING APPROACHES TO THIS CASE

There are two possibilities, micro or macro. Ask students to identify and analyze JSMC's problems. Early in a course this could be done by sector in the ETOP and SAP. What solutions can be recommended? It is apparent that functional areas could be improved. Then ask how well the hospital operates. It prospers, but it does so almost in spite of itself. Will it continue to do so? Possibly, but that may be doubtful. Which way is JSMC going? No one knows, and no one seems to care. The macro approach is to ask what JSMC's preeminent problem is and go from there.

CASE ANALYSIS

STRATEGIC MANAGEMENT ELEMENTS: MISSION, GOALS AND OBJECTIVES

None of these is stated. We presume then that JSMC's <u>mission</u> is to provide hospital care, to include acute care, to those in Hopkinsville and surrounding communities. <u>Goals</u> are unknown, unless cost consciousness can be taken as one. An unspoken <u>objective</u> is growth.

STRATEGISTS

A volunteer board of trustees governing the hospital ostensibly does planning. Its role in governance proper is not described. The hospital administrator, James Walker, admittedly is not well schooled in hospital administration but believes himself to be a capable manager. At the same time he enjoys a "shabby" relationship with the professional staff. Since the employee attitude is why bother to change, it follows that Walker must accept that attitude. He may lack force and finesse, or perhaps he does not know people. We say that in view of the fact that although JSMC has hired marketing and PR personnel, some of its clientele are unaware of its services. Walker himself impresses as more of a PR man who will portray everything in the best possible light. Walker does no strategic planning, nor apparently do the trustees, so perhaps there really are no strategists whatsoever at JSMC.

ENVIRONMENTAL ANALYSIS

<u>SOCIOECONOMIC SECTOR</u>. JSMC is witnessing rising health care costs due to inflation, a population that is aging, growth in the use of third party insurers, increasing use of both expensive medical equipment and procedures, rising demand for more widespread medical care plus the ability to pay for it, and higher costs per unit of service. The <u>economic pressures</u> of rising costs have led to measures calculated to contain costs. Hospital stays are fewer and shorter. Overall occupancy rates have also declined. Costs and cost containment are bedeviled by a desire for more and better care and then the very best available, but at less cost. <u>Economic cycles</u> do affect expenditures for health care, though to what extent is not known because of the many reimbursement schemes such as Medicare, Medicaid, Blue Cross, and private insurers. JSMC has responded to these pressures by cutting costs wherever possible, yet at the same time it has attempted to meet rising demands for more and better health care.

<u>TECHNOLOGICAL SECTOR</u>. Apparently not a factor in this case.

<u>GOVERNMENT SECTOR</u>. Governmental interest in health care is a matter of some age, both for social and for financial reasons. Reducing the fiscal barriers to health care for all has long been a governmental objective, but at the same time

207

rising costs generated DRG's, a set fee for a specific procedure. At the same time the government has moved to reduce its involvement in health care and to de-regulate the hospital industry to encourage competition. Although the government once encouraged hospital construction through the Lister-Hill Bill, it later came to effectively discourage new construction through the 1974 National Health Planning and Resources Development Act where new hospital construction was made contingent upon the issuance of a certificate of need. JSMC has mastered costs, at least for now, but its increasing uncollectibles appear to reflect either an inability to meet DRG cost targets or a necessity to treat a growing number of the wholly uninsured medically indigent.

INDUSTRY THREATS AND OPPORTUNITIES. Threats come from competitors as hospitals vie for patients. A declining occupancy rate, a lower admission rate, walk-in clinics, and outpatient surgery formerly done on inpatient basis must all bother JSMC. There are still opportunities, however, if JSMC can recognize them. A growing number of elderly people will require more care. There is a demand for less expensive outpatient services. New technologies constantly appear, and the demand for the best treatment rises concomitantly. JSMC boasts it has the "most modern medical technology available," yet local people and those in the surrounding area go elsewhere, believing they can do better elsewhere.

STRATEGIC ADVANTAGE PROFILE

CORPORATE RESOURCES AND PERSONNEL. JSMC has an image problem, we conclude, because potential clients favor more distant facilities. We note that while the Phase III project has modern medical technology, no mention is made of the remainder of the hospital. Its decentralized organizational structure is of the double deputy type (admin and supply) and is effective enough to have given JSMC a very favorable cost structure when compared to other hospitals, so a survey reported. Facilities are more than adequate; JSMC is actually overbedded. There is no strategic management system and no long range planning. Computer systems are unknown, so management information probably is not timely and is of uncertain accuracy. Walker is of doubtful capability as an administrator, admitting a shaky relationship with his doctors, so top management quality is questionable. Employees are largely local, and there are many older employees. Change thus is difficult, given an attitude which breeds contentment with the status quo. This makes us wonder - when is medical equipment replaced: when it becomes unserviceable, or when something better becomes available?

FINANCE AND ACCOUNTING. The case does not describe financial systems. Tables show increasing revenues and income in 1984 and 1985. JSMC has been profitable since 1981, even though uncollectibles increased more than $800,000 between 1982 and 1985. CR and QR are favorable. A major liability is $19.8 million in long term construction bonds; JSMC has had no obvious difficulty in paying either debt or interest on debt. We say "obvious" because with a manual accounting system and just one bookkeeper, Tables 1 and 2 are somewhat suspect.

MARKETING AND DISTRIBUTION. Despite hiring marketing and PR personnel, JSMC has admitted problems in selling the public on its virtues. The hospital advertises on the radio and TV, in newspapers, and through interest groups, but something has to be lacking when JSMC remains a virtual unknown to local people.

PRODUCTION AND OPERATIONS MANAGEMENT. JSMC has built well if not wisely. 247 beds for a town of 27,000 are excessive, and Walker talks of adding a new wing. This is more than odd, since we learn that the 190 bed acute care facility is underutilized, and patient numbers are decreasing. Wisely, JSMC has opened outpatient services around the clock. Construction is at a temporary halt, but new equipment acquisition is not. The hospital is cost conscious, shutting down underutilized wings and cutting employee hours. Its costs compare favorably with other hospitals in the region.

STRATEGIC ALTERNATIVES AND CHOICE

There are no present alternatives. JSMC has had and still espouses a strategy of growth.

RECOMMENDED DISCUSSION QUESTIONS

1. What problems confront JSMC?

2. What should be done?

3. Is JSMC overbedded? If so, why?

4. How can the administrator maintain that JSMC "is equipped with the most modern medical technology available" when local clients have to travel to Nashville for treatment?

5. How can you account for JSMC's apparent marketing problem?

6. What is JSMC's central problem?

ANALYSIS AND DISCUSSION

1. What problems confront JSMC?

There are more than a few, so you should hear most. Leadership, people, systems, internal relationships, attitudes, capacity, and uncollectibles, to name a few.

2. What should be done?

Leadership - Staff the Board of Trustees with professionals who are more qualified in health care, not just those who volunteer. People - Improve personnel selection and development. Encourage early retirement in favor of fresh blood and younger, better trained employees. Retire Walker, too, in favor of someone truly trained in hospital administration. Systems - computerize data. This should greatly improve recordkeeping, billing, and collections. Internal relationships - The administrator and his doctors should iron out their differences and meet regularly to deal effectively with their differences. Attitudes - Hard to change. Takes better leadership to crack the "Why change, we're doing OK" attitude. Capacity - A problem everywhere. Shut down wings permanently. Reduce overhead permanently and provide greater stability of personnel assignment. Uncollectibles - Again a persistent problem everywhere. Someone has to get a handle on this one; as Medi- payments are capped at lower levels in the future, the problem might grow out of hand. Also, in recessionary times, the numbers of indigent tend to rise, so how is this non-payment problem to be handled?

3. Is JSMC overbedded? If so, why?

Yes, probably due to a lack of planning. This is a good one to do some homework on. How many beds per capital in your town, and do those represent a surplus? For example, Manhattan, Kansas has a population of 38,000 not including 20,000 students (Kansas State University), two hospitals aggregating 155 beds, and is considered to be overbedded.

4. How can the administrator maintain that JSMC "is equipped with the most modern medical technology available" when local clients have to travel to Nashville for treatment?

Two possibilities: a. He doesn't know what he is talking about. b. Potential clients are unaware of JSMC's capabilities. We tend to believe a. in view of JSMC's advertising efforts. Someone may mention the 72 doctors who enjoy professional privileges and say that they would demand the most modern technology. Agreed, but Walker doesn't do all that well with the doctors, and if something is lacking, what can a doctor do but quit. Remember, Walker runs the only show in town.

5. How can you account for JSMC's apparent marketing problem?

We don't have a good answer here, but with all its promotional efforts, it shouldn't have to admit to problems. This implies either a lack of personnel competency or a lack of leadership. JSMC's new hire is director of community relations, we note, to reach business and civic leaders. That's not creative - JSMC needs a marketeer, not a gladhander for town leaders.

6. What is JSMC's central problem?

We think it is a lack of strategic management. No overall design is detectable, and no one is inclined to look at the future. Unpleasant surprises lie ahead.

SAUNDERS SYSTEM, INC. (SS)

TEACHING NOTE

TEACHING OBJECTIVES

SS, an old line transportation company, was just too set in its ways to compete in a deregulated, competitive environment and therefore decided to sell out. Specific objectives:

See the impact of deregulation on an industry

See the acquisition process

Understand the complexity of strategic management in a turbulent environment

Grasp the costs of expansion

Propose alternative strategies for SS

USING THIS CASE

The case reads easily and is well complemented by the Industry Note. Since both ought to be read, SS is just too much for an inclass exam. It is suitable for either a short report or a long report. It is at least moderately difficult and probably too much so to be used early in a course. It falls better in mid-course when the objective is to frame alternatives or later in a course when reformulation accepts the sale of SS and wonders how it could have been avoided.

SYNOPSIS

SS was an early, early name in vehicle renting, first for cars, then trucks, and eventually to doing everything with trucks. SS shared in the post WWII boom after falling apart during the Great Depression. The company was known for quality service. It weathered the higher fuel costs and inflation of the 1970s by differentiating itself by its service record and image. It came to offer a full line of transportation services and became one of the country's largest leasing companies, yet it lacked the strength of an industry leader. Deregulation in the 1980s brought a more competitive market where low costs had to be if one were to persevere, yet SS simply did not pay attention to its costs. Its leasing interests faltered. Industry consolidations made the playing field more uneven. SS, though it expanded, was not achieving its objective of 16% ROI. "The boys" were tired and just not interested in a game where success was only possible without major changes, changes which to them just looked like too much. It was time to go, and go SS did.

As stated in case.

TEACHING APPROACHES TO THIS CASE

Split the discussion into two parts. First, assign the reading of the Industry Note. Discuss the trucking industry, whose complexity may be surprising, to bring out the strategies of industry leaders and to convey some understanding of the industry. Then ask students to develop a new strategy which repositions SS in the market. Saunders' size makes only a niche strategy feasible, if it is to enjoy a continuing competitive advantage. Deregulation, Saunders' competitive disadvantage in cost, its capital structure, and alternatives to acquisition should surface. Another approach is to dissect the decision to sell; having isolated the reasons, then ask if there were any other ways out. If so, which and why, and how could it best be achieved.

CASE ANALYSIS

STRATEGIC MANAGEMENT ELEMENTS: MISSION, GOALS, AND OBJECTIVES

We believe Saunders' <u>mission</u> was to provide a broad range of transportation services as effectively and efficiently as possible. No <u>goals</u> are apparent. <u>Objectives</u> are growth, survival and 16% ROI.

STRATEGISTS

The case does not directly describe the Saunders brothers. We're led to believe, however, that they are astute opportunists, hard working, not above risk, sometimes not too perceptive, and rather resistant to change. The retained president, Shelfer, is bright and capable and able to plan well but is hobbled by a lack of means.

ENVIRONMENTAL ANALYSIS

<u>SOCIOECONOMIC SECTOR</u>. As in the prior case of Drexell Burnham Lambert, the socioeconomic sector dominates here, too. SS was an early beneficiary of the car rental business. In those days not everyone owned a car, even when prices were $777 FOB Detroit. Renting was the next best thing. World War II popularized air travel. The railroads gradually gave up passenger service and turned more and more to freight. A rising national income and a far more comfortable way of life bred need after need. Consumer wants multiplied. Not all factories were served by rail. More and more traffic came to be carried by truck. Saunders was a beneficiary of this, too, and its major focus came to be on truck leasing.

The fuel crisis of 1973 put a new face on transportation as fuel costs rose unbelievably. Inflation was a problem. <u>Costs</u> went up faster than <u>prices</u>, especially in regulated industries. However, rising prices could be passed on to customers, so price <u>competition</u> was minimal. Firms could only differentiate themselves by image and by service record. Not only did regulated prices cover rising exogenous costs, but they masked inefficiencies, too, and served to keep in business those who otherwise would not be able to compete.

Leasing was popular. Tax structures and a stable (regulated) environment were further urgings to lease. Shippers needed little capital going in and escaped all the attendant headaches. Leasors profited, too. If undercapacity in the trucking industry existed in the 1970s, it did not in the 1980s. The Motor Carrier Act of 1980 brought deregulation. Interest rates and truck prices declined, as did fuel prices. Ownership now looked better than leasing, and leasing was half of Saunders' business. The used truck market went flat as deregulation acted to create overcapacity in the industry. The industry consolidated and began a massive shakeout. No longer protected by the regulatory umbrella, the inefficient or the weak went out of business via acquisition or bankruptcy. Trucking became a buyers' market where all three generic strategies mattered: differentiation, cost, and focus, with firms zeroing in on profitable market segments.

With low barriers to entry, more carriers entered the industry. With rates largely freed, price competition became a major market factor. There was a scramble for market share; coupled with the demise of the empty backhaul was the realization that many smaller cities were now wholly dependent on the trucking industry for carriage. Increased competition held down costs, but business failures rose when many firms could not ride out the squeeze falling rates put on margins. The big got bigger, the small tended to disappear into niches if not from the scene, and the medium sized firms were squeezed. SS was caught in the middle of all this. While it had to be aware of the strategies needed for success, cited at the close of the Industry Note, SS had lost sight of its costs. SS CEO, Shelfer, noted that not having one's costs in line would tend to highlight weaknesses, and it did exactly that.

GOVERNMENTAL SECTOR. Regulation and deregulation are the principal actors here. The Motor Carrier Act of 1935 put the trucking industry in the same regulatory straightjacket as confronted the railroads. The ability of a truck to go anywhere there was a road, was not recognized. Protected by the ICC, the industry kept rates high, as noted in the preceding sector. Cost and inefficiencies were passed on to the customer. The consolidation was helped along by the 1982 Staggers Rail Act, which made for greater efficiencies, more favorable rail rates for shippers, and a smaller price/service differential rail vs. truck. Deregulation also fostered new methods of competition which had formerly been forbidden. The 1982 Surface Transportation Assistance Act also influenced the industry by permitting wider, heavier, and/or multiple trailer trucks on federal highways.

TECHNOLOGICAL SECTOR. Not an apparent factor in this case.

INDUSTRY THREATS AND OPPORTUNITIES. Deregulation fathered threats as industry overcapacity became apparent. Shippers could bargain for and demand lower rates and better service, once deregulation took hold. Competition increased. While market entry was easier, it was equally easier to disappear as an operating entity. The effects of deregulation and lower costs for former shippers made leasing difficult. Opportunities still existed for those who were able to follow Porter's three generic strategies (noted above).

STRATEGIC ADVANTAGE PROFILE

CORPORATE RESOURCES AND PERSONNEL. Saunders is an older company, widely known and well respected. Its image is favorable. The firm is functionally organized. Management has been streamlined and is alert, emphasizing performance, cost reduction, quality, and market segmentation. The Industry Note shows SS to be the smallest of its industry group. It trails that same group in nearly every measure of performance. A planning system is evident, though by the CEO's admission SS was "reacting rather than planning" by the mid 80s, so a strategic management system apparently does not exist. The CEO has installed excellent staff support systems. The computer system is advanced and invaluable to a far flung operation where details are all important (when to grease a truck, when to replace it, etc.) Employees are not directly described, but we gather that they are skilled; SS moreover has an HRM department, and top management's urging to get into the field has increased employee loyalty and understanding of SS as a business. Top management is well qualified; the Saunders brothers have a wealth of experience, and the new CEO has a handle on the problems of SS. However, the values of the brothers stand in the way of progress.

FINANCE AND ACCOUNTING. Saunders is not in its financial grave. It has not run at a deficit during the period 1979-84, but it does seem to trail the biggies in its motor/carrier leasing group (Gelco excepted) in ROE, ROA, and ROR. Its performance is called sluggish, but we would characterize it as being erratic since its EPS varies considerably. SS has never reduced its dividend, and 51% of its stock is family owned. That has to say something. As aforesaid, SS had trouble reducing costs, so while 1985 revenues were a record, 1985 EPS were lower than in 1984, when EPS was 85¢ and operating expenses somewhat greater. The decrease was ostensibly due to the greater expenses of depreciation and interest. Shelfer complains of being unable to achieve the objective of 16% ROI, but SS has not done that since 1980, so we wonder about that figure. Saunders in a relative sense is small, hence does not share the cost advantages of volume buying which their competitors hold. When SS needed capital for expansion, it took no action. Equity was not acceptable, and the objective was to reduce debt, not add to it. Borrowing at a reasonable rate looked infeasible. In consequence, a lot of growth bypassed SS, and its relatively smaller size added insult to injury by the interest SS would be required to pay, compared to its larger competitors. Its financial condition could be described as relatively weak, its capital structure restrictive and resistant to change.

MARKETING AND DISTRIBUTION. Saunders has always had an eye for its customers. Shelfer made a mighty effort to emphasize marketing, even replacing 70% of his sales force with more aggressive types. That sales force had the advantage of an advanced computer system, a good common net and supportive top management. Before deregulation marketing in the industry was almost unknown, but after deregulation the reverse was true. SS apparently had an effective market research system, judging from its extensive product-service risk. Shelfer emphasized "Client Tailored services," which meant simply that SS would tailor its services to whatever needs SS identified for a customer. And SS segmented the market, catering to some unique requirements like bulk common carriage.

Marketing focused on consumer satisfaction, but at a profit, and price appeared to be the major marketing variable. Shelfer's answer was to appoint a marketing VP and to emphasize cost reduction and market segmentation. Saunders' product line widened in response to the "buyer's market" of deregulation which sought better service and lower rates. SS could tackle the service aspect, but cost, which Shelfer identified as the real issue facing the industry, was a different matter.

Saunders' leasing market started to disintegrate, and the used truck market flattened. Shelfer had inherited an unfavorable overhead cost picture. Although he pursued cost reduction, he had to live with the diseconomies of smaller size, plus rising exogenous costs (insurance, for one) over which he had no control. His streamlining of management reduced costs, and lowered fuel costs, inflation, and interest costs helped, too, but not enough. As costs rose SS found itself not performing to its satisfaction and realized that marketing notwithstanding, it had a problem beyond its present reach.

Leasing, its cash cow, was increasingly less cost effective: leasing was in the mature stage, and thus there was extensive pressure on being the low cost producer. Saunders could not milk the cow, and its margins were too narrow to afford to grasp new opportunities, even though deregulation offered it potential for growth in easing restrictions on markets and services. Lower barriers to entry meant that some of its new competitors could chase those opportunities instead.

PRODUCTION AND OPERATIONS MANAGEMENT SECTOR. Here one must note that SS is dedicated to meeting market demands, though its prices may not be competitive. It has a name for quality service. Management in this sector is active and capable. Its truck fleet is relatively new, and its facilities are efficient and well dispersed. Its communications network and computer systems are advanced. Despite a growing market, industry overcapacity and SS' cost disadvantage toward competitors put it at a disadvantage. SS does everything right - we just wonder if it has done the right things.

STRATEGIC ALTERNATIVES AND CHOICE

Stability accepts present conditions, but this is at best slow death. Expansion is an answer, but this requires capital raised by debt or equity, neither of which is acceptable to SS. Retrenchment by sale represents the only choice. A combination strategy is not feasible.

RECOMMENDED DISCUSSION QUESTIONS

1. Was deregulation a factor in the sale of Saunders? Explain.

2. Where was Saunders at a disadvantage with its competitors?

3. Why did Saunders not expand after deregulation, when acquisitions were easily available?

4. Was Saunders following an end-game strategy? If not, what strategy was it following?

5. What strategy would you have recommended?

6. What was the greatest single factor influencing the sale?

7. What principal reasons underlay the sale?

8. Was the sale handled well?

9. If you were Shelfer, would you have recommended accepting Ryder's offer?

10. How might Saunders have stayed competitive in the industry?

11. What will the industry look like in 1995?

ANALYSIS AND DISCUSSION

1. Was deregulation a factor in the sale of Saunders? Explain.

It was, of course. It shook up the industry and fostered competition. Many could not stand being deprived of the regulatory security blankets. What this meant was a brand new world where marketing strategies and cost containment were key. Saunders was having difficulty in making the transition.

2. Where was Saunders at a disadvantage with its competitors?

SS was not dominant in terms of volume; it could not match operating costs with large competitors, and it was not a price leader. All else it had. It just didn't have what counted most.

3.Why did Saunders not expand after deregulation, when acquisitions were easily available?

Saunders was constrained by its capital structure. The family's reluctance to use equity let Ryder pass it in leasing; in the early 70s both were about the same size, but Ryder financed and grew. The dividend policy paid out what should have been growth funds, in order to make the stock attractive. The policy was continued into the 80s. Since "the boy's" holdings were not well diversified, they wanted a regular dividend from SS.

4.Was Saunders following an endgame strategy? If not, what strategy was it following?

Not really. An endgame strategy is for declining industries. It is hard to conceive of trucking as declining. True, SS had relative corporate weaknesses and the industry traits for the endgame were unfavorable, but endgame strategy does not fit here. Students may claim that SS acted precisely by the book, but there was more here than met the eye. With greater accuracy one could say that SS was attempting an amalgam of Porter's generics - cost leadership, differentiation and focus - but it was deficient in cost leadership.

5.What strategy would you have recommended?

Shelfer followed a combination strategy of retrenchment and growth, but he was forced to compete out of his depth with the big boys since expansion could not be achieved. That's wrong. Smaller companies need to find a niche for themselves.

6.What was the greatest single factor influencing the sale?

Various answers will be heard here. We maintain that the values of management put the handwriting on the wall years before with the family policy, perhaps unspoken but still evident, of capital restraint. The family now was motivated to sell. The world was so much more complex. The brothers were after less work, rather than more. Challenge no longer had that old allure. To grow would take money and a lot of time and energy. It was just time to go on to other things, and the tax laws made a sale sooner more attractive financially than one later.

7.What principal reasons underlay the sale?

a. A belief that the company could be sold as a unit and at a good profit with its management intact.

b. Mistaken belief that tax loss carryforward and ITC would have good value.

c. Belief that capital gains tax treatment would make the sale more advantageous in 1986 than later.

d. Belief that the company could not achieve in the next three years or so the values possible in a sale.

8. Was the sale handled well?

This will flush out some divided opinions. We say no because Kidder, Peabody drew over $1 million and really produced nothing. SS wanted the company to survive intact with its management and thus looked for someone to bring forth a noncompetitor. Selling to a trucking firm meant the end of SS as an operating entity. Kidder, Peabody's locating Ryder was as useful as hiring a scientist to see if a fish knows that water is wet. The Saunders brothers knew most of the industry figures personally, and if they had wanted to sell to a competitor, they could easily have done so. We believe that since SS did not qualify as a failing company, the horizontal merger could have taken place only under the relaxed antitrust attitude of the Reagan administration.

9. If you were Shelfer, would you have recommended accepting Ryder's offer?

Yes. This gives the instructor a chance to ask what a company is worth and to discuss ways of determining company values and acquisition prices. There the price of some $100 million was about 20 times earnings, a good figure, and 1.63 times book value, an amount much more than continuing operations over several more years would have brought.

10. How might Saunders have stayed competitive in the industry?

Shelfer couldn't make it work because his actions may have been too little and too late. He thought SS could have survived as a smaller company, $150-$175 million. Market segments needed to be nearer home, for lower costs and better defense. Geographically smaller, SS could have reduced personnel considerably. His first objective had to be retrenchment, to get costs down so SS could be more competitive. Then to concentrate on profitable niches - bulk common carriage, even if immediate growth there might not be in order; equipment cleaning for bulk chemical haulers, and other services already created. SS could have used its leadership position in these to provide for differentiated pricing and higher returns.

11. What will the industry look like in 1995?

We don't know, but we felt this would make a good discussion question. We conceive of it as concentrated and growing. Since industry ROEs and profits fell in the 80s, firms couldn't buy new equipment. Low spending, if continued into the early 90s, may well produce a capacity shortage. The rewards should be substantial for the survivors of the deregulation shakeout.

SPRINGFIELD BALLET COMPANY, INC. (SBC)

TEACHING NOTE

TEACHING OBJECTIVES

The Springfield Ballet Company has struggled for years. An outgoing member has shepherded the SBC board of directors in the drafting of a mission statement and goals, yet the outgoing president of the board is uncertain of the fulfillment of those goals. Specific objectives:

See the operations of a not for profit (NFP) organization

Understand the involvement of a board of directors

Accept the necessity for strategic management in a NFP organization

USING THIS CASE

SBC is a relatively simple case which logically falls in the early part of a course. It is easy to read and easy to discuss. It is never too early for students to learn that strategic management is not solely for profit making organizations. It could easily be used for an inclass exam, a short report, or a long report. It would be a poor candidate for a final problem. SBC reads easily, everything comes out in simple language, and the issues are clear. What may not be clear to those new to strategic management is what should be done.

SYNOPSIS

SBC started in 1976 in Springfield, Missouri, now a town of some 157,000. The case follows its tenuous existence noting that its financial wellbeing was a matter of concern as far back as 1981. SBC plays against a stormy backdrop of uncertain direction and lackluster image. Its board of directors is active in its affairs, perhaps too active. In 1987 its board produced a mission statement and some goals. However, the outgoing president has his reservations that all will come to pass as dreamed, so he wonders what recommendations should be made to his successor and the incoming board.

OUTCOME

The Baryshinokov performance netted about $40,000 which SBC used to pay its debt and to establish the small endowment fund. The artistic director was terminated by "mutual agreement," so SBC has established a search committee to find another director.

This Note draws on an excellent prior Note by the casewriters.

219

Joe Fisk says at the outset that SBC has an uncertain future, so a logical approach is to ask what reason or reasons he has for pessimism. If these are charted, they probably fall in the one of three areas: marketing, personnel, and management, or more properly, the role of the board of directors. Do these problems also visit themselves on profit making organizations? They do, of course. This is an entre to discussing the need for strategic management in NFP organizations. Are there differences between strategic management in NFP and for-profit organizations? Some should certainly emerge, not the least of which is the role of the board of directors of SBC as compared to the GM board of directors. The casewriters point out that the Epilogue could be used to discuss possible changes in SBC's future. The performance received wide, favorable coverage. Is this the time to conduct another community survey? Students occasionally need to be reminded that there are many nonprofit and not for profit organizations in society, so their chances of involvement as they move along in the world of business are more than slight. Given that, SBC would be a good case to remember.

CASE ANALYSIS

STRATEGIC MANAGEMENT ELEMENTS: MISSION, GOALS, AND OBJECTIVES

SBC's <u>mission</u> is "to educate students and the public in the techniques of dance, to perform at the highest level possible, and to present the finest dance available for southwest Missouri." Its <u>objective</u> is that of "building a dedicated ballet company and expanding public awareness of the arts through dance." Its 12 <u>goals</u> seem less to be goals and more to be work assignments for the board of directors.

STRATEGISTS

None is described. It is instructive to note, however, that with more than a little insight Fisk wonders if SBC's board of directors has the ability to come up with the strategies necessary for success. The board then are SBC's strategists. Many are said to know little about ballet; they presumably are volunteers who represent a cross section of the community and bring a "particular expertise" to the board. Strategic management in our view does not fall into that aggregation of expertise.

ENVIRONMENTAL ANALYSIS

<u>SOCIOECONOMIC SECTOR</u>. SBC commenced in 1976 when a local business man and his wife created a place where their child could learn ballet. Others of like interest joined what was to be from the outset a closely managed organization. Efforts to unite ballet instructors from small local schools into a strong regional ballet company failed because some instructors feared the competition. However cyclical its early days were, SBC was a beneficiary of a general feeling that the arts deserve to be supported, and that Springfield ought to have a thriving ballet. SBC received periodic financial injections from the Springfield Junior League, Missouri Arts Council and community fund raisers. Ballet may not

appeal as widely as other activities to the fine arts public, but society is loath to cut off support for the fine arts, appeal notwithstanding. SBC exists only because of the efforts of a few who are determined that ballet shall be, and lack of general support seems not to daunt that few. Support varies with the economic cycle, but the variance is indeterminate.

GOVERNMENT SECTOR. Tax policies influence fine arts support. Donations are tax deductible, there is greater impetus to give, and support seems a self-solving problem. Also, lack of federal funding support for say, the National Endowment for The Arts, meant the demise of numerous such activities that could no longer make it a reduced local support alone.

INDUSTRY THREATS AND OPPORTUNITIES. SBC has to fight for its existence since it is not the only occupant of the arts scene. Other than the continuing threat of underfunding, it must contend with competitors like the Symphony, the Art Museum, the Regional Opera, the Chameleon Puppet Theatre, and the Little Theatre. Two of Springfield's fine colleges also provide arts performance. If the Little Theatre is SBC's model, its success can be attributed to the fact that it gives the supporting public what it wants. SBC's opportunities seem scant. Its low school enrollments indicate a general lack of interest. Essentially, SBC has little to offer and exists through the financial sufferance of a relative few. If it can turn itself around, it does find itself in a growing area where there is community support of the arts. It can work with the colleges in Springfield, though that seems unexplored as yet. There is a degree of synergism in centrally-housed arts groups. Grants are available; the National Association of Regional Ballets can assist, and there is always the possibility of publicity and profit from sponsoring well known performances.

STRATEGIC ADVANTAGE PROFILE

CORPORATE RESOURCES AND PERSONNEL. There is little to cheer about here. SBC has a poor image and low prestige. There is no formal organizational structure, so SBC functions on an ad hoc basis. There is no strategic management system; though the outgoing member has left a legacy of mission and "goals", the outgoing president indicates that getting there is yet a different matter. A training session for new board members is fine, but that alone is no guarantee of success. Either from within the board or from the faculty of one of the city's colleges must come the talent necessary to glue together a comprehensive strategy. Personnel policies seem to be inadequate, and employee qualification is unknown.

FINANCE AND ACCOUNTING. SBC is bone poor. Its revenues have never met its expenses. It has managed to lead a hand to mouth existence on grants; community support activities, one of which phases out in 1987; donations and memberships; tuition and admission fees from fund raisers like the holiday favorite, the Nutcracker Ballet. Table 4 shows an illusory operating surplus because SBC has some unlisted liabilities; even so, we read that the financial situation is improving. Ratio analysis is meaningless, but some solace can be derived from an abrupt rise in membership fees. The board is rightly concerned about measures to promote a stable level of revenue. The Baryshinokov bonus may be a one time affair that will prove difficult to equal in the future.

MARKETING AND DISTRIBUTION. SBC wants for lack of a sound marketing effort. The arts are given to believing that marketing is not necessary, that their very being is marketing enough. However, SBC has come to realize that perhaps its marketing has to crank up and best the competition, but how? Past promotional efforts are regarded as "lackluster" and match the 1985 survey which said SBC suffered from low visibility, low prestige, limited variety of performances, and low performance quality. Essentially its marketing efforts, despite competitive pricing, have been inadequate. A full blown dance company is out of reach because of low enrollment at the dance school - yet that could hardly be a surprise because an interest survey showed almost 60% preferred to learn modern or jazz dancing. Ballet ranked with tap dancing at 16%. All this indicates the SBC is set on doing what the board wants rather than responding to the indicated desires of the market. The means of salvation seem at hand, but the board seems oblivious to these opportunities. None are so deaf as those who will not hear. The new mission may be corrective, however, since it speaks of dance, not ballet to the exclusion of all else.

STRATEGIC ALTERNATIVES

Stability has little to recommend it since it literally means standing still. Growth is essential if SBC is to come even close to reaching its objective. Retrenchment cannot be considered since SBC is already close to the bone in every possible way. A combination strategy could be considered.

CHOICE

A combination strategy of stability and growth in sequence.

IMPLEMENTATION

We see the role of SBC's board of directors as the key to SBC's survival. While the group is willing, it does not follow that the group ergo is able as well. The SBC needs some leadership, but that quality is hard to come by when the board micromanages operations. Volunteers will bring what they can and do what they can, but that is not enough because there is no real responsibility here. There ought to be a higher degree of expertise on the board. Putting up posters or moving scenery or staging a fund drive are all necessary in their time, but SBC needs actions like that far less than it needs a board which can make something of the mission statement and its accompanying "goals." At least SBC now has a sense of direction - but someone still has to get the boat away from the dock.

SBC needs an artistic director who has some tenure. That will continue to be uncertain until the board knows what it wants, puts that in writing, and merely holds the incumbent to those duties without interference from the board. The present job description seems inadequate. The inveterate propensity to take over the details blinds the board to the bigger picture - the nuts and bolts assume such fearsome dimensions that the true reason for being is forgotten, if indeed it is ever acknowledged.

The position of the general business manager should become full time so that someone is in charge at all times. In conjunction with the board, that manager needs to see to an overall strategy for the SBC. Unquestionably, marketing and personnel need attention, but finance can't be forgotten. Strategy is a seamless garment. Each functional area needs at least the rudiments of an objective, pertinent policies, a general plan for reaching that objective, and some idea of how to fund what programs emerge. If this isn't done, then the manager and/or artistic director must continue to put fingers in the dike without a chance to realize any real progress.

RECOMMENDED DISCUSSION QUESTIONS

1. What is SBC's preeminent problem? How can it be solved?

2. How has SBC come to its present position?

3. What suggestions would you make to SBC?

4. What is SBC's greatest need now? Justify.

5. What differences do you see in strategic management in NFP organizations as opposed to for-profit organizations?

6. What marketing strategies would you suggest? Refer to the 4P's and describe a strategy for each.

7. How would you improve the turnover in the artistic director position?

8. Are job descriptions important to an organization like SBC?

9. What use would you make of the market survey results mentioned in the case?

10. What are the advantages and disadvantages of having a very involved board of directors? What do you recommend for SBC and why?

11. How will the Baryshinokov performance affect SBC? How best can SBC most effectively use the performance for its own benefit?

ANALYSIS AND DISCUSSION

1. What is SBC's preeminent problem? How can it be solved?

This will allow you to put a finger on the pulse of the class. Some will ask what "preeminent" is supposed to mean. Take it as the problem which must be solved if SBC is to succeed. We believe the problem to be that of a lack of strategic management since there is no overall strategy, and SBC has never really thought to follow one. The problem can be solved if the board recognizes its existence. Problems in finance and marketing are really symptoms of the preeminent problem.

2. How has SBC come to its present position?

This is not a replay of the first question. SBC has simply done whatever it wanted with little apparent regard for the environment and no attention to the marketing aspects of its existence. It does say that SBC has no strategy, true, but in the absence of even that, it says even more, that SBC simply disregarded that for which it had no liking.

3. What suggestions would you make to SBC?

This should provide numerous answers. You might want to arrange them on a blackboard by functional area and then refer back to them in some of the later questions. See our remarks under Implementation.

4. What is SBC's greatest need now? Justify.

This is subjective, to be sure, so you will hear a bit of everything. We would hope that a basic strategy would have been covered in Question 1 above, or certainly Question 2. We believe that SBC will continue to drift, even with a strategy, unless some true leadership emerges. Its system of governance makes leadership difficult - but who ever built a monument to a committee? The start of a strategy - mission certainly and goals perhaps - has been laid down, so the need now is for someone to grab the ball and start running.

5. What differences do you see in strategic management in NFP organizations as opposed to for-profit organizations?

It would be hard to catalog them all, so we won't pretend to do so. Most businesses, as opposed to NFPs, follow some sort of defined strategy, probably with one or more quantifiable goals and perhaps even an objective. Responsibility is vested in the CEO, picked for his qualifications for the job. Boards of directors do not micromanage but restrict themselves to selecting CEO's, approving strategy, passing on major strategic changes in direction or operation, levels of executive compensation, etc. Far greater use is made of marketing research. Finance gets priority attention and usually does not depend on somewhat shakey sources of revenue like memberships and grants.

6. What marketing strategies would you suggest? Refer to the 4P's and describe a strategy for each.

SBC needs to improve its marketing strategies, especially as evidenced by the market surveys. Some suggested strategies for the 4 P's are as follows:

Services offered (Product): Continue to offer a variety of dance classes at the school. Offering just one type of dance instruction would not be a wise move. Product offerings should be scheduled at acceptable times throughout the day (such as after school, early evening, etc.). Because of the downtown location of SBC's studies, they might want to consider offering a lunch hour dance/exercise class to appeal to individuals who work downtown. Dance performances by SBC need to include elaborate costumes, scenery and sets. Stick with familiar ballets. Developing a theme for a season's offerings might be worth a try.

Price: The price decision for dance performances is fairly well established. SBC's season ticket prices are in line with other Springfield arts organizations' season ticket prices. Special corporate rates might be considered to encourage volume sales. Prices for the ballet school need to be examined closely to insure a competitive price that will better cover the expenses of operating the school.

Place: Again, the place decision for dance performances by SBC and/or by visiting dance companies does not need to be changed. These typically take place in the Vandivort Center or in the adjacent Landers Theatre where facilities are available. However, based upon market survey information, SBC might want to consider offering some classes (such as modern and jazz) in a southwest or southeast Springfield location. SBC should consider another market survey before committing to this action.

Promotion: Because of SBC's perceived low visibility, much attention should be given to more effective promotions. If a theme for the dance season is developed, promotions could carry out the theme. Working within a limited budget, SBC should develop "attention-getting" promotions. Dance is an art--use its artistic "license" to develop unusual advertising. Also, SBC should promote its performances at the colleges within the community. Dance does not appeal to everyone but SBC can and should develop a more effective promotional approach. Try lecture/slide presentations/demonstrations at Springfield elementary schools.

7. How would you improve the turnover in the artistic director position?

There is no question that the turnover in artistic directors is quite high. This may not be too unusual for performing arts organizations; however, many ballet groups have maintained their artistic director for extended periods of time. (As an added note, ballet company performers generally have long tenures with their companies.) A part of the problem in turnover stems from a lack of effectively analyzing the organization's current personnel situation. Conducting a meaningful analysis of jobs is a detailed, time-consuming process that involves trained human resource specialists. SBC board members have never performed a job analysis. No one on the present board has training in human resource management that qualifies him/her to conduct a meaningful analysis. Without clear understanding of job expectations from management and from the artistic director, there is likely to be turmoil and strong feelings that the job is not being performed as anticipated. The artistic director reports to the president of the board. The frustrating part of the director's job is that the executive committee of the board, composed of board officers and the past president, is also involved in supervision activities. With a large number of "chiefs" all at the same level, it is easy to see why job expectations vary, and why different signals may be transmitted to the artistic director. Clearly, the kind of performances, teaching approaches, etc. will vary by individual. In addition, the officers change yearly. Consequently, philosophy changes from one year to the next. In fact commitments by one president to the artistic director are not necessarily commitments to be followed by the next president, since no employment contracts have been used in the past.

8. Are job descriptions important to an organization like SBC?

Job descriptions are relevant to any type and size of organization. Unfortunately, small organizations do not take the time to provide accurate job descriptions to their workers. The importance of job descriptions to any organization can be to (1) find the right people for the job, (2) establish the criteria for employee appraisals, and (3) determine equitable compensation levels. Given these points, a job description can be a very useful document in developing an employment contract. Many of the items in the contract can be carried into a handbook describing the specific benefits and requirements of the position.

9. What use would you make of the market survey results mentioned in the case?

Both market surveys in the case gave interesting and useful information. As SBC develops appropriate short and long run strategies, it should employ the results of other surveys. As an example, one survey showed the SBC had low visibility and low prestige in the community. In order to overcome or change this perception, SBC needs to develop more sophisticated, appealing promotions. The Baryshinokov appearance should be instrumental in providing both visibility and prestige.

10. What are the advantages and disadvantages of having a very involved board of directors? What do you recommend for SBC and why?

The board of directors is a very important part of an NFP organization. SEC has a working board. Board members not only function as management but help solic funds, usher at performances, and put up posters in store-front windows. Management functions are performed by board members, but they hold no position as officers within the corporation. The board's president provides direct, day-to-day supervision. Furthermore, all policy decisions and any activities having a financial or other impact on the ballet are made by the president in concert with the executive committee.

The board's members are all outside directors but serve without pay or title. This arrangement is quite different from that of a board of directors of a proprietary firm where the directors are composed of corporate officers (including the chief executive officer and the president) and several qualified outside directors. Yet in the corporate business world, the reason for a board's being is "to manage and control the affairs of the enterprise." The advantages of having a very involved board in the daily affairs of the organization are: (1) The board becomes responsible for the strategic planning of the organization. It is not delegated to an operating manager. The board alone has the responsibility for setting the direction and course to be followed by the organization. (2) Outside knowledge possessed by the board can be applied to strategic and operational management decisions. By having members who have a vast array of knowledge outside of the SBC, decision making can be more objective and rational.

The disadvantages of a very involved board are: (1) The board becomes extremely large for the organization to survive. There may be no exact number for an effective board, but boards with more than 15 people are often considered cumbersome and might be restricted in effectiveness. (2) Board members do not have sufficient time to engage in active management and perform operational tasks. Since board members are selected for their knowledge, insight and expertise in a variety of areas, they by their very nature are busy and involved in their own professions and occupations. Having to give time for operational tasks may cause the most highly qualified outside board member to consider twice before accepting an appointment.

Stanley Vance in his book Corporate Leadership: Boards, Directors and Strategy, notes some of the frailties and potential boardroom problems of corporate governance. Some of the more severe:

(a) Lack of entrepreneurial leadership. Many directors are like the eminent French naturalist, Jean-Henri Fabre, who described how certain caterpillars, when enticed to the rim of a large flower pot, would follow one after the other in endless circling. Here, there is a lot of activity but not much accomplishment. Boards must be composed of people willing to express opinions and to challenge decisions that may not be in the best interests of the organization. A strong board member of SBC should be a person who can sit across the table from others and feel comfortable in providing information as he/she sees it, no matter how difficult it may be for others to accept. The person should be one who can persuade and encourage others to do the necessary planning, organizing, directing and evaluating long before it is too late.

(b) Maintaining secrecy of board operations, when there is nothing to be gained from doing so.

(c) Staying on the board just for the prestige or money that can be earned. The SBC board is not paid, nor are its members provided any perks. In fact, each board member is required to purchase a membership to the ballet through a tax deductible contribution, the minimum of which is $50. In short, members of the SBC board serve in a complimentary capacity. The board meets monthly with many outside committee assignments, all of which are done free with little or no direct vested interest.

(d) Corporate directors abdicate their strategic management responsibility.

> *11.How will the Baryshinokov performance affect SBC? How best can SBC most effectively use the performance for its own benefit?*

The Baryshinokov performance will doubtlessly have a major impact upon the organization. Since Baryshinokov is a famous dance personality, his troupe's coming to Springfield is an important community arts event. The potential for increasing SBC's prestige and visibility via this event is high. SBC needs to get the most mileage out of Baryshinokov's appearance by linking its name with Baryshinokov's as often and as much as possible. Posters, billboards and other "reminder" forms of advertising are needed. Promotions should not be oriented toward selling tickets (since the performance has sold out) but should be aimed at getting the most out of Baryshinokov's name and reputation.

In addition, the revenues from the Baryshinokov appearance should allow the organization to get out of debt and to establish a small endowment fund. Revenues from ticket sales alone amount to $135,000. Any additional revenue gained from the sale of promotional items at the concert could increase the actual revenues. A $100,000 cost of performance would net SBC $35,000, which could be used to pay off debt and establish a small endowment fund. The Baryshinokov appearance will serve to enhance SBC's prestige and visibility as well as to strengthen its financial position.

NOTES

NOTES

NOTES

NOTES

NOTES

NOTES